THE BEST IN TENT CAMPING:

WISCONSIN

A Guide for Car Campers Who Hate RVs, Concrete Slabs, and Loud Portable Stereos

Other Books By Johnny Molloy

Beach & Coastal Camping in Florida
The Best in Tent Camping: The Carolinas
The Best in Tent Camping: Colorado
The Best In Tent Camping: Florida
Best in Tent Camping: Georgia
The Best in Tent Camping: Southern Appalachian & Smoky Mountains
The Best in Tent Camping: Tennessee and Kentucky
The Best in Tent Camping: West Virginia
Day & Overnight Hikes in the Great Smoky Mountains National Park
Day & Overnight Hikes in Shenandoah National Park
Day & Overnight Hikes in West Virginia's Monongahela National Forest
From the Swamp to the Keys: A Paddle Through Florida History
The Hiking Trails of Florida's National Forests, Parks, and Preserves
Land Between the Lakes National Recreation Area Handbook
Long Trails of the Southeast
Mount Rogers Outdoor Recreation Handbook
A Paddler's Guide to Everglades National Park
60 Hikes Within 60 Miles: Nashville
Trail By Trail: Backpacking in the Smoky Mountains

Visit the author's website:
www.johnnymolloy.com

THE BEST IN TENT CAMPING:

WISCONSIN

---

*A Guide for Car Campers Who Hate RVs, Concrete Slabs,
and Loud Portable Stereos*

1st Edition

Johnny Molloy

Menasha
Ridge
Press, Inc.

This book is for Ellie Connolly, who loves the Wisconsin outdoors.

Library of Congress Cataloging-in-Publication Data
available from the Library of Congress

ISBN 0-89732-541-9

Cover design by Grant Tatum
Cover photo by Johnny Molloy

Menasha Ridge Press
P.O. Box 43673
Birmingham, Alabama 35243
www.menasharidge.com

CONTENTS

ACKNOWLEDGMENTS

I would like to thank the following people for helping me in the research and writing of this book: All the land managers of Wisconsin's state parks and forests, the folks at Nicolet and Chequamegon national forests, and the people who administer the many county parks throughout the state. Specifically I would like to thank Ron Campbell, Niki Robinson, Melissa Parker, and B.J. Farra at Wildcat Mountain State Park; Pat and Cindy Hummer at Wildcat Mountain; Brian Hefty, Paul Ahlen, and Barry Fetting of Hartman Creek for their captivating commentary; Geoffrey Cooke and Garrett Meador at Rock Island State Park; Scott Johnson and Neal Kephart at Wyalusing State Park; and Jim and Paul Volz and their families at Starrett Lake. Thanks also to P. Lynn, Amp I. Tay, Bruce, and Melinda at White Deer Lake; and to Darin Williams and Allen Middendorp of Lake Wissota State Park.

Thanks to Lisa Daniel for camping with me and keeping me company at campgrounds and at home. Thanks to Ellie Connolly for canoeing with me on the St. Croix, and advising me on her favorite tent camping destinations. Thanks to Jackie White for her help, too. Thanks to Linda Grebe at Eureka! for providing me with a great tent, the Mountain Pass X2. Thanks to Silva for their compasses and to Camp Trails for their packs. Thanks to Jean Cobb and Brooke Wilson at Freebairn & Co. for their help.

The biggest thanks of all goes to the people of Wisconsin who have a beautiful state in which to tent camp.

MAP LEGEND

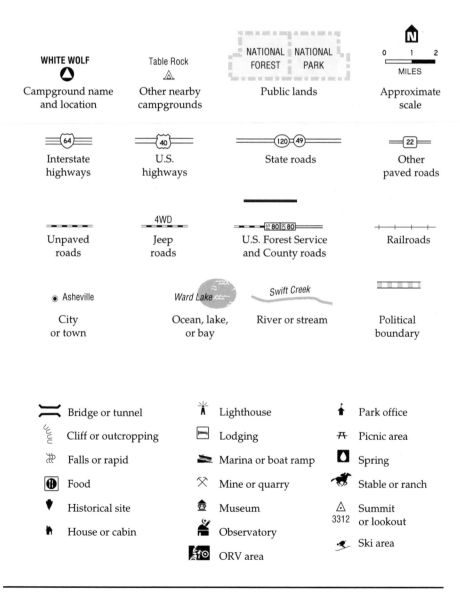

WHITE WOLF
Campground name
and location

Table Rock
Other nearby
campgrounds

NATIONAL FOREST | NATIONAL PARK
Public lands

0 1 2 MILES
Approximate
scale

64
Interstate
highways

40
U.S.
highways

120 49
State roads

22
Other
paved roads

Unpaved
roads

4WD
Jeep
roads

80 80
U.S. Forest Service
and County roads

Railroads

● Asheville
City
or town

Ward Lake
Ocean, lake,
or bay

Swift Creek
River or stream

Political
boundary

Bridge or tunnel
Cliff or outcropping
Falls or rapid
Food
Historical site
House or cabin

Lighthouse
Lodging
Marina or boat ramp
Mine or quarry
Museum
Observatory
ORV area

Park office
Picnic area
Spring
Stable or ranch
3312 Summit
or lookout
Ski area

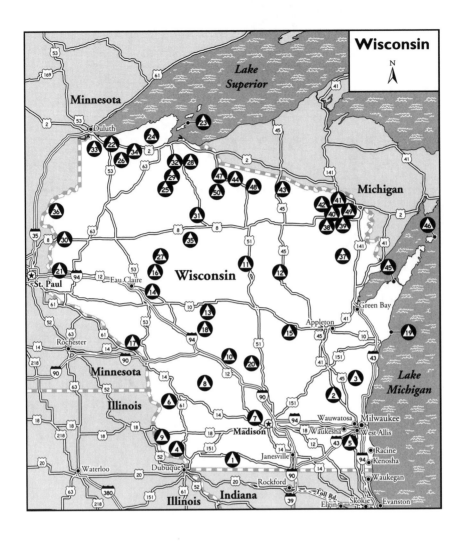

Southern Wisconsin
1. Blackhawk Memorial Park
2. Horicon Ledges County Park
3. Long Lake Recreation Area
4. Nelson Dewey State Park
5. Pine Woods
6. Sidie Hollow County Park
7. Tower Hill State Park
8. Wildcat Mountain State Park
9. Wyalusing State Park

Central Wisconsin
10. Buckhorn State Park
11. Council Grounds State Park
12. Dells of Eau Claire County Park
13. East Fork
14. Harstad County Park
15. Hartman Creek State Park
16. Lake Wissota State Park
17. Perrot State Park
18. Pigeon Creek
19. Point Beach State Forest
20. Roche-A-Cri State Park
21. Willow River State Park

Northwestern Wisconsin
22. Amnicon Falls State Park
23. Big Bay State Park
24. Birch Grove
25. Black Lake
26. Bois Brule
27. Brunet Island State Park
28. Copper Falls State Park
29. Day Lake
30. Interstate State Park
31. Lake of the Pines
32. Lake Three/Beaver Lake
33. Pattison State Park
34. Perch Lake
35. Spearhead Point
36. St. Croix

Northeastern Wisconsin
37. Bagley Rapids
38. Bear Lake
39. Goodman Park
40. Laura Lake
41. Lauterman Lake/ Perch Lake
42. Lost Lake
43. Luna Lake/ White Deer Lake
44. North Trout Lake
45. Potawatomi State Park
46. Rock Island State Park
47. Sandy Beach Lake
48. Starrett Lake
49. Twelve Foot Falls Park
50. Twin Lakes

PREFACE

L ife is so interesting—you just never know where it will lead you. I certainly would not have known just how unique and beautiful Wisconsin is if it weren't for serendipitous fortune. Way back when, I met Tom Rodgers, who was moving from Madison, Wisconsin to Knoxville, Tennessee to further his wife Kathleen's college teaching career. He waxed eloquent about the beauty of the Badger State. I had been stopping there some on trips, but I hadn't explored it fully. Tom introduced me to his friend Ellie Connolly, who talked up Wisconsin even more. Then the opportunity arose to write this book. I grabbed my tent and laptop and hopped in my Jeep, exploring the state by day and typing up literal on-site campground reports by night.

The first surprise came at Wyalusing State Park. The view from the bluffs of the Wisconsin River rivaled any mountain vista, as did views from the walk-in tent sites at Nelson Dewey State Park. Next, I headed east to the glacially carved features of Kettle Moraine State Forest. Glaciers had a hand in molding much of Wisconsin, but the concentration of features at Kettle Moraine made for a good geological lesson and scenic beauty. Big lakes border parts of the Badger State, so I went to enjoy the cool breezes at Point Beach State Forest, on the shores of Lake Michigan. The tan sand squished beneath my toes as I looked up at Rawley Point lighthouse. In the central state were two of the biggest surprises of them all, Dells of Eau Claire and Hartman Creek. Hartman Creek is an exemplary state park: an attractive, relaxing campground with lots of nearby natural features to enjoy. The Dells of Eau Claire, a county park east of Wausau, is a rocky natural feature on the Eau Claire River that is a must for all those who want to know their state well. Speaking of rocks, have you seen the view from the top of Roche-A-Cri? That is one amazing natural feature with a nice campground within walking distance. More bluffs waited at Perrot State Park, astride the Mississippi River.

And then there are the North Woods. It seems tent campers from Wisconsin and points beyond like to go "up Nort," as it is often said. And there are so many fine campgrounds up north—it was difficult to choose the best. Not only were there many state parks, but also county parks, state forests, and national forests, too. Two common themes to the campgrounds of the North Woods were water and natural beauty, from Big Bay State Park in the Apostle Islands of Lake Superior, to Amnicon Falls in Douglas County to serene Laura Lake, where the loons provided the background music to those long, long summer days. And I can't forget the fantastic rivers of the North Woods, the Bois Brule, the Flambeau, and the Peshtigo. But to single out the North Woods rivers would be to leave out many fine paddling rivers throughout the state. Wisconsin is paddling country—from the East Fork Pecatonica down south, to the Black River of the central state, to the federally preserved St. Croix astride the Minnesota border. And there are still other rivers, the wild lower Wisconsin, the Kickapoo, the Chippewa, and the Eau Claire near the city of Eau Claire. Campgrounds in this book are along or near all the above rivers.

The days began to shorten—fall was on its way as I explored more campgrounds. And with the joy of completing a book and the sadness of an adventure ended, I finished my research. But I will continue putting my lessons to work, enjoying more of Wisconsin in future outdoor adventures.

THE BEST IN TENT CAMPING:

WISCONSIN

A Guide for Car Campers Who Hate RVs, Concrete Slabs, and Loud Portable Stereos

INTRODUCTION

A Word about this Book and Wisconsin Tent Camping

Wisconsin is rich in both human and natural history. Originally settled by aboriginal Americans who used the ample rivers and lakes for travel, French voyageurs and United States pioneers followed, exploring a land shaped by glaciers and time. Green Bay and Prairie du Chien were settled first as furs, lead, and lumber attracted more settlers. The vast and varied landscape was evident to all who came to the Badger State. They saw sand dune–laden shores of Lake Michigan, lake-studded highlands of the North Woods, the ridges and valleys of the southwest, where the Wisconsin and Mississippi rivers cut deep swaths through the land, and the deep gorges cut by dark, fast-flowing rivers forming waterfalls striving for Lake Superior.

Today tent campers can enjoy these parcels, each distinct regions of Wisconsin. You can explore the surprisingly hilly terrain of Sidie Hollow, near the Illinois border. The bluffs of Perrot State Park overlook Minnesota. The central state has the remote and wild Black River State Forest, where timber wolves have reclaimed their old domain, with the quiet of East Fork campground returning you to nature. Here also are the big waters of Castle Rock Flowage, where Buckhorn's numerous walk-in tent camping sites await. A tent camper has to take two ferries to reach Rock Island State Park, Wisconsin's "furthest northeast" point. So many lakes dot Wisconsin's North Woods that you can literally camp on two lakes at once, such as Birch Grove campground in the Chequamegon National Forest, or Luna Lake/White Deer Lake campground in the Nicolet National Forest. And then there are the waterfalls of the North Woods. Marinette County calls itself the waterfall capital of Wisconsin. Two campgrounds in this book are situated along falls in Marinette County, with many other cascades nearby. Yet other falls are featured at other parks in this book.

All this spells paradise for the tent camper. No matter where you go, the scenery will never fail to please the eye. Before embarking on a trip, take time to prepare. Many of the best tent campgrounds are a fair distance from the civilized world and you want to be enjoying yourself rather than making supply or gear runs. Call ahead and ask for a park map, brochure, or other information to help you plan your trip. Visit the campground's website. Make reservations wherever applicable, especially at popular state parks. Inquire about the latest reservation fees and entrance fees at state parks and forests.

Ask questions. Ask more questions. The more questions you ask, the fewer surprises you will get. There are other times, however, when you'll grab your gear and this book, hop in the car, and just wing it. This can be an adventure in its own right.

The Rating System

Included in this book is a rating system for Wisconsin's 50 best tent campgrounds. Certain campground attributes—beauty, site privacy, site spaciousness, quiet, security, and cleanliness/upkeep—are ranked using a star system. Five stars are ideal, one is acceptable. This system will help you find the campground that has the attributes you desire.

Beauty

In the best campgrounds, the fluid shapes and elements of nature—flora, water, land, and sky—have melded to create locales that seem to have been made for tent camping. The best sites are so attractive you may be tempted not to leave your outdoor home. A little site work is all right to make the scenic area camper-friendly, but too many reminders of civilization eliminated many a campground from inclusion in this book.

Site privacy

A little understory goes a long way in making you feel comfortable once you've picked your site for the night. There is a trend in planting natural borders between campsites if the borders don't exist already. With some trees or brush to define the sites, everyone has his or her personal space. Then you can go about the pleasures of tent camping without keeping up with the Joneses at the site next door—or them with you.

Site spaciousness

This attribute can be very important depending on how much of a gear-head you are and the size of your group. Campers with family-style tents and screen shelters need a large, flat spot on which to pitch a tent with more room for the ice chest to prepare foods, all the while not getting burned near the fire ring. Gearheads need adequate space to show off all their stuff to neighbors strolling by. I just want enough room to keep my bedroom, den, and kitchen separate.

Quiet

The music of the lakes, rivers, and all the land between—the singing birds, rushing streams, waves lapping against the shoreline, wind whooshing through the trees—includes the kinds of noises tent campers associate with being in Wisconsin. In concert, they camouflage the sounds you don't want to hear—autos coming and going, loud neighbors, and so on.

Security

Campground security is relative. A remote campground with no civilization nearby is usually safe, but don't tempt potential thieves by leaving your valuables out for all to see. Use common sense, and go with your instinct. Campground hosts are wonderful to have around, and state parks with locked gates are ideal for security. Get to know your neighbors and develop a buddy system to watch each other's belongings when possible.

Cleanliness/upkeep

I'm a stickler for this one. Nothing will sabotage a scenic campground like trash. Most of the campgrounds in this guidebook are clean. More rustic campgrounds—my favorites—usually receive less maintenance. Busy weekends and holidays will show their effects; however, don't let a little litter spoil your good time. Help clean up, and think of it as doing your part for Wisconsin's natural environment.

Helpful Hints

To make the most of your tent camping trip, call ahead whenever possible. If going to a state or national park, call for an informative brochure before setting out. This way you can familiarize yourself with the area. Once there, ask questions. Most stewards of the land are proud of their piece of terra firma and are honored you came for a visit. They're happy to help you have the best time possible.

If traveling to the Chequamegon National Forest or Nicolet National Forest, call ahead and order a forest map. Not only will a map make it that much easier to reach your destination, but nearby hikes, scenic drives, waterfalls, and landmarks will be easier to find. There are forest visitor centers in addition to ranger stations. Call or visit and ask questions. When ordering a map, ask for any additional literature about the area in which you are interested.

In writing this book I had the pleasure of meeting many friendly, helpful people: local residents proud of the unique lands around them, as well as state park and national forest employees who endured my endless questions. Even better were my fellow tent campers, who were eager to share knowledge about their favorite spots. They already know what beauty lies on the horizon. As this state becomes more populated, these lands become that much more precious. Enjoy them, protect them, and use them wisely.

SOUTHERN WISCONSIN

---

1. *BLACKHAWK MEMORIAL PARK*

Argyle

Blackhawk Memorial Park isn't exactly the most publicized place around. This Lafayette County Park, located on the small but canoeable East Branch Pecatonica River, contrasts mightily with ultra-busy Yellowstone Lake State Park, which lies upstream a few miles in the Pecatonica River watershed. The only way you might find out about this quiet park is by word of mouth, or maybe from a curious guidebook writer on the lookout for the best tent camping destinations in Wisconsin. And yes, Blackhawk Memorial Park is one of them. Here, you can camp along the river in a very large, secluded campground. Once here, you can do a little canoeing, fishing, and relaxing; or you can visit Yellowstone Lake, then return to your quiet retreat. You might even paddle the Pecatonica proper, which flows through nearby Darlington.

The access road rolls through farmland then dips into the East Branch Pecatonica Valley as it approaches the park. Just beyond the entrance, pass a shelter, water spigot, and bathrooms. Beyond that point, campsites are spread all over the place amid grassy areas broken by copses of trees and wooded wetlands. Solitude and spaciousness prevail in this little-used locale. Horseshoe Lake lies below to your left. The road ahead divides. The right fork leads to the upper canoe landing on the East Branch Pecatonica and a small grassy

CAMPGROUND RATINGS

Beauty:	★★★
Site privacy:	★★★★★
Site spaciousness:	★★★★★
Quiet:	★★★★
Security:	★★★
Cleanliness/upkeep:	★★★

This quiet county park on the East Branch Pecatonica River is sure to have an open campsite.

flat where four secluded campsites are set against a line of trees along the river. The left fork leads to another camping area near the Dead River, a small lake once part of the East Branch of the Pecatonica.

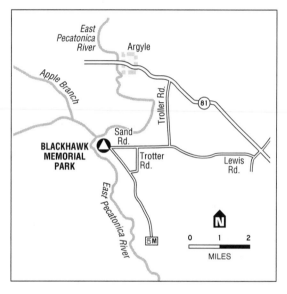

Dead River is also known as Bloody Lake—site of a battle between the United States Army and the Sac and Fox tribes. In 1832, Blackhawk, the leader of the Sac and Fox tribes, tried to reclaim his treaty-ceded land near the site of present-day Rock Island, Illinois. He was unsuccessful, and as a result, fled to Wisconsin while pursued by the United States Army. There were numerous battles along the way (one of which is memorialized by a plaque at site #14), but on June 16, 1832, Blackhawk and his followers were defeated near Bad Axe Creek, Wisconsin, not far from the Mississippi River.

Follow the road to reach several shaded sites by the still waters. The campground road curves onward toward two coveted sites, #15 and #16, on the shore of pretty Horseshoe Lake. Return to the East Branch Pecatonica River, a good bit downstream of the upper landing. Here, the lower canoe landing is set amid several open sites along the riverbank. Reach a couple of secluded shady sites, #31 and #32, then curve away from the river back to the shore of Bloody Lake, across from the Blackhawk Memorial. This campground road curves more than a snake climbing a tree. A few other, well separated, well scattered sites are on Bloody Lake.

Want to camp on a holiday weekend? Come here, and a site should be available. Want privacy? This is the place. Want a big site? This is the place.

However, the wooded marshes and lakes here create ripe conditions for mosquitoes—be prepared from mid–May through June. The fishing here is purportedly good: walleye, bass, panfish, and a few northern pike are in the river. Paddlers can float the East Fork Pecatonica from Argyle down to the campground, or downstream toward South Wayne and the main Pecatonica River. The main Pecatonica offers paddling opportunities of its own, especially from Darlington downstream. Make a gentle float past woods, prairie lands, and farm country. You will also see bluffs and rock outcrops. Darlington is so proud of the paddling opportunities here that they hold a canoe festival the second week of June! Also in Darlington is the Cheese Country Recreational Trail, a 47-mile rail trail corridor leading from Mineral Point to South Wayne. You could combine a float down the river with a bike trip. Call (608) 328-9430 for more info on the rail trail.

The very small and quiet hamlet of Woodford is just a mile to the south of Blackhawk. If you are looking for some busy outdoor action, head to Yellowstone Lake State Park, north of Argyle. The 450-acre Yellowstone Lake is the park centerpiece. The state park offers fishing, swimming, boating, and has ten miles of hiking trails. After your visit to Yellowstone, you will be glad everyone else hasn't heard about Blackhawk Memorial.

KEY INFORMATION

Blackhawk Memorial Park
2995 County Road Y
Woodford, WI 53599

Operated by: Lafayette County Sportsman Club Alliance

Information: (608) 776-4830

Open: Year-round, roads not plowed in winter

Individual sites: 38

Each site has: Fire grate, most have picnic table

Site assignment: First come, first served, no reservation

Registration: Self-registration on-site

Facilities: Water spigot, vault toilets

Parking: At campsites only

Fee: $5 per night Sunday–Thursday, $10 per night Friday–Saturday

Elevation: 800 feet

Restrictions

Pets—On leash only

Fires—In fire rings only

Alcoholic beverages—At campsites only

Vehicles—None

To get there: From Argyle, take WI 81 east for 2.5 miles to Trotter Road. Turn right on Trotter Road and follow it for 2.5 miles to a "T" intersection. Turn right, staying on Trotter Road for 1 mile to Sand Road. Stay forward on Sand Road (Trotter Road veers left) and follow it 1 mile to the park, on your right.

2. *HORICON LEDGES COUNTY PARK*

Horicon

The Horicon Ledges are a western extension of the Niagara Escarpment, the same ancient rock formation over which Niagara Falls flows. In this case, the escarpment is a wooded hilltop bordered with rock bluffs that overlook Horicon Marsh and the surrounding countryside. At 32,000 acres, Horicon Marsh is the largest freshwater cattail marsh in the country. The marsh is situated along the Canada geese flyway, with 200,000 birds passing through in spring and fall. Many other creatures call the marsh home.

Horicon Ledges County Park makes for a good jumping-off point to explore both the ledges at the park and the marsh below. The campground, a little rough around the edges, has some good tent sites and some electric sites that will make the case for why you are a tent camper. The tent sites have their own loop and you will be satisfied calling this county park home for a night. But don't expect a bunch of sedate bird watchers here. Your fellow tent campers are likely to be fun-loving families and others out to enjoy the warm days of summer.

Pass the office and enter the electric loop. Pass campsites #1 and #2, which overlook a volleyball court and a field beyond. Climb a hill and pass by a string of campsites with electricity that are shaded but too close together, with nothing but grass and dirt between them. The

CAMPGROUND RATINGS

Beauty:	★★★
Site privacy:	★★
Site spaciousness:	★★★★
Quiet:	★★★
Security:	★★★
Cleanliness/upkeep:	★★★★

Camp under the tall oaks and maples from this vista-top campground overlooking wildlife-rich Horicon Marsh.

best aspect of the electric loop is the kid's playground. The good loop, the nonelectric loop, spurs right. Tall oaks and maples shade the hillside. Last year's leaves carpet the campsites. These sites are lettered A–W. If you are going to reserve a site here, only ask for a "letter" site. Site A and B are behind one another. C through J are strung along the road well away from one another with young trees adding campsite privacy. Campsite E is all alone. A mini loop

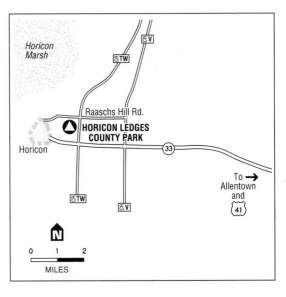

houses sites K, L, and M. The loop curves around toward the Horicon Ledge. Campsites N, O, and P are also backed against the ledge on the outside of the loop while Q, R, and S are on the inside of the loop. Campsites T and U are closer to the ledge on a mini loop. All these sites are well shaded and suited for a tent. V is the only poor tent site, being shaded but with no privacy. I stayed in W because it was so close to a cleared view of the land beyond the ledge.

The Horicon Rocks Hiking Trail runs along the escarpment winding through woods and along rocks where you can see below. In places, boulders have fallen from the bluff, forming mini-caves with trails going under and around them. In other places, paths lead from boulder to boulder, and hikers have to step over deep crevices to continue their journey. A virtual maze of trails connects the escarpment to another trail running along the bottom of the escarpment past the Contemplation Tree, a huge oak, and on to a spring. Other paths interconnect in the deep woods opposite the ledge. A handy trail map is available at the campground office.

Now that you have seen the marsh from above, it's time to see it up close. Visit the Horicon Marsh International Education Center, just north of the town of Horicon on Highway 28. It has lots of interpretive information, a boardwalk, and nature trails about this wildlife refuge. The visitor center, adjacent to Bachuber Flowage, is a regular outdoor laboratory for visitors who want to learn about the marsh. The lake levels of the flowage are regulated to enhance wildlife habitat. The Dike Trail circles the flowage. The Headquarters Trail leaves from North Palmatory Road near the DNR Field Station and loops through woods, fields, and the marsh. Bikers and hikers can enjoy the Wild Goose State Trail. It follows an old rail corridor along the west side of Horicon Marsh for 34 miles between Juneau and Fond du Lac. The best place for Horicon Ledge campers to pick up the trail is at Minnesota Junction, four miles west of the campground off Highway 33.

The waters of Horicon Marsh offer another venue to see the preserve. Canoes are available for rent at Blue Heron Landing in Horicon. You may want to take a pontoon boat tour. A guide will lead the tour and dish out a lot of information. They also lead birding tours. Call (920) 485-4663 for information about Blue Heron offerings. After coming here, you will have seen two natural features that make Wisconsin so special.

To get there: From the junction with US 41, take Highway 33 west 13 miles to County Road V. Turn right on County Road V and follow it 1 mile to Raasch's Hill Road. Turn left on Raasch's Hill Road. Follow Raasch's Hill Road 2 miles to Park Road, entering the park.

KEY INFORMATION

Horicon Ledges County Park
N7403 Park Road
Horicon, WI 53032

Operated by: Dodge County Parks

Information: (920) 387-5450

Open: April through October

Individual sites: 24 non-electric, 22 electric

Each site has: Picnic table, fire ring

Site assignment: First come, first served, and by reservation

Registration: At park attendant station

Facilities: Vault toilets, water spigots

Parking: At campsites only

Fee: $10 per night, $13 per night w/electricity; rates decrease with length of stay

Elevation: 950 feet

Restrictions

Pets—On leash only

Fires—In fire rings only

Alcoholic beverages—At campsites only

Vehicles—Two vehicles per site

Other—No radios after 9 p.m.

3. *LONG LAKE RECREATION AREA*

Dundee

The northern unit of Kettle Moraine State Forest covers 30,000 acres of recreation opportunities, ranging from boating, biking, and hiking, to fishing, swimming, and wildlife watching. Centrally located in the forest, Long Lake has 200 campsites, most of which are fine for a tent camper. Campsites fill quickly on weekends during the warm season, due to being close to greater Milwaukee. But if you make reservations ahead of time, you can get in here and check out Kettle Moraine. Book as far in advance as you can.

Having 200 sites can be imposing, but Long Lake Campground has the campsites divided among five loops. The "600s Loop" is one of the three best loops. The campsites here are laid out beneath a hardwood forest mixed with sumac and occasional locust. Tall brush and small trees offer good campsite privacy. Campsite #620 is very big. The campsites on the inside of the loop are closer together. A center road splits the loop. However, these sites offer good privacy. The "700s Loop" has sites shaded by evergreens on the inside of the loop. Consider even numbered sites #714–#722. Campsites #708–#710 are walk-in sites.

The "800s Loop" is larger. It has some good and many less-than-good sites. Many sites are open to the sun overhead. Interestingly, a marsh lies in the center of the loop, which could pose bug problems.

CAMPGROUND RATINGS

Beauty: ★★★
Site privacy: ★★★
Site spaciousness: ★★★
Quiet: ★★★
Security: ★★★★
Cleanliness/upkeep: ★★★★

Long Lake is your HQ for exploring Kettle Moraine State Forest North Unit.

The best sites in this loop are from #807–#822. The south end of the loop has two cross roads and is too open, but does have some hills. Campsites #844 and #845 are walk-in tent sites. The "Lower 900s Loop" with sites #901–#921, has well shaded sites among evergreens, but are only average in spaciousness. The "Upper 900s Loop" with sites #922–#967 is the least recommended. Many of these sites have little or no shade and limited privacy. The best sites here are #966 and #967.

Four of the five loops have showers. Water spigots and vault toilets are spread throughout the campground.

There are several activity options at this recreation area. You passed the Ice Age Visitor Center on the way in. Go back there to learn about the glacial history of the area, and about the forest's complete recreation opportunities. Naturalist programs are held at the visitor center and at Long Lake.

The marked Kettle Moraine Scenic Drive traverses the length of the northern unit and heads a complete distance of 115 miles to and through the southern unit of Kettle Moraine. Scenic drivers can see first-hand many features left behind from the retreating glaciers as they changed the land. Dundee Mountain, a world famous feature known as a kame (a conical mound of sand, pebbles, and boulders) is just south of Long Lake.

Long Lake is popular with boaters. During high summer, folks will be out skiing, tubing, and generally having a good time on the water. However, this can be disruptive to the fishing. If you want to try your hand at Long Lake, consider fishing in the early morning and late evening. A fishing pier extends into the water from near the campground where you can go for bluegill, crappie, pike, walleye, and largemouth bass. A swim beach is provided at Long Lake for those who want to cool off on a hot summer day.

Of course, this forest is full of trails. The one-mile Dundee Mountain Summit Trail leads to the top of this physical feature and leaves near campsite #944. The Butler Lake Trail area is just three miles distant from Long Lake and offers a three-mile loop through the Butler Lake State Natural Area. This path circles the spring-fed Kettle Lake. Part of the loop is shared with the Ice Age Trail, which makes a 31-mile traverse through the forest. Bikers and hikers share the Greenbush and New Fane trail areas. The Greenbush area is more challenging to pedalers as the ten miles of paths wind in a terminal moraine. The New Fane Trails offer gentler, more rolling terrain. After considering all the above activities, it is easy to see why the words "Recreation Area" are after "Long Lake" here at Kettle Moraine north.

To get there: From Kewaskum, drive north on US 45 for 5 miles to Highway 67. Turn right on Highway 67 and follow it 4 miles to County Road F. Turn right on County Road F and follow it 1 mile to Division Road. Turn left on Division Road and follow it 1 mile to Long Lake Recreation Area, on your left.

KEY INFORMATION

Long Lake Recreation Area
N1765 Highway G
Campbellsport, WI 53010

Operated by: Wisconsin Department of Natural Resources

Information: (920) 533-8612, www.wiparks.net, reservations (888) WIPARKS, www.reserveamerica.com

Open: May through mid–October

Individual sites: 195, plus 5 walk-in campsites

Each site has: Picnic table, fire ring

Site assignment: By phone, internet, or first come, first served

Registration: At visitor center

Facilities: Hot showers, flush toilets, pit toilet, water spigots

Parking: At campsites only

Fee: Memorial Day weekend through Labor Day weekend Friday–Saturday $9 residents, $11 non-residents; weekdays and all days rest of year $7 residents, $9 non-residents; $3 extra for electricity

Elevation: 1,050 feet

Restrictions

Pets—On leash only

Fires—In fire rings only

Alcoholic beverages—At campsites only

Vehicles—Two vehicles per site

Other—21-day stay-limit

4. NELSON DEWEY STATE PARK

Cassville

The campground is the star of this desti-nation. It has most of the qualities a tent camper desires: not too big with widely spaced sites; large sites with near maximum privacy, and a beautiful forest. And that's just the regular campground! Nelson Dewey also has four walk-in tent campsites that have all the above plus ridgetop views of the Mississippi River and across to Iowa that any tent camper would be proud to call home. This state park is also blessed with amenities both within and nearby that will keep you busy when you are not standing around admir-ing your campsite.

Usually, any campground has a few dud sites. Not this one. By the way, all camp-sites here are reservable, so make your plans. The campground is set on a bluffline peering down on the Mississippi River. From the park entrance, follow the camp road to reach the camping loop on the left, situated beneath a cathedral-like hardwood forest dominated by oak trees. Younger trees and heavy brush form a privacy-delivering understory. Pass camp-sites #1 and #2. These large, shaded sites are typical of the campground with good sites on either side of the loop. Campsite #3 is even larger. A vault toilet for both sexes is located past a double site. The Woodbine Nature Trail lies across the campground road. Pass a few electric sites, along with an all-access site, to reach a

CAMPGROUND RATINGS

Beauty:	★★★★★
Site privacy:	★★★★★
Site spaciousness:	★★★★
Quiet:	★★
Security:	★★★★★
Cleanliness/upkeep:	★★★★

The views from the walk-in tent sites are among the best anywhere.

spur road leading left. You'll find a few electric sites on this mini-loop as well as some real winners. Site #18 has a view of the river below. Site #17 sits all alone and is highly recommended. A short foot trail in between these two sites leads to the walk-in tent sites.

Handy pull carts are provided to transport your gear from your vehicle to the walk-in campsites. These bluff-side sites have been leveled with landscaping timbers. Walk-in site D is first. It offers a stunning

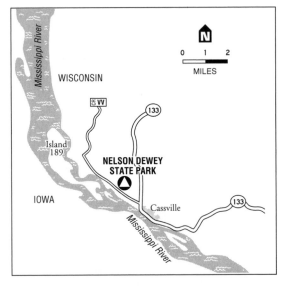

view to the southeast and is partially shaded by locust trees. Site A offers an excellent view also and is more shaded. A portable toilet is located near Site B. A final spur trail leads to site C, arguably the best of the best. It looks far to the southwest at the end of the ridgeline. Shade trees overhang the site. Be apprised that you can hear trains traveling the riverside tracks at the base of the bluff, whether you are in the walk-in sites or not. They didn't bother me a bit.

The main campground loop continues beyond the spur roads and circles past a modern bathhouse. It then reaches another spur loop housing sites #24–#31. This is the domain of the electricity-loving big rigs and the only place a tent camper wouldn't want to be. But even these sites are attractive and would work just fine. Pass the firewood shed. A series of non-electric sites graces the loop as it circles to an end. The large sites are very well separated.

This smallish state park offers some trails along the Mississippi River bluff. The Prairie Trail features rocky points with fantastic vistas of their own. The Cedar Trail offers overlooks, too. Once the home of Wisconsin's first governor,

Nelson Dewey, the park preserves his home, which you can tour. Other than that, the park serves as a jumping-off point for nearby attractions. Just across the road is the Stonefield Historic Site, owned and operated by the State Historical Society of Wisconsin. Originally a farm started by Dewey, the area now includes the Wisconsin State Agricultural Museum and a 1900 village exhibit. The museum houses farm implements of the past and rare, one-of-a-kind machines. It also follows the history of farming in the Badger State. The turn-of the-19th-century exhibit features 30 reconstructed buildings displaying a small farm community from the early 1900s. Stonefield is open from Memorial Day through early October.

Some campers will be using private facilities in nearby Cassville to fish the Mississippi River. Kids will want to swim in the Cassville public pool, which charges a small fee. Consider canoeing or tubing the nearby Grant River, down by Beetown. It offers a quiet, scenic small river experience. A rental and shuttle service operates on the Grant during the warm season. For more information on the Grant River, call Grant River Canoe Rental at (608) 794-2342.

To get there: From downtown Cassville, head north on Wisconsin 133 for 0.5 mile to County Road VV. Turn left on County Road VV and follow it for 1.2 miles to the state park, on your right.

KEY INFORMATION

Nelson Dewey State Park
P.O. Box 658
Cassville, WI 53806

Operated by: Wisconsin State Parks

Information: (608) 725-5374, www.wiparks.net, reservations (888) WIPARKS, www.reserveamerica.com

Open: Year-round, bathhouse and spigots open May through October

Individual sites: 4 walk-in sites, 41 other

Each site has: Picnic table, fire grate, 16 also have electricity

Site assignment: By phone, internet, or first come, first served

Registration: At park office or self-registration if office is closed

Facilities: Hot showers, flush toilets, pit toilets, water spigots

Parking: At campsites only

Fee: Memorial Day weekend through Labor Day weekend during weekends $10 residents, $12 non-residents; weekdays and all days rest of year $8 residents, $10 non-residents; $3 extra for electricity

Elevation: 900 feet

Restrictions

Pets—On leash only

Fires—In fire rings only

Alcoholic beverages—At campsites only

Vehicles—None

5. *PINE WOODS*

Wales

Everybody has heard that many of Wisconsin's landforms were glacially created. However, you will be hard-pressed to find someplace with so many glacial features in one area, as here at the South Unit of the Kettle Moraine State Forest. A forest visitor can see everything from the obvious kettle depressions and knobby hills to rare prairie marsh environments and springside wetlands called fens. Pine Woods Campground, located in the north end of the forest, makes for a quiet and attractive camp from which to explore these features.

Enter the campground and reach Loop 1. This loop is a 24-hour quiet zone and no pets are allowed. Sites #6–#36 are reservable. Campsites #16, #25, and #28 are walk-in sites. The last two require an uphill hike but are worth it for solitude. The beginning of Loop 1 is in a mix of field and forest. The loop then drops into white pine woods after campsite #11. Thick underbrush screens campers from one another. Hilly terrain adds vertical variation to the widely separated sites.

Loop 2 houses sites #150–#179. The first two sites, #150 and #151, are walk-in campsites. Drive a bit more and reach the rest of the loop. Heavy shade and thick woods of hickory-oak and other hardwoods characterize this site. Campsites #168–#171 are somewhat open. The loop enters thick pine woods after campsite #172.

CAMPGROUND RATINGS

Beauty:	★★★★
Site privacy:	★★★★
Site spaciousness:	★★★
Quiet:	★★★★
Security:	★★★★
Cleanliness/upkeep:	★★★★

The glacially altered landforms here offer many sites to see at Kettle Moraine South State Forest.

Of the three loops, Loop 3 covers the most area, though it only has 36 camp-sites. This indicates how widespread sites #263–#299 are. Pine trees loom over an understory that is dense here, so dense in places it diminishes the size of the campsite itself. Overall, these are great campsites. Campsites #270–#299 are reservable on this loop. A large and modern shower building is available for all campers. Keep in mind that Pine Woods has a tendency to fill on summer weekends.

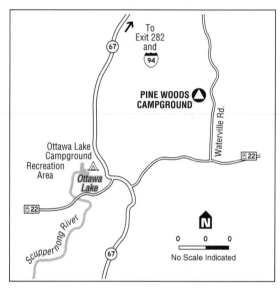

There are many means by which to explore the forest: by foot, bike, water, even horseback! Specific information on each option is available at the Ottawa Lake entrance station or the forest visitor center on Highway 59 between Palmyra and Eagle. The Swinging "W" Ranch offers rides through the forest ranging from one hour to overnight treks. Call (262) 594-2416 for reservations. More conventional means include hiking, which can be done directly from the campground. A total of 54 miles of trail are available for hikers. Take the Green Trail south from the campground road to meet the Ice Age Trail, which travels 30 miles though the forest. The Green Trail is part of the Scuppernong Trail System that adds 12 miles of campground-accessible paths in addition to the Ice Age Trail. Of special interest is the nearby Scuppernong Springs Nature Trail, one of seven nature trails in the forest. This path explores the springs that have drawn people to the forest for centuries. Pass through Scup-pernong Marsh, a wet prairie in the midst of restoration, then past a marl works, where men extracted marl soil for fertilizer. An ancient campsite lies next to Indian Springs. Other springs here have stories, such as Hotel Spring.

Also in the historical vein are three frontier logs cabins in the forest that have been restored and can be visited. Old World Wisconsin is a 576-acre rural museum run by the Wisconsin State Historical Society. It has more than 60 old structures and other features. Old World Wisconsin is located south of Pine Woods on Highway 67.

Road bikers will be pedaling the country lanes that run through and around the forest. The Emma Carlin and John Muir trail systems are available for hikers and bikers. Drivers will want to tour the lower half of the Kettle Moraine Scenic Drive that passes directly by Pine Woods Campground.

On hot days, campers will be heading to Ottawa Lake, a kettle lake formed when a huge chunk of ice slowly melted, creating a depression that filled with water. A swim beach lies along this body of water. This "no gas motors" lake is also an angling destination. Paddlers can follow the self-guided canoe trail to learn more about Ottawa Lake and its relationship to the time of glaciers. No matter your mode of transportation, the South Unit of Kettle Moraine State Forest makes for an interesting destination, especially with a campground as nice as Pine Woods.

To get there: From Exit 282 on I-94, take Highway 67 south for 9 miles to Ottawa Lake Camground. You must register here. From Ottawa Lake, take 67 south 0.4 mile to Highway ZZ. Turn left on Highway ZZ and follow it 1.6 miles to Waterville Road. Turn left on Waterville Road and follow it 1.2 miles to Pine Woods campground, on your left.

KEY INFORMATION

Pine Woods
S91–W39091, Highway 59
Eagle, WI 53119

Operated by: Wisconsin Department of Natural Resources

Information: (262) 594-6200, www.wiparks.net, reservations (888) WIPARKS, www.reserveamerica.com

Open: Early May through mid–October

Individual sites: 101

Each site has: Picnic table, fire grate

Site assignment: By phone, internet, or first come, first served

Registration: At Ottawa Lake Campground

Facilities: Hot showers, flush toilets, pit toilets, water spigots

Parking: At campsites only

Fee: Memorial Day weekend through Labor Day weekend Friday–Saturday $9 residents, $11 non-residents; weekdays and all days rest of year $7 residents, $9 non-residents

Elevation: 1,000 feet

Restrictions

Pets—On leash only and prohibited in Loop 1

Fires—In fire rings only

Alcoholic beverages—At campsites only

Vehicles—Two vehicles per campsite

Other—21-day stay limit

6. SIDIE HOLLOW COUNTY PARK

Viroqua

Do you ever get to the point where if you get in one more traffic jam, see one more TV commercial, get one more unsolicited e-mail, or hear one more co-worker say one more stupid thing you are going to tear your hair out? Then it's time for a tent camping trip. Time to get away from the rush, rush, rush madness of our modern era. And I have the place for you—somewhere that exudes relaxation, somewhere tucked away in the hills of southwestern Wisconsin, that even if you were from the area, you might not even know it was there. It is called Sidie Hollow.

Some destinations are so packed with paths to walk, rivers to float, rail trails to pedal, and natural things to see that you feel compelled to "do" them. This "go there, do that" pressure sometimes kills the relaxing intent of a camping trip. There is no pressure at Sidie Hollow. It is scenic for sure—and you can fish, float your canoe around the lake, and maybe walk in the valley, but all that seems an after-thought to just kicking back and watching the sun move across the sky. Or maybe taking a nap in the lounge chair. This slow-paced Vernon County park outside the town of Viroqua is so relaxed, they give turtles speeding tickets!

Set on the shores of Sidie Hollow Lake, an impoundment of a feeder branch of the South Fork of the Bad Axe River, this campground has three distinct sections.

CAMPGROUND RATINGS

Beauty:	★★★
Site privacy:	★★★
Site spaciousness:	★★★
Quiet:	★★★★★
Security:	★★★
Cleanliness/upkeep:	★★★★

Sidie Hollow is a great "get-away-from-it-all" destination.

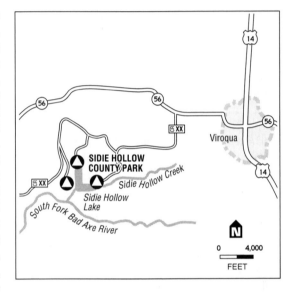

Tall, forested hills add a remote touch to the setting. Coming from Viroqua, leave County Road XX and turn left to reach the first section, at the head of the lake. Sites #1–#3 are set beneath tall trees beside a wooded stream, Sidie Hollow Creek. These are the best sites in this hollow and are great for tent campers. The next 12 sites are along a dead end road and have electricity. The sites away from the creek are sun-whipped. A playground, picnic shelter, water spigot, and vault toilet serve this area better suited for big rigs. The boat launch for this "no gas motors" lake lies near this area.

The second area lies 0.8 mile farther down County XX. This is the largest camping area. A small, clear trout stream forms the hollow. The first sites are banked against hardwood trees by the stream and have a grassy understory. Some sites may get too much sun, but all are well spaced from one another. The campground stretches down the hollow, with sites on both sides of the road. Wooded hills give the clean campground an intimate feel. Mixes of trees shade the grassy tent sites. One section near the office has electrical sites favored by larger rigs.

Pass the campground office and come to a picnic shelter with a nice lake view. To the left of the shelter are four good tent sites that require a short walk from the parking area. Surprisingly, these sites are lesser used, though the campground as a whole has a lightly used look. Water spigots and vault toilets are set in this hollow.

The third area rests on a ridgetop. The left turn, Campsite Road, is four miles after getting on County Road XX. This heavily wooded hilltop camp is much less used than the others. I will personally guarantee this third camp never fills! The 20 shaded sites lie on either side of the road. They are literally cut into a hickory, cherry, oak, and aspen forest and are ideal for the solitude seeker. This area is a getaway from the "get-away-from-it-all" destination that is Sidie Hollow. Water spigot and vault toilets are located up here, too.

Trails leave every camping area and connect to a master path circling Sidie Hollow Lake. You can use this path for bank fishing or to merely stretch your legs. Anglers try their luck for panfish and trout in Sidie Hollow Lake. Others will fish the small creeks feeding Sidie Hollow Lake. Supplies can be had in nearby Viroqua. My advice to you is get everything you need, set up camp, and go into relaxation mode. We could all use more of that.

KEY INFORMATION

Sidie Hollow
220 Airport Road
Viroqua, WI 54665

Operated by: Vernon County Parks Administration

Information: (608) 637-7335

Open: April 15–October 15

Individual sites: 74

Each site has: Picnic table, fire grate

Site assignment: First come, first served, no reservation

Registration: At camp office

Facilities: Water spigots, vault toilets

Parking: At campsites only

Fee: $7 per night; $10 per night for sites with electricity

Elevation: 675 feet

Restrictions

Pets—On leash only

Fires—In fire rings only

Alcoholic beverages—At campsites only

Vehicles—None

To **get there:** From downtown Viroqua, take Highway 56 west for 1.7 miles to County Road XX. Turn left on XX and follow it 2.0 miles to a left turn to the first camp area, 2.8 miles to the second camp area, and 4.0 miles to the third camp area, all marked with signs.

7 . *TOWER HILL STATE PARK*

Spring Green

How Tower Hill State Park came to be is mix of location, history, and chance. Lead was discovered in southwestern Wisconsin in the mid-1820s. Sometime later, an entrepreneur from Green Bay named Daniel Whitney hired a fellow to build a shot tower, an operation for making musket balls from lead, near the village of Helena on the banks of the Wisconsin River. The river made transporting the shot quite convenient. The hamlet of Helena grew as a result of the shot tower, but when the tower went out of business in 1864, Helena died. In 1889, a Unitarian minister, Jenkin Lloyd Jones, bought the Helena site for 60 bucks. Jones built some cottages before dying himself in 1918. Four years later, his wife deeded the land to the state of Wisconsin for a park. Today, we have a preserved slice of beauty and history with a good but small campground. You can visit the shot tower, canoe the Lower Wisconsin State Riverway, and enjoy some other nearby attractions.

First the campground. It has vastly different sites for a campground so small. Pass the park office and the remains of a stone barn. The first six campsites split left on an access road to Mill Creek, which immediately flows into the Wisconsin River. The first two sites on the left are mostly grassy, and receive afternoon shade from a line of trees. Across the road is a fine site shaded by pines and maples.

CAMPGROUND RATINGS

Beauty:	★★★★
Site privacy:	★★★
Site spaciousness:	★★★
Quiet:	★★★
Security:	★★★★
Cleanliness/upkeep:	★★★★

This small and quiet campground lies along the banks of the Lower Wisconsin State Riverway.

Another site is situated below it. The best site of this bunch is #3, on the banks of Mill Creek, offering maximum in privacy. A canoe landing lies at the end of this road. A canoe rack is available for campers by the water.

The next group of sites is set along a loop road. A grassy picnic area shaded by trees occupies the middle of the loop. Between the loop and Mill Creek stand two nice sites on a level flat shaded by pines. The next site, #9, is all alone in a grassy area divided by trees. Two vault toilets are across the road from #10, which offers pine needles for a tent spot. Grassy campsite #11 offers a stone fireplace and is also shaded with trees. This was my choice. Campsites #12 and #13 are a bit open in a grassy area. Campsite #14 lies beneath a majestic white pine, but is a bit sloped. Campsite #15 has been leveled, and is a well-shaded walk-up site.

Start your Tower Hill adventure with a visit to the shot tower. Imagine this park through its various transformations as you take the short trail to the tower. Next, you may want to canoe the Lower Wisconsin State Riverway. From nearby Sauk City, the last 93 miles of this river to the Mississippi River are undammed and offer surprisingly natural scenery, as land continues to be purchased along the waterway. The ten-mile canoe run from Arena to nearby Spring Green is popular. The farther you go down the river, the more remote your experience. Several canoe liveries make trips easy, even if you don't have your own canoe. Use their shuttles if you have your own boat. A list of liveries is available at the park office.

Both Mill Creek and the Wisconsin River have quality fishing at normal water levels. Mill Creek can be fished for trout by foot. Return to WI 18 and turn left, then left again on County Road T, and look for the signs indicating the public fishing areas. A hot day will find careful swimmers at Peterson Landing on the Wisconsin River, across the WI 18 bridge toward Spring Green. Watch out for the river, though, it can flow deceptively fast.

Just down the road from Tower Hill is an array of attractions from sophisticated to hoaky. The House on the Rock is an unusual house that has transformed into a display of anything out of the ordinary, from the world's largest carousel to a miniature circus. The Frank Lloyd Wright Visitor Center and his nearby Taliesin house give insight into the architectural genius. Wright described the house and its furnishings as his autobiography. The American Players Theatre offers outdoor Shakespearean plays. Just north of Tower Hill is the town of Spring Green, which has turned into a cultural Mecca from the influence of the Frank Lloyd Wright house. I can't help but wonder what this whole area would be like today if the shot tower hadn't been built on the banks of the Wisconsin River at the confluence of Mill Creek.

To get there: From Spring Green, head south on WI 23, crossing the Wisconsin River after 2 miles. Turn left on County Road C and follow it 1 mile to the park, on your left.

KEY INFORMATION

Tower Hill State Park
5808 C.T.H. C
Spring Green, WI 53588

Operated by: Wisconsin State Parks

Information: (608) 588-2116, www.wiparks.net

Open: May through October

Individual sites: 15

Each site has: Picnic table, fire ring, wood bench

Site assignment: First come, first served, no reservation

Registration: At entrance station

Facilities: Water spigot, vault toilet

Parking: At campsites only

Fee: $7 per night Sunday–Thursday, non-residents $9; $9 per night Friday–Saturday, non-resident $11

Elevation: 450 feet

Restrictions

Pets—Allowed only at campsites #7–#15 and then on leash only

Fires—In fire rings only

Alcoholic beverages—At campsites only

Vehicles—None

Other—21-day stay limit

8. WILDCAT MOUNTAIN STATE PARK

Ontario

The campground at this state park is really on top of a mountain. The view from the observation area will attest to that. Furthermore, the lack of water up top makes it one of the least buggy campgrounds in the state. Remember that when you are enjoying the mountain breezes in your folding chair while others are pouring on the bug dope and diving headlong into their tents. However, odds are you will be engaging in the many activities here—hiking the steep and challenging trails, canoeing the famed Kickapoo River, or bicycling some of Wisconsin's most famous rail trails.

Enter the campground after chugging uphill from Ontario. The campsite numbering system is a little backwards. You'll first reach a line of campsites, #17–#27, in a grassy flat broken by white pines, sugar maples and other planted trees. Most of the sites are on a level, grassy slope. What they lack in privacy they make up for in spaciousness. The planted trees are far enough along to provide shade for most any tent. Campers drive onto the grassy area to park.

The main road then ends. Turn right and pass four more sites that are even larger than the previous ten sites. The campground host occupies one of these sites. Reach the modern bathhouse with hot showers and water spigots. The loop portion of the campground offers an entirely different setting. The sites, #1–#13, are perched on the cusp of Wildcat Mountain.

CAMPGROUND RATINGS

Beauty:	★★★
Site privacy:	★★★
Site spaciousness:	★★★★
Quiet:	★★★★
Security:	★★★
Cleanliness/upkeep:	★★★★★

Wildcat Mountain is an active camper's destination.

Trees mostly block views, but the land dropping off from the campsites has a mountain atmosphere. The sites on the inside of the loop are more open, but the sites on the outside of the loop are mostly shaded and the campground's best. Campsite #1 is all alone. Pass a vault toilet for either sex. Reservation makers coming in blind should consider sites #6, #7, #9, and #11. Pass a set of vault toilets, then reach a mini-loop with a road so narrow that no big rig would dare drive in.

Campsite #14 has a mountain view through the trees. Campsite #16 is on the inside of this mini-loop and is the only site in the park I do not recommend.

Wildcat Mountain will fill on nice summer weekends, so I encourage visitors to make reservations when they decide to come. This place will make you rethink just how appealing this area of the state can be if you didn't already know. The primary draw is the Kickapoo River. A canoe landing is down the mountain in the state park. Several liveries in nearby Ontario make renting a canoe or getting a shuttle easy. The park office has a list of operators. The water is swift enough to make the float fun but do-able by most everyone, and makes unending twists and turns among sandstone cliffs and thick woods.

The hiking trails here will test you. The Hemlock Trail cruises along the Kickapoo River and enters old growth woods before switchbacking up to the top of Mount Pisgah and a great vista. It then drops steeply to the water again. The Old Settlers Trail starts near Observation Point (a must) and goes up and down through hardwood forests, pine woods, small creeks, and past small rock formations. The Ice Cave Trail provides a short walk to the mouth of a rock overhang where a spring makes ice formations in winter. Bicyclers have already heard of the Elroy–Sparta State Trail. This 32-mile rail trail was one of the nation's first. It passes through three tunnels on the way, the longest being 3,810 feet long! Bring your flashlight. The "400" State Trail travels 22 miles between Elroy and Reedsburg, passing small villages along the way. The La Crosse River Trail extends 21 miles across the La Crosse River Valley. The park office and state park website are full of information about these rail trails.

And if that isn't enough to keep you busy, fish Billings Creek, a quality trout stream on Wildcat Mountain and Kickapoo Valley Reserve property. It has some fine brown trout. The Kickapoo Valley Reserve is 8,500 acres of state-owned wilderness adjacent to Wildcat. Hiking and mountain biking trails await in this lower portion of the Kickapoo River valley. Tributaries of the Kickapoo provide more angling opportunities. Grab a reserve map at the Wildcat park office or visit kvr.state.wi.us for more information on Kickapoo Valley Reserve, then head for Wildcat Mountain.

To get there: From Ontario, take Highway 33 two miles south to the park, on your left.

KEY INFORMATION

**Wildcat Mountain State Park
Highway 33 E, Box 99
Ontario, WI 54651**

Operated by: Wisconsin State Parks

Information: (608) 337-4775, www.wiparks.net, reservations (888) WIPARKS, www.reserveamerica.com

Open: Year-round, water and bathhouse open May through October

Individual sites: 30

Each site has: Picnic table, fire ring

Site assignment: By phone, internet, or first come, first served

Registration: At visitor center

Facilities: Hot showers, flush toilets, pit toilets, water spigots

Parking: At campsites only

Fee: Memorial Day weekend through Labor Day weekend Friday–Saturday $10 residents, $12 non-residents; weekdays and all days rest of year $8 residents, $10 non-residents

Parking: At campsites only

Elevation: 1,265 feet

Restrictions

Pets—On leash only

Fires—In fire rings only

Alcoholic beverages—At campsites only

Vehicles—Two vehicles per site

Other—21-day stay limit

9. *WYALUSING STATE PARK*

Prairie du Chien

It is easy to see why Wyalusing was among the first candidates for a state park in Wisconsin. Was it the aboriginal mounds, settler history, or the incredible views of the Mississippi River/Wisconsin River confluence? No matter the actual reason, the reasoning was sound. Wisconsonians should be proud of this trail-laced jewel with two good yet different campgrounds.

Homestead Campground and Wisconsin Ridge Campground offer distinctly different reasons to pitch a tent. The views from Wisconsin Ridge will astound you. Enter a long, narrow loop with a fine bathhouse. The first few sites on the outside of the loop have no view but are heavily shaded with hardwoods and would make a fine tenter's camp. A steep hill drops sharply away from the camps. The inside loop sites have limited views and no privacy. The loop curves past the Knob Picnic Shelter, one of many attractive stone structures built by the Civilian Conservation Corps. The sites with views start with #119. And they are million dollar views. The last 11 sites on this loop are first come, first served. If you reserve a site here, make sure and ask if it is on the outside of the loop with a number higher than #118.

A price is paid for this view. The sites with a view are small and have no privacy. Some have limited shade. But it seems campers are nearly always looking out to the vastness below and beyond. The other

CAMPGROUND RATINGS

Beauty:	★★★★★
Site privacy:	★★★
Site spaciousness:	★★★★
Quiet:	★★★
Security:	★★★★★
Cleanliness/upkeep:	★★★★

Choosing among the two excellent campgrounds is only the first among several win-win decisions here.

---

downside: This camp-
ground and Homestead
Campground are sure to fill
during high summer week-
ends. Consider coming
some early fall weekend or
during the week anytime.

What Homestead Camp-
ground lacks in views, it
makes up in being an all-
around great place to camp,
with its large, grassy campsites well spaced from one
another and broken with
thick brush for maximum
privacy. Fours spur roads
with mini-loops emanate
from a larger center loop.

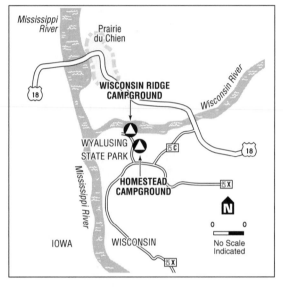

The center loop has a bathhouse, water spigot, and pit toilet. The first spur,
with sites #201–#219, offers a mix of sun and shaded sites beneath pine, oak,
sumac, and cherry trees. Site #211 offers excellent shade and solitude. The second spur is smaller and on a hill. Site #225 also has good shade and solitude.
The third spur, with sites #229–#244, has heavy brush for privacy but limited
shade. The sites at the end of the spur are first come, first served in deep dark
woods. The final spur, with sites #245–#255, features a mix of sun and shaded
sites. The Turkey Hollow Trail leaves from the back of this spur.

The Turkey Hollow Trail is but a portion of 22 total miles of feature-packed
paths at Wyalusing. All the trails are interconnected, so you can start hiking
directly from either campground. Want to see some of the Indian mounds?
Take the Sentinel Ridge Trail, which circles some mounds on the way down to
the Mississippi River and gives added historical information about the
mound builders, voyageurs, Black Robes, and others who passed this way.
The Bluff Trail passes Treasure Cave, Signal Point, and Point Lookout, where
you are sure to get an eyeful. Check out a waterfall and Pictured Rock Cave on

the Sugar Maple Nature Trail. Sand Cave Trail also has a waterfall. Pass through the Keyhole on the Bluff Trail.

The above is just a sampling of the trails. Some paths are open to bicycles, too, so check the comprehensive park trails map. If you don't feel like hiking, how about a canoe trip? A signed six-mile canoe trail circles through sloughs on the Mississippi and then down the mighty river itself. Many watery wild-flowers bloom during summer. A concessionaire rents boats from the nature center, located near Wisconsin Ridge Campground.

Wyalusing is popular with bird watchers. They invade the campgrounds from late April through mid-May. More species can be seen here than any other park in the state. A full-time naturalist leads programs about birds and much more. Call ahead for exact programs and schedules. Anglers will be scouring the backwaters of the Mississippi and Wisconsin rivers for panfish, bass, northern pike, and walleye. A fishing pier is located at the park's boat landing. Hot days will find campers driving two miles south to Wyalusing Recreation Area, a Grant County park that has a swim beach and boat landing on the Mississippi River. Finally, a group called the Starsplitters has installed observatories at the park. They will be glad to introduce you to astronomy—only at night, though. With all the things to do at Wyalusing, choosing your campground doesn't seem quite as difficult.

To get there: From Prairie du Chien, head east on US 18 for 7 miles to cross the Wisconsin River. Turn right on County Road C and follow it for 3 miles to County Road X. Turn right on County Road X and follow it for 1 mile to the state park on your right.

KEY INFORMATION

Wyalusing State Park
13081 State Park Lane
Bagley, WI 53801

Operated by: Wisconsin State Parks

Information: (608) 996-2261, www.wiparks.net, reservations (888) WIPARKS, www.rserveamerica.com

Open: Wisconsin Ridge open year-round; Homestead open May through October

Individual sites: Wisconsin Ridge 54, Homestead 54

Each site has: Picnic table, fire ring; 34 sites also have electricity

Site assignment: By phone, internet, or first come, first served

Registration: At visitor center

Facilities: Hot showers, flush toilets, pit toilets, water spigots

Parking: At campsites only

Fee: Memorial Day weekend through Labor Day weekend Friday–Saturday $10 residents, $12 non-residents; weekdays and all days rest of year $8 residents, $10 non-residents; $3 extra for electricity

Elevation: 1,100 feet

Restrictions

Pets—On leash only

Fires—In fire rings only

Alcoholic beverages—At campsites only

Vehicles—None

Other—21-day stay limit

CENTRAL
WISCONSIN

10. *BUCKHORN STATE PARK*

New Lisbon

Buckhorn is an evolving park in a wild area that keeps improving over time. For starters, it has "backpack" campsites. I call them "extended walk-in" sites. These walk-in sites range from under 100 feet from car to campsite to over a mile to the camp. However, don't mark this park off your list because you don't have a backpack; Buckhorn provides carts to carry your gear from the parking area to the campsite (you still have to walk, though). There is also another option. Since these sites are on the shores of Castle Rock Lake, you can "boat-in" your gear! If you are still not convinced this park is for you, Buckhorn does have some conventional drive-up campsites. Wherever you choose to camp, you can enjoy the wilderness surrounding Wisconsin's fourth largest lake.

The sites at Buckhorn are located in five clusters (six if you count the groupcamping area) that are spread throughout the peninsula-shaped park. Campsites are numbered but do not follow any numerical order. Starting in the northeast section and going around the peninsula in a clockwise fashion, the first cluster includes sites #1–#3, located just off 22nd Avenue. The name belies the gravel road's true rustic nature. These sites are mostly wooded and share a small sandy beach ideal for kids. About 100 yards south is the second cluster. Also located just off 22nd Avenue, campsites #20–#22 have lake access.

CAMPGROUND RATINGS

Beauty: ★★★★★
Site privacy: ★★★★
Site spaciousness: ★★★★★
Quiet: ★★★
Security: ★★★★
Cleanliness/upkeep: ★★★★

*Most of the camps here
are lakeside walk-in sites!*

Skipping past the seven-site group camp, the next cluster encountered is located on the southwest side of the peninsula—sites #4–#7, #13–#15, and #17–#19. Campsites #4–#7 sit on a small peninsula overlooking the lake and require a mile walk, but they are worth the effort. Of special note is #6, located on a lakefront point beneath a stand of white pines. Campsite #7 is for solitude lovers. Campsites #13–#15 are set in heavier woods along the shore and also require a one-mile walk. Campsites #17–#19 are the farthest—1.25 miles—and are often reached by boat.

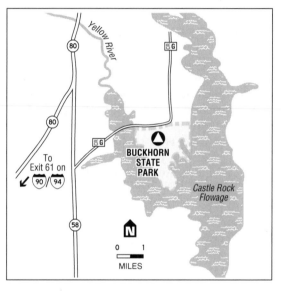

Continuing north around the peninsula, you'll find the fourth cluster: #8–#12, #16, and #23–#25. Campsites #8, #9, #16 have a very short walk—#8 even has a paved path to the site for disabled campers. Campsites #10–#12 and #25 are set on an open peninsula after a 200-yard walk. Shade is scarce here, but a small wood shelter keeps campers out of the elements. Campsites #23–#24 share a lightly wooded point with a great lake view. The final cluster includes campsites #26–#29. Campsite #26 is a short walk-in site. The other three are drive-up sites shaded by river birch trees.

Each campsite cluster has a portable toilet within an easy walk. Water can be had at the main "backpack" parking area and park office. Showers can be had outside the park for a fee; check at the park office for location and directions. Be advised that late spring and early summer can be buggy at Buckhorn. Call ahead for the latest mosquito report. Bugs or not, these sites will fill on summer weekends. No wonder—these are some of the best tent campsites in the state. The lakeside setting is simply beautiful. Most campers set up and enjoy the park from their little havens. Fishing and boating are just steps away. Castle Rock Flowage, as this dammed reservoir on the Wisconsin River is also known, is famous for its walleye fishing. But that is only the beginning. Try your luck with bass (largemouth and smallmouth), plus toothy pike and panfish. Bank-fish from your campsite or use the pier at the North Picnic Area. Whether you are on your feet or in a motorboat or canoe, the angling is quite scenic here.

Canoeists have an additional venue to stroke their paddle—the Canoe Interpretive Trail. This marked route plies one of the many sloughs that make up the park. And if you don't have a canoe, the park will be glad to rent you one at the start of the paddle trail. They will also loan you a fishing rod free of charge. If you are into games, borrow a volleyball for use at the court near the 300-foot-long swim beach, or borrow some horseshoes.

Campers will quickly learn the trails here—they are used to access the campsites. I walked them all on my visit. Learn about the sands of the central state on the Nature Trail. Traverse wetlands on wood bridges. A hiker is just about guaranteed to see deer and turkeys here. Check out the short Sandblow Walk. Just don't let the lack of a backpack keep you from tent camping at Buckhorn.

To get there: From Exit 61 on I-90/94, take Highway 80 north for 7 miles to Highway 58. Turn right on 58 and follow it 3 miles to County Road G. Turn left on County Road G and follow it 3 miles to Buckhorn, on your right.

KEY INFORMATION

Buckhorn State Park
W8450 Buckhorn Park Avenue Necedah, WI 54646

Operated by: Wisconsin State Parks

Information: (608) 565-2789, www.wiparks.net, reservations (888) WIPARKS, www.reserveamerica.com

Open: May through October, 3 sites open year-round

Individual sites: 36

Each site has: Picnic table, fire grate, lantern post, wood bench

Site assignment: By phone, Internet, or first come, first served

Registration: At park office or self-registration if office is closed

Facilities: Pump well, vault toilet, carts for toting gear to campsites

Parking: At campsites and walk-in site parking

Fee: Memorial Day weekend through Labor Day weekend Friday–Saturday $10 residents, $12 non-residents; summer weekdays and all days rest of year, $8 residents, $10 non-residents

Elevation: 885 feet

Restrictions

Pets—On leash only

Fires—In fire rings only

Alcoholic beverages—At campsites only

Vehicles—None

Other—21-day stay limit

11. *COUNCIL GROUNDS STATE PARK*

Merrill

Council Grounds State Park lies on a bend of the upper Wisconsin River just outside the town of Merrill. The park is so close to Merrill that it exudes a suburban park atmosphere. The ground upon which Council Grounds lies was actually a city park before Merrill deeded the land over to the state of Wisconsin in 1978. Most suburban parks can't make the cut in this book, but Council Grounds offers a shady and attractive campground with complementary lake and riverside natural offerings along the banks of the Wisconsin River. Showers and instant access to town make a tent-camping adventure to Council Grounds a "light" version of roughing it. Solitude seekers will camp elsewhere—Council Grounds has that busy feel. Families and sociable campers will enjoy the hustle and bustle of this park.

The campground is laid out in a long oval near the Wisconsin River. The forest overhead offers is a thick agglomeration of evergreens that give a North Woods ambience to the campground, though technically the Merrill area lies in what may be called the "tension zone," an area where tree and plant species of southern Wisconsin and the North Woods meet and mingle. In some areas of this campground, the evergreens grow so densely as to keep understory plants from thriving. Here, the trunks of the conifers themselves give campsite privacy. Most of the campsites

CAMPGROUND RATINGS

Beauty:	★★★
Site privacy:	★★★
Site spaciousness:	★★★
Quiet:	★★★
Security:	★★★★
Cleanliness/upkeep:	★★★★

This busy park offers a shady campground to beat the summer heat.

are adequately spaced from one another, and shade can be found at most. Nineteen of the 55 campsites have electricity; they are all on the inside of the loop and are the first to go.

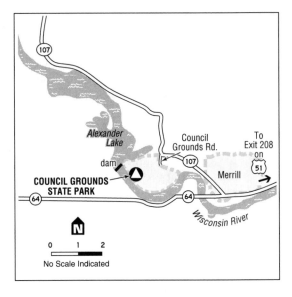

After entering the campground areas, travel right around the loop, passing the first few sites, which are non-reservable. A campground host at one of these sites makes everyone's stay better. The shower building is near campsite #4. The small Kienitz Nature Center is located just past campsite #15. The loop curves around toward the Wisconsin River past campsite #28. The river is visible downhill through the trees. The sites toward the river on the outside of the loop are very popular, but they do not have direct access to the river. The campsites here are also very shady. Recommended reservable campsites include #15, #19, #25, #33, #37, #39, #41, and #51.

Merrill is an ideal location for a summertime respite, so reserve a site well in advance here. The campground is cool, dark, and shady, and watery recreation opportunities are immediately accessible The park swim beach is busy with campers and day-use visitors. A boat launch makes tooling around Lake Alexander—an impoundment of the Wisconsin River—an easy proposition. Folks engage in all manner of water sports here. There is even a water ski take-out and drop-off area near the swim beach. An all-access fishing pier makes angling fun for kids and those with disabilities. Northern pike is the primary game species, with walleye, smallmouth bass, and panfish following behind.

Council Grounds, purportedly the site of Ojibwe Indian gatherings, has its quiet, natural side, too. The Big Pines Nature Trail offers a loop hike with interpretive information. More trails pass through the Krueger Pines Natural Area. The Fitness Trail makes a loop of its own. Other folks like to walk the main park road, especially during winter when the gates are closed. Kids and adults on bikes can pedal along the road during the warm season. Canoers often start below the Alexander Lake dam and float the Wisconsin River, which offers some rapids. From Memorial Day to Labor Day, campers can conveniently convene at the Kienitz Nature Center located in the campground and enjoy programs about the park's wild side every Friday and Saturday. Visits to nearby Merrill for supply runs and more activities are a pleasant advantage for this suburban park.

To get there: From Exit 208 on US 51, take WI 64 west for 3 miles, passing through the town of Merrill to WI 107. Take WI 107 north for 1.8 miles to Council Grounds Road. Turn left on Council Grounds Road and follow it a short distance to enter the park.

KEY INFORMATION

**Council Grounds State Park
N1895 Council Grounds Drive
Merrill, WI 54452-8704**

Operated by: Wisconsin State Parks

Information: (715) 536-8773, www.wiparks.net; reservations (888) WIPARKS, www.reserveamerica.com

Open: May through October

Individual sites: 55

Each site has: Picnic table, fire grate, 19 also have electricity

Site assignment: By phone, internet, or first come, first served

Registration: At visitor center

Facilities: Hot showers, flush toilets, pit toilets, water spigots

Parking: At campsites only

Fee: Memorial Day weekend through Labor Day weekend Friday–Saturday $10 residents, $12 non-residents; summer weekdays and all days rest of year $8 residents, $10 non-residents; $3 extra for electricity

Elevation: 1,300 feet

Restrictions

Pets—On leash only

Fires—In fire rings only

Alcoholic beverages—At campsites only

Vehicles—One wheeled camping unit per site

Other—21-day stay limit

12. DELLS OF EAU CLAIRE COUNTY PARK

Wausau

All Wisconsinites should see the Dells of Eau Claire. After all, the state deemed them significant enough to be preserved as a state natural area. The park's name might confuse folks trying to locate it. This is not "the Dells" that are so well-known in Wisconsin; those Dells are located on the Wisconsin River and are surrounded by tourist traps. No, the Dells of Eau Claire are located on the Eau Claire River, just east of Wausau in Marathon County, which operates the campground, trails, and swim beach. The name "Eau Claire" can also add to the confusion—there is an Eau Claire County, the city of Eau Claire, and three Eau Claire rivers in Wisconsin. Regardless of the confusion, visiting this park is well worth your time. Visitors will see amazing rock formations surrounded by cascading water and unusual plants. This recreational development has enhanced the work of Mother Nature, making these dells easier for tent campers to enjoy.

I don't want to mislead you—the natural landscape is the star of the show here. It was two million years in the making. The campground works, but it is no destination unto itself. It—like the rest of the park—is well kept, neat, and in good shape. Enter the campground, which is laid out in a loop. Pass the telephone, pump well, and vault toilets. The first 16 sites are equipped with electricity and are

CAMPGROUND RATINGS

Beauty: ★★★
Site privacy: ★★★
Site spaciousness: ★★★
Quiet: ★★★
Security: ★★★★
Cleanliness/upkeep: ★★★★★

These dells deserve their designation as a state natural area.

reservable. These smallish sites may contain pop-ups, but not a whole lot of big rigs will fit in. The first few sites on the inside of the loop are surrounded by forest but are open overhead where a telephone line cuts through the campground. The good sites begin with #8. If you want to reserve a site, go with #8, #9, or #10.

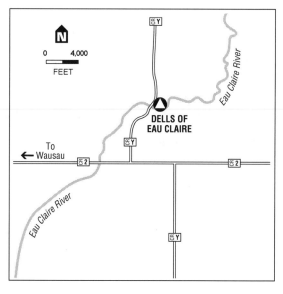

The loop curves around, and the sites become shaded and private. Grass and/or sand covers the campsite floors. Sites from #16–#26 are first come, first served and are as good and generally better than the reservable sites. However, this campground fills on holidays and nice summer weekends. The park manager lives on the premises during the camping season, enhancing campsite security, which can be questionable at some county parks.

Like much of the Wisconsin landscape, the dells themselves are of glacial origin. The frothy waters of the Eau Claire crash, twist, and work their way among broken boulders, outcrops, crags, and step-like platforms, forming waterfalls and cascades. Visitors hopping from rock to rock near the river will also notice "potholes," smooth depressions carved into the rock back when the glaciers were melting. Rock-hopping isn't the only thing you can do on your feet here. A network of interconnected trails has been laid out in this geologically significant valley. The High Bridge downstream from the Dells of Eau Claire enables hikers to make a loop through rich fern woods along both sides of the river. The forest's dark "fairyland" nature contrasts with rocky dells open to the sky overhead. The high ground is covered in pine. Even a short section of the Ice Age Trail passes through the Dells of Eau Claire. The entire trail network can be accessed directly from the campground.

One trail leads from the campground to the picnic area/swim beach on the banks of the Eau Claire River above the dells. A grassy lawn with both sun and shade stands above steps leading down to the beach. Changing rooms are conveniently close. The park urges campers to dip at the swim beach and not take their chances in the swiftly moving waters near the dells.

Another picnic area features a large playground for kids near some rustic-looking open-sided shelters. As you look around, you will agree this park is so well maintained that Marathon County should receive kudos. Remember, the natural scenery here outstrips any shortcomings the campground may have. So put the Dells of Eau Claire on your "must do" list of natural Wisconsin, now that you know where they are.

To get there: From downtown Wausau, take Franklin Street east and stay with it as it becomes County Road Z. Follow Franklin Street/County Road Z for 14.5 miles to County Road Y. Turn left on County Road Y and follow it for 1.7 miles to the park.

KEY INFORMATION

Dells of Eau Claire County Park
County Courthouse
500 Forest Street
Wausau, WI 54403

Operated by: Marathon County

Information: (715) 261-1550, reservations (715) 261-1566 between 9 a.m. and 3 p.m.

Open: May through October

Individual sites: 26

Each site has: Picnic table, fire grate, 16 have electricity

Site assignment: By reservation and first come, first served

Registration: Park manager will come by and register you; self-registration before Memorial Day and after Labor Day

Facilities: Pump well, vault toilets

Parking: At campsites only

Fee: $9 per night, $3 electricity

Elevation: 1,300 feet

Restrictions

Pets—On leash only

Fires—In fire rings only

Alcoholic beverages—At campsites only

Vehicles—None

Other—21-day stay limit between June 1 and Labor Day

13 . *EAST FORK*

Black River Fall

The timber wolf has returned to the forests of the Black River in Jackson County. So should you, especially with a campground as nice as East Fork, set on the banks of East Fork Black River. From here, you can explore some 67,000 acres of the Black River State Forest, which offers everything from excellent canoeing and fishing to hiking and wildlife-watching.

The timber wolf was extirpated from Wisconsin in the late 1950s, about when Black River State Forest was established. Since then, things have really looked up for both the timber wolf and the state forest. The wolves have returned. You may even hear the call of a pack of wolves roaming the Black from your campsite on the East Fork Black River.

Reach the convenient campground canoe ramp at the end of Campground Road, then turn into the campground, which lies along a road paralleling the beautiful East Fork to your left and a marsh to your right. Pass a vault toilet for each gender and a firewood shed. A mix of sugar maple, red pine, white pine, oak, and scattered birch trees shade the campground. Younger trees, brush, and ferns galore provide privacy. The sites themselves are sand and mown grass. Pass by a pump well; another pump well is located about 0.25 mile back on Campground Road.

Most of the sites on the left-hand side of the road offer river views and river access,

CAMPGROUND RATINGS

Beauty: ★★★★★
Site privacy: ★★★★
Site spaciousness: ★★★★★
Quiet: ★★★★
Security: ★★★
Cleanliness/upkeep: ★★★★

East Fork is your base camp for exploring the north side of the Black River State Forest.

at least enough to grab a view or toss in a line. The sites away from the river are less used and offer more privacy. But don't get the idea this is a used and abused campground—no way. It is clean, well kept, and naturally beautiful. A mini-loop at the end of the campground road has three sites, of which the most private is #23. A short nature trail departs up the East Fork from the end of the loop.

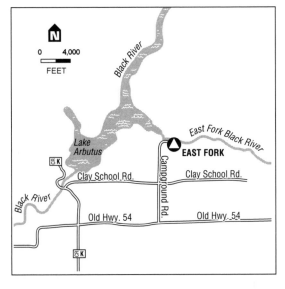

This is a first come, first served campground, and you will almost certainly be served—even someone arriving late Friday on a holiday weekend will most likely get a site. I was the only person there during my weekday visit. But, just like the timber wolf, once you come here, you will return. The timber wolf returned to Wisconsin around the late 1980s, a result of timber wolf protection in neighboring Minnesota during the early 1970s, which led to offspring expanding their range. The first wolves were spotted in the Black River State Forest in 1994. Don't expect to see one, but just knowing they are there gives a little extra verve to the forest.

You can expect to enjoy canoeing the East Fork Black River with its mild rapids. The stream has good fishing for bass and walleye. A popular excursion starts from Pray Road and meanders to the campground landing—a trip of about 10 miles. Shorter runs can be made from Waterbury Road or East Fork Road to the campground landing. You can also canoe down from the campground to East Arbutus County Park, on Lake Arbutus. This county park also has a swim beach. The Black River below Lake Arbutus is good for canoeing, but check ahead about water releases from Lake Arbutus. The forest also has numerous lakes for paddling and fishing. Of special note is the Dike 17 Wildlife Area, which is managed for waterfowl. Ducks, geese, and sandhill cranes can be seen from the observation tower. The Wildcat hiking trails are in the south end of the forest. You may not even mind the drive there since so much of the Black River State Forest is primitive and scenic. If you are very, very, very lucky, you may even see a timber wolf.

To get there: From Black River Falls, drive east on Highway 54 for 5 miles to County Road K. Turn left on County Road K and follow it for 5.1 miles to Old Highway 54. Turn right on Old Highway 54 and follow it 2 miles to Campground Road. Veer left and follow Campground Road for 2 miles to dead end at East Fork.

14. HARSTAD COUNTY PARK

Fall Creek

By the time I chugged into Harstad Park, the temperature had soared into the 90s. The noon sun was blaring overhead. The only things moving were a few lazy mosquitoes. Sweat poured off me as I set up camp. It was time for a dip in the Eau Claire River, so I walked down to the riverside canoe landing. Bridge Creek flowed shallow into the deep, dark waters of the Eau Claire, forming a large tan sand bar. My toes squished in the sand as I tore off my shirt and splashed into the river. What relief! I spent much of the afternoon on the sand bar, reading beneath a river birch and taking a swim while ol' Sol cranked out the rays.

Harstad Park is definitely an overlooked destination. The amenities aren't immediately obvious on first arrival. While other parks might have a buoyed swim beach with a groomed, grassy lawn for swimmers, Harstad Park has a sandbar at the confluence of Bridge Creek and the Eau Claire River. Instead of a fishing pier, anglers fish from the bank and the canoe landing. This is a place to visit for the simple and rustic pleasure of the outdoors.

The park doesn't harbor any unique physical formations, but the campground lies in an attractive forest. As you enter the campground loop, you'll notice widely branched oaks complemented by jack pines growing over a thick understory. White pine and cherry trees also thrive here. Grass

CAMPGROUND RATINGS

Beauty:	★★★
Site privacy:	★★★★
Site spaciousness:	★★★★★
Quiet:	★★★★
Security:	★★★
Cleanliness/upkeep:	★★★

This out-of-the-way park is on the Eau Claire River, a quality canoeing destination.

generally covers the camp-sites. Some campsites have concrete benches, others have wood benches. The metal fire rings are dug into the ground. Campsites #1–#5 are very large but open to the noonday sun. Ascend a rise, then loop past the wood lot and recycling station. The campground signboard has information on canoe put-ins and take-outs. The next set of sites are large, too, and even more open to the sun. The openness reveals the bluff upon which the campground rests. However, no campsites

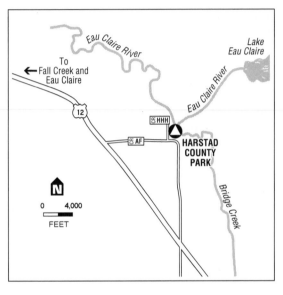

offer river views. The oaks crowd in and shade all the campsites from #20–#27.

Harstad Park, on the eastern edge of Eau Claire County, is virtually unused during the week, but it can get busy on nice-weather weekends. The pump well is deep, and it can take a little while to get water. Be patient as you pump. Grassy spur trails cut through the center of the woods leading to two vault toilets.

The park land was donated to Eau Claire County back in 1927 by a fellow named Ole Harstad. The Eau Claire River borders Harstad's land, making this a canoer's park. Much of the Eau Claire here runs through Eau Claire County Forest, giving the river a real wilderness feel. Occasional shoals and rocky rapids add another touch to the paddle. It is but two miles from the outflow of Lake Eau Claire to Harstad Park. Many paddlers make the six-mile run down the Eau Claire from Harstad Park to Big Falls County Park. Big Falls is the most scenic feature of the river, as it descends 15 feet over granite ledges. Do not try to canoe Big Falls! Instead, use the established portage trail. A second day trip runs from Big Falls down to Altoona Lake Park.

At Harstad Park, a groomed day-use area overlooks a noisy river rapid, adding an audible feature to the park. The day-use area houses a large shelter with picnic tables that could be a dry campers' refuge on a rainy day. A horseshoe pit, sandy volleyball court, and playground complement the shelter. If you are looking for more organized action, head to Coon Fork County Park, eight miles east of Harstad, on County Road 12. Turn left on County Road CF, and follow CF to this 80-acre lake with a swim beach, bike trail, fishing pier, and too-busy campground. The park rents paddleboats, rowboats, and canoes on this "no gas motors" impoundment. Anglers fish here for muskellunge, walleye, and smallmouth bass. Though fishing wasn't on the agenda during my visit, the Eau Claire River was a pleasure, especially on that hot day. Hopefully it won't be quite so hot during your visit to Harstad Park.

KEY INFORMATION

Harstad County Park
227 1st Street West
Altoona, WI 54720

Operated by: Eau Claire County Parks and Forests Department

Information: (715) 839-4738

Open: May 15 through September 15

Individual sites: 27

Each site has: Picnic table, fire ring, bench

Site assignment: First come, first served, no reservation

Registration: Self-registration on site

Facilities: Pump well, vault toilet

Parking: At campsites only

Fee: $7 per night, $35 per week

Elevation: 925 feet

Restrictions

Pets—On leash only

Fires—In fire rings only

Alcoholic beverages—At campsites only

Vehicles—No more than two vehicles per site

Other—14-day stay limit

To get there: From Fall Creek, 9 miles east of Eau Claire, drive east on Highway 12 for 4.3 miles to County Road AF. Turn left on AF and follow it 1.6 miles to County Road HHH. Turn left on County Road HHH and follow it for 0.3 mile to the county park, on your right.

15. HARTMAN CREEK STATE PARK

Waupaca

If you want to pass on the tent camping tradition to your kids, other family members, or friends, take them to Hartman Creek State Park. Camping here is sure to be good with myriad attractive sites. The campground has showers to break in those less used to roughing it in the great outdoors. And this state park has great outdoor activities—hiking trails, biking trails, and five lakes for your enjoyment. The fishing is good and suitable for both kids and adults. So do a little sweet-talking to the reluctant ones close to you, and after coming to Hartman Creek, they may be the ones urging you to tent camp next time!

The campground is situated along the south side of Allen Lake, an impoundment of Hartman Creek. The campground is laid out in a classic loop with two spur roads. Nearly all the campsites are large, and privacy can be found in the occasional areas of hardwoods (actually remnants of an old apple orchard) amid towering white and red pines over a floor sprinkled with needles. The first 22 sites of the camping area are first come, first served. Campsites #1–#16 are in pines with some brushy understory. You'll hit an area of deciduous trees before nearing Allen Lake. Campsites #22, #25, and #28 have lake views from the elevated flat. The loop swings around and climbs a little, staying in the pine zone. The piney sites are preferred though campsite privacy is often limited.

CAMPGROUND RATINGS

Beauty:	★★★★
Site privacy:	★★★
Site spaciousness:	★★★★
Quiet:	★★★★
Security:	★★★★
Cleanliness/upkeep:	★★★★

This attractive family campground moves as slow as a summer day.

Here, the two cross roads lead left to bisect the loop. The first cross road leads to sites #75–#87. The first few sites in this section are in pines, and the rest are in hardwoods for privacy seekers. These sites are also close to the Orchard Shower Building. The second cross road contains sites #88–#100. Thick underbrush in sites #95–#100 gives privacy, but the sites are open to the sun overhead.

The main loop continues around to reach sites #39–#74. Most of these are in the pines. Some sites on the outside of the loop are backed against a hill. The Pine Shower Building is located near campsite #44, as is the campground host. Campsites #54–#64 are underneath the hardwoods. The last ten sites are open under the pines.

Hartman Creek will fill on nice summer weekends. However, campsites #22–#100 are reservable. So call ahead and start relaxing early.

The park is blessed with numerous lakes. Allen Lake, near the campground, is fun for kids and adults for catching panfish and bass. The Deer Path Trail circles the lake, making for easy access. A fishing pier makes angling even easier. Hartman Lake has a 300-foot swim beach with a grassy shoreline and shaded areas, too. Marl Lake, Pope Lake, and Manomin Lake can be accessed from the Whispering Pines Picnic Area.

The Ice Age Trail, Wisconsin's premier long-distance path, makes part of its extended trek through Hartman Creek. Four miles of the trail pass directly through the park. Faraway Valley, along Emmons Creek just south of the park, is especially scenic. The trail keeps on for nine miles north beyond the park border. However, there are plenty of trails inside the park. You can make a near loop on the Dike Trail. Mountain bikers and hikers share the Glacial Bike Loop and the Windfelt Trail. The Oak Ridge Trail is for hikers only. The Pope Lake Trail makes a one-mile loop through the pines.

All of the above are only suggested activities. You may just want to tool around the campground on your bike or pedal the park roads. Better yet, you may want to sit around the fire and pass on those all-important fishing tips to the next generation. After a few adventures at Hartman Lake, they will be carrying on the tent-camping tradition at this fine state park.

To get there: From Waupaca and the junction of US 10 and Highway 54, take Highway 54 west for 4.4 miles to Hartman Creek Road. Turn left on Hartman Creek Road and drive 2 miles to enter the park.

KEY INFORMATION

**Hartman Creek State Park
N2480 Hartman Creek Road
Waupaca, WI 54981**

Operated by: Wisconsin State Parks

Information: (715) 258-2372, www.wiparks.net, reservations (888) WIPARKS, www.reserveamerica.com

Open: Year-round; bathhouse and water available May–October

Individual sites: 100, plus 1 tipi

Each site has: Picnic table, fire grate

Site assignment: By phone, internet, or first come, first served

Registration: At entrance station

Facilities: Hot showers, flush toilets, pit toilets, water spigots

Parking: At campsites only

Fee: Memorial Day weekend through Labor Day weekend Friday–Saturday $10 residents, $12 non-residents; weekdays and all days rest of year $8 residents, $10 non-residents; tipi $25 per night

Elevation: 925 feet

Restrictions

Pets—On leash only

Fires—In fire rings only

Alcoholic beverages—At campsites only

Vehicles—Maximum 2 vehicles per site

Other—21-day stay limit

16. *LAKE WISSOTA STATE PARK*

Chippewa Falls

Lake Wissota State Park is close to the city of Chippewa Falls—too close I feared, before coming to check it out. But after overnighting here, I came to appreciate its rustic nature despite its proximity to town. On the shores of big Lake Wissota, the park offers the watery recreation associated with a big lake, yet also has lots of trails for hikers and mountain bikers in a restored prairie. The campground is heavily wooded and well kept and offers a great natural respite for tent campers, including those from Chippewa Falls and Eau Claire. It's a good sign when locals use a campground just minutes from home.

The campground is set on a bluff well above Lake Wissota and is divided into two loops. The first loop contains sites #1–#41. A campground host fronts the first loop. Basswood, white pines, maple, and oaks loom overhead. Thick brush not only divides the sites but often runs along the paved campground road, adding extra privacy. The electric sites are on the inside of both loops (it was easier to run the electric line without crossing the paved campground road). Some recommended reservable sites here include #11, #15, #17, #19, and #40. Campsites closest to the lake start with #24. You can sense the lake's presence, but thick woods prevent lake views. Also, the Lake Trail runs between the campsites and the edge of the bluff.

CAMPGROUND RATINGS

Beauty: ★★★
Site privacy: ★★★★
Site spaciousness: ★★★
Quiet: ★★
Security: ★★★★★
Cleanliness/upkeep: ★★★

You will be surprised at the combination of developed and rustic recreation opportunities here.

A field and playground with a shelter nearby lie between the two loops. The second loop holds campsites #42–#81. The first few sites are a little too open, but the woods thicken as you near the lake. Recommended reservable campsites are #57, #60, #61, and #68. Beyond #61, the loop enters a red pine plantation. It offers very large sites with pine needles for a floor, but there's no campsite privacy due to a lack of understory brush. Lake Wissota is a busy park during the summer. Reservations are recommended on weekends. Campsites #10–#81 are reservable.

Water is the star of the show here. Boaters of all stripes use the park. Campers and day users flock to the large swim beach, located on an arm of 6,300-acre Lake Wissota. A picnic area and bathhouse are located at the beach. Also near here is a boat landing that can accommodate most any boat a camper would bring. Canoes are for rent in case you are boatless. A fishing pier enables shore anglers to try their luck, along with a few other access points scattered throughout the park. Anglers most often go for walleye and smallmouth bass here, but muskie, pike, largemouth bass, panfish, and catfish are also caught.

If you are only going to hike one trail here, take the one-mile Beaver Meadow Nature Trail. I enjoyed this path that travels through a marsh and offers interpretive information along the way. Most campers like the Lake Trail, since it runs directly on the bluff overlooking Lake Wissota and connects to the campground. The Staghorn Trail is two miles long, and like the three previous trails, is hiker-only. Mountain bikers have many other paths available (11 miles worth) that are also open to hikers and horses. The terrain is mostly level, but the prairie and woods scenery will keep your eyes plenty busy, instead of looking down for roots and rocks. Bikers also ply park roads and the paved campground loops.

If the trails of Wissota State Park aren't enough for you, try out the Old Abe State Trail. This 20-mile paved rail trail runs north to reach Brunet Island State Park, also included in this book (campground #27). People like to hike, bike, and even inline-skate this path that runs through agricultural and forest land beside the Chippewa River. To reach the southern terminus of the Old Abe Trail, turn left from the park onto County Road O, and follow it for two miles to the trailhead at the intersection of County Road O and County Road S. You can just bike from the park, since County O was widened to enable bike access from the park. With the town of Chippewa Falls so near, why not take advantage of it? Supplies are close by, and you might consider touring the Leinenkugal Brewery. Wisconsin's most notable label has been brewing beer since 1878.

To get there: From downtown Chippewa Falls, take Highway 178 east for 3 miles to County Road S. Turn right on County Road S and follow it for 2.2 miles to County Road O. Turn right on County Road O and follow it for 2 miles to the park, on your right.

KEY INFORMATION

Lake Wissota State Park
18127 County Highway O
Chippewa Falls, WI 54729

Operated by: Wisconsin State Parks

Information: (715) 382-4574, www.wiparks.net, reservations (888)WIPARKS, www.reserveamerica.com

Open: Year-round, water on from last frost of spring to first frost of fall

Individual sites: 81

Each site has: Picnic table, fire ring, 17 also have electricity

Site assignment: By phone, Internet, or first come, first served

Registration: At visitor center

Facilities: Hot showers, flush toilets, pit toilets, water spigots

Parking: At campsites only

Fee: Memorial Day weekend through Labor Day weekend Friday–Saturday $10 residents, $12 non-residents; summer weekdays and all days rest of year $8 residents, $10 non-residents; $3 extra for electricity

Elevation: 950 feet

Restrictions

Pets—On leash only

Fires—In fire rings only

Alcoholic beverages—At campsites only

Vehicles—None

Other—21-day stay limit

17. PEROT STATE PARK

Trempealeau

The land upon which Perrot State Park lies has been popular for a long, long time. This upper–Mississippi River valley area of bluffs, thick forests, deep valleys, and flowing waters was first occupied by mound-building ancients as far back as 7,000 years ago. Later, French voyageur Nicholas Perrot made a winter camp here in 1685 while building trade with the Dakota and Iowa tribes. In 1731, a French fort was built on this very site. Fast forward to 1927, when the scenic spot was taken over by the state of Wisconsin and built into a park that offers land- and water-based recreation, as well as a quality spot to pitch your tent.

The campground matches the park's natural beauty. It offers both electric and non-electric sties on hilly terrain. Tent campers should know that the electric areas are generally congregated together, keeping the big rigs separate from the good campsites. Enter the campground and immediately reach the main electric loop (sites #1–#23). These sites are well spaced apart but are usually filled with RVs. Fear not; drive right and reach a spur road heading left to access the loop with campsites #51–#86. This spur road bisects the loop and has the best sites (#51–#59). Hilly terrain and heavy vegetation offer private sites beneath a shady hardwood forest. Campsites #61–#69 offer a mix of sun and shade in pines, sumac, and hickory. The sites are

CAMPGROUND RATINGS

Beauty: ★★★
Site privacy: ★★★
Site spaciousness: ★★★★
Quiet: ★★★★
Security: ★★★
Cleanliness/upkeep: ★★★★

Enjoy both hilly and watery environments at this state park.

well separated. Campsites #70–#86 start out with too much sun but them become completely shaded after campsite #75.

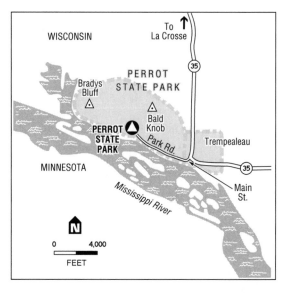

If you head left instead of right at the main electric loop, you'll come to sites #30–#50. Of these, #36–#48 are the most coveted in all the park, as they offer a view of Trempealeau Bay in an ever-expanding woodland (#40, #42, #46, and #48 are opposite the road from the water). Beyond here is a mini-loop with several sites: #24–#27 are on a small mini-loop and are too sloped for a good night's sleep; #28–#29 are electric and should be bypassed A final area houses the "upper sites" which number from #87–#95 and are second in demand to those on Trempealeau Bay. These sites are widespread, like the entire campground, and shaded by white pines. The Great River State Trail comes in near here.

Perrot will fill on most Saturday nights during summer. You can generally squeeze in on Friday night, save for holiday weekends. I suggest eliminating the worry and calling ahead, since all sites are reservable. Water, showers and toilets are spread throughout the campground.

Hiking is popular here. Seven miles of hiking paths cruise along the river and to heights such as Brady's Bluff, where you can gain a good view of your camping paradise. Another view can be had on Perrot Ridge. The Black Walnut Nature Trail makes its loop near rock formations and in deep woods. For a lower, more watery perspective, take the 2.5-mile Riverview Trail. Seven miles of other trails are open to mountain bikers and hikers. The main path starts near park headquarters and makes several smaller loops before returning to the park office. The major attraction for bikers is the Great River State Trail. This 24-mile rail trail starts in North La Crosse and travels through the upper Mississippi River valley amid prairie and bottomland. The trail traverses 20 bridges, including the 287-foot trestle over the Black River. It also passes by some Hopewell Indian mounds before entering the Upper Mississippi Wildlife Refuge, home to eagles. Perrot State Park offers a spur path connecting to the Great River State Trail directly from the campground.

Other attractions include canoeing Trempealeau Bay. The Voyageurs Canoe Trail starts at the park canoe launch and makes a 3.4-mile loop around the bay, offering great views of Trempealeau Mountain. The French word "trempealeau" roughly translates to "mountain in the water," and you will see that this is true. Anglers can catch anything from pike to bass to crappie to walleye and panfish. The park has a boat launch in lower Trempealeau Bay. Another way to enjoy the water is at the town of Trempealeau's public pool. Perrot State Park nature center is also by the river and houses information on archeology, fish, and the mound builders of the region. Your history lesson here, along with a little exploration of your own, will make clear why this location has been popular for thousands of years.

To get there: From I-90 near La Crosse, take Exit 4 to US 53. Head north on US 53 for 9 miles to Highway 35. Turn left on Highway 35 and follow it 8 miles into the town of Trempealeau. Turn left on Main Street and follow it 0.1 mile to Park Road. Turn right on First Street and follow it to enter the park.

KEY INFORMATION

Perrot State Park
P.O. Box 407
Trempealeau, WI 54661

Operated by: Wisconsin State Parks

Information: (608) 534-6409, www.wiparks.net, reservations (888) WIPARKS, www.reserveamerica.com

Open: Year-round; showers and water mid-April through mid-October

Individual sites: 98

Each site has: Picnic table, fire ring, 36 also have electricity

Site assignment: By phone, Internet, or first come, first served

Registration: At ranger station

Facilities: Hot showers, flush toilets, pit toilets, water spigots

Parking: At campsites only

Fee: Memorial Day weekend through Labor Day weekend Friday–Saturday $10 residents, $12 non-residents; summer weekdays and all days rest of year $8 residents, $10 non-residents; $3 extra for electricity

Elevation: 675 feet

Restrictions

Pets—On leash only

Fires—In fire rings only

Alcoholic beverages—At campsites only

Vehicles—Two vehicles per campsite

Other—21-day stay limit

18. PIGEON CREEK

Black River Falls

Campgrounds located within quick driving access from an interstate are often overcrowded with RVs and overrun in general. Pigeon Creek bucks that trend. Located just a few miles off I-94 near Black River Falls, this destination within the Black River State Forest is actually underutilized. Sure, they get a few travelers wandering off the interstate, but the lack of hookups or showers keeps the big-rig set away for the most part. This campground offers a near-ideal setting for tent campers and has all sorts of fun stuff to do nearby, yet it won't even fill on July 4th. Frankly, I'm stumped as to why!

But never mind the "whys." Just appreciate the fact that you can throw your tent in the car, hit I-94, and be guaranteed a campsite! And once you come here, you will be coming back for more. Folks that discover Pigeon Creek become regulars who swear by the place. The campground is situated in an attractive forest near Pigeon Creek Flowage, a dark-water impoundment (Pigeon Creek is just a little stream that feeds the lake). Enter the paved campground loop road to beautiful white pine stands mixed with mostly maple trees. Oaks, aspen, and jack pine are also represented. Ferns, brush and young trees between campsites make for ample campsite privacy. Campsites are also spaced well apart from one another. Furthermore, you most likely won't have any neighbors

CAMPGROUND RATINGS

Beauty:	★★★★
Site privacy:	★★★★
Site spaciousness:	★★★★
Quiet:	★★
Security:	★★★
Cleanliness/upkeep:	★★★★★

Pigeon Creek is the most underutilized campground in this entire guidebook.

camping beside you! The only drawback I see—er, hear—is the low hum of cars from I-94, but I didn't find it bothersome during any of my three stays here.

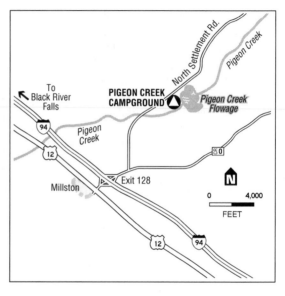

The main loop contains sites #1–#29. Pass the pump well at the loop's beginning then pass many great campsites. Most are well shaded and have a grass or sand floor to make staking your tent a breeze. A giant white pine grows near campsite #1. Another majestic pine shades campsite #7. A mini-loop spurs off the main loop past campsite #10, which houses campsites #30–#38. Campsite #34 is at the back of the mini-loop. Wooden barriers separate the parking spur from the camping area. Back on the main loop, campsites #12, #14, #18, and #20 have pull-through parking. Most sites on the outside of the loop are above average in size. The last two sites, #27 and #29, are the most popular, since they are closest to the water. A pump well and two pairs of vault toilets serve the campground.

The 34-acre Pigeon Creek Flowage is mostly bordered in brush and grass. While bass, panfish, and catfish call it home, the flowage is not a destination for serious anglers. Geared more toward family fun, the lake is quiet (thanks to the "electric motors only" rule) and is a perfect place for kids to explore by canoe. The lake also enjoys one of the largest swim beaches in the state parks and forests; the sloped sandy shore is nearly 100 yards wide and leads up to a grassy picnic area with scattered shade trees, picnic tables, and grills. The lake is fairly shallow and good for swimming. A grassy "island" connected by a narrow peninsula lies in the middle of the lake. Yert another swimming experience can be had at Robinson Beach, just a short car trip away. Robinson Beach is an old quarry now filled with crystal-clear groundwater. This beach also has a picnic area.

Mountain bikers will really enjoy this campground. The Pigeon Creek Mountain Bike Trail leaves directly from the campground, passes over Pigeon Creek Flowage dam, then heads right 1.8 miles to North Settlement Road and left 2.9 miles to Smrekar Road. Just a half-mile on Smrekar Road is the Smrekar Mountain Biking and Cross-Country Ski Trails parking area. Combined with the Wildcat Trails on the north side of North Settlement Road, fat-tire enthusiasts have over 24 miles of paths to pedal! Hikers often use these trails, too. Backpackers will tent camp at Pigeon Creek Campground, then take off on overnight treks in this loop-laden trail system. Whether you are backpacking on not, toss your tent in the car and head out on a camping trek at Pigeon Creek.

To get there: From Exit 128 on I-94, head east on County Road O for 0.3 mile. Turn left on North Settlement Road and follow it for 2 miles to the campground, on your right.

KEY INFORMATION

Pigeon Creek
910 Highway 54 East
Black River Falls, WI 54615

Operated by: Wisconsin Department of Natural Resources

Information: (715) 284-4103, www.wiparks.net

Open: May 15 through October 1

Individual sites: 38

Each site has: Picnic table, fire grate

Site assignment: First come, first served, no reservation

Registration: Self-registration, on site

Facilities: Pump well, vault toilets

Parking: At campsites only

Fee: $7 per night Wisconsin residents, $9 per night non-residents

Elevation: 950 feet

Restrictions

Pets—On leash only

Fires—In fire rings only

Alcoholic beverages—At campsites only

Vehicles—No more than two vehicles at each campsite

Other—Use of generators prohibited

19. *POINT BEACH STATE FOREST*

Two Rivers

Point Beach State Forest is your best bet for a beachfront camping experience in southeastern Wisconsin. Point Beach can be cool in the early season, busy later in the summer, and mosquito-ish at times, but a stroll along the tan sands on Lake Michigan more than compensates for any of these ills. From the beach, you will see Rawley Port Lighthouse, a century-old beacon to ships on Lake Michigan. Hikers and bikers can enjoy inland trails totaling 10 miles in distance. A word of caution: As a whole, the campground is a winner, but the sheer number of electric campsites brings in the big rigs. However, the electric sites are generally segregated, effectively leaving tent campers to their own loops. And there are some great tent-camping sites here.

The campground sits back about 100 yards from Lake Michigan, situated on undulating old dunes that are now heavily forested. While it may not be directly beside the shore, it does get the cooling lake effect. That is why early summer can be less busy—campers fear a freeze-out. A paved park road lies between the lake and the campground, but fortunately for campers, thick evergreens and underbrush mostly screen out the road.

On first inspection, the campground seems like a maze. The first loop houses sites #1–#16. It offers widely separated sites with thick brush between them in an

CAMPGROUND RATINGS

Beauty:	★★★
Site privacy:	★★★★
Site spaciousness:	★★★★
Quiet:	★★★
Security:	★★★★
Cleanliness/upkeep:	★★★★

Six miles of waterfront on Lake Michigan attract campers to Point Beach.

oak-white pine forest. These are first come, first served sites. The next loop offers sites #17–#30. It is a little too close to the main park road, has a few electric sites mixed in, and is not recommended. Next comes the loop that offers the best in tent camping at Point Beach. Remember this loop for reservations: #31–#62. Pass the campground shower area and enter a narrow road that specifically forbids RVs. This narrow road twists and undulates beneath a pretty forest of sugar maple, birch,

oak and white pine. The sites are widely spaced and have thick brush between them, offering good campsite privacy. Some of the sites have fences, prohibiting vehicles from driving up or down a hill to reach the actual site, effectively making them walk-in campsites. Both sides of the loop have good sites, and due to the twisting road and elevation changes, there is a variety of sites and situations. You won't go wrong choosing any of the sites, though after your first visit, you may find one you prefer for next time.. During the week, the campground never fills; just come and take your chances.

With a few exceptions, sites #63 to #125 are electric. Of special note are #120, a non-electric site offering solitude, and #119, which is near the Ridges Trail. The electric sites are strung out on a long loop that is nicely forested, but I prefer to stay away from the big rigs with the lights strung on them like it was Christmas. The electric sites are first to fill. Make reservations after mid-June thorough mid-August if coming on a weekend. Remember, the mosquitoes can be troublesome here. Many campers bring screen shelters. Most campsites can accommodate a screen shelter, tent, and other gear. The Lodge, located near the entrance station, serves hamburgers and such.

The beach is the big draw here. Six miles of lakefront give beachcombers plenty of room to crunch their feet as clear, cool Lake Michigan laps against the shoreline. Swimmers can tackle the chilly waters, but be advised that lifeguards are not provided. Try to get up and watch sunrise from the beach—it's quite a sight. Everyone likes to visit Rawley Point Lighthouse. The original brick lighthouse was built in 1853. It was later cut down and made into the light keeper's house. The second tower was built in 1894 and at 113 feet is one of the largest and brightest on the Great Lakes. Other sights can be seen on the forest's 2,900 acres. Campers can pedal along the campground and forest roads, but they should be careful, as the roads can get busy on warm weekends. A bicycle trail plies the inland woods. The hiking trails loop south from the campground all the way to Molash Creek. The Red Pine Trail makes a 3-mile loop inland from the campground. You will enjoy these trails, but like most tent campers, you will be enjoying all that sand on Lake Michigan.

To get there: From Two Rivers, drive north on County Road O for 5 miles to reach the forest, on your right.

KEY INFORMATION

Point Beach State Forest
400 County Trunk O
Two Rivers, WI 54241

Operated by: Wisconsin Department of Natural Resources

Information: (920) 794-7480, www.wiparks.net, reservations (888) WIPARKS, www.reserveamerica.com

Open: Year-round, water on from last frost of spring to first frost of fall

Individual sites: 127

Each site has: Picnic table, fire ring, 70 have electricity

Site assignment: By phone, internet, or first come, first served

Registration: At visitor center

Facilities: Hot showers, flush toilets, pit toilets, water spigots

Parking: At campsites only

Fee: Memorial Day weekend through Labor Day weekend Friday–Saturday $10 residents, $12 non-residents; summer weekdays and all days rest of year $8 residents, $10 non-residents; $3 extra for electricity

Elevation: 600 feet

Restrictions

Pets—On leash only

Fires—In fire rings only

Alcoholic beverages—At campsites only

Vehicles—None

Other—21-day stay limit; 6 individuals per campsite

20. ROCHE-A-CRI STATE PARK

Friendship

Roche-A-Cri is quite a landmark on the Wisconsin landscape, as is the state park that surrounds and protects it. Roche-A-Cri itself is a rock prominence uplifting from the central Wisconsin landscape. Its 300 feet of elevation allow a view of ten counties and up to 60 miles distant! First discovered by aboriginals who left petroglyphs to prove their find, the flat-topped cliff-sided perch was dubbed by Frenchmen the "crying rock." Later, American soldiers and explorers let their presence be known with their own rock inscriptions. Today, visitors can camp in an attractive, wooded campground at the base of Roche-A-Cri, get a view from the top, and make their own memory that needs no inscription. The park's proximity to the Wisconsin Dells, 30 miles south, makes for a sane basecamp and respite to explore the tourist madness that is the Dells.

Before you hit the Dells or climb the 303 wooden steps to the top of Roche-A-Cri, find a site at the campground. Your biggest problem will be choosing from the many ideal tent sites. The campground is laid out in a classic loop with a side road splitting the loop in half. Tall pines and oaks shade the loop. Smaller trees and thick brush provide ample campsite privacy. Enter the loop and pass a pump well. Immediately appreciate the large, mostly level sites. A bathroom building lies on the inside of the loop after campsite #7. Just

CAMPGROUND RATINGS

Beauty:	★★★★
Site privacy:	★★★
Site spaciousness:	★★★★
Quiet:	★★
Security:	★★★★
Cleanliness/upkeep:	★★★

This is the nearest sane tent campground within driving distance to the Wisconsin Dells.

past here is a handicapped-accessible site, and then the loop begins to turn away from Highway 13. A side road containing 8 ultra-shady sites splits the main loop. A small, sandy play area lies near here.

The west part of the loop, with sites #26–#41, curves toward the base of Roche-A-Cri. Some of the sites against the base of the outcrop are sloped, but most are level and have the added scenery of red pine, jack pine, and boulders as their backyard.

The only drawback here? Roche-A-Cri was a state holding that started as a roadside park, then expanded to become a real park. In a sense it still is a roadside park, since Highway 13 is within earshot for the first half of the loop. An upside is campsite availability—Roche-A-Cri fills only on summer holiday weekends. All sites are reservable. Showers can be had two miles south in Friendship. Check the park office for shower sites and directions.

Some great trails are walkable directly from the campground. The Acorn Loop circumnavigates Roche-A-Cri Mound and passes amid some thick and open forests along the way. It also passes Chickadee Rock, a neat formation, but the rock lacks a view. In the fields of the Turkey Vulture Trail, you can see these big carrion-eating birds drifting between Roche-A-Cri and Friendship Mound, a half-mile south. For some vertical variation, make the climb to the top of Roche-A-Cri. Plaques atop the outcrop tell you exactly what you are looking at in the distance. This is the sheerest rock face in Wisconsin, left standing after the waters of ancient Lake Wisconsin broke from their ice dam at the end of the last ice age. The campground road and the one mile paved loop around Roche-A-Cri make for fun and casual bicycling. Carter Creek, a good trout stream, is within walking distance to the campground. This watercourse has been manipulated to make it better habitat for fish. Friendship Lake, 1.5 miles south of the park, has a nice swim beach for cooling off on a hot day.

And then there is the Wisconsin Dells. Love it or hate it, the area is a draw. Here, you can float the Wisconsin River on a double-decker boat or a "duck," an amphibious boat that traverses both land and water. And the man-made amusements are endless. After a hectic day down at the Dells, you will really appreciate the sanity and serenity found at Roche-A-Cri.

To get there: From Friendship, head north on Highway 13 for 2 miles to the park, on your left.

Roche-A-Cri State Park
1767 Highway 13
Friendship, WI 53934

Operated by: Wisconsin State Parks

Information: Summer phone # (608) 339-6881, # November–April (608) 565-2789, www.wiparks.net, reservations (888) WIPARKS, www.reserveamerica.com

Open: May through mid-October

Individual sites: 41

Each site has: Picnic table, fire grate, wood bench

Site assignment: By phone, Internet, or first come, first served

Registration: At park office or by self-registration if office is closed

Facilities: Vault toilets, pump well

Parking: At campsites only

Fee: $7 per night Sunday–Thursday, non-residents $9; $9 per night Friday–Saturday, non-residents $11

Elevation: 1,000 feet

Restrictions

Pets—On leash only

Fires—In fire rings only

Alcoholic beverages—At campsites only

Vehicles—None

Other—21-day stay limit

21. WILLOW RIVER STATE PARK

Hudson

With its close proximity to the Twin Cities, you might expect Willow River State Park to be kind of beat-up and overused. Quite the contrary. I found over 3,000 acres of well-preserved land here in St. Croix County, with a great campground set on the shores of a large yet quiet lake. Sure, this park can get busy, but dedicated park staffers keep it in good shape. So whether you are into waterfall viewing, swimming, hiking, fishing, or canoeing, head this way, grab your private campsite, and be as surprised as I was.

This campground is a winner. A bluff atop Little Falls Lake is the setting for the 72 campsites found in the main campground. (Another six campsites with electricity are in the parking lot by the swim beach. Don't even bother—they are for RVs.) A lush woodland of oak trees with widespread gnarled branches give shade to the main campground, along with some basswood and enough brush to give the campground the maximum privacy rating. The campground loop has two crossroads. A red pine plantation shades the southeastern part of the loop, but is the only part of the campground that lacks a thick understory. The piney campsites have needles for a floor and airiness not found at the rest of the heavily vegetated campground.

As you enter the campground, you'll see campsites #1–#6 straight ahead, located on one of the crossroads. The very thickness

CAMPGROUND RATINGS

Beauty:	★★★★
Site privacy:	★★★★★
Site spaciousness:	★★★
Quiet:	★★★
Security:	★★★
Cleanliness/upkeep:	★★★

Willow Falls and a quality campground will surprise visitors at this Twin Cities getaway.

of the forest here barely allows a car to enter the campsites from the narrow but paved campground road. This narrow road discourages the big rigs too, although many pop-up campers will be found, especially on the electric sites found on the inside of the loop. The main loop circles the bluff's edge overlooking Little Falls Lake, an impoundment of Willow River. Many campsites are perched along the edge of the bluff. Most every site here is desirable. Recommended reservable bluffside campsites include #17, #18, #20, #53, #55, #57 and #59. While part of the loop away from the lake has many fine secluded sites, avoid sites #64–#72, as you may end up on a double site. Other recommended reservable sites not along the lake are #30, #45, #49, #51, and #62.

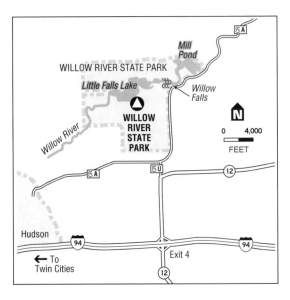

The second crossroad includes campsites #22–#27. Most of these sites are electric. The most important part of this crossroad is the shower facility to wash off the post-hike sweat. If you wish to camp among the red pines, these are campsites #34–#45. Reservations are recommended, as Willow River Campground fills on summer weekends.

Willow Falls, in my opinion, is the most impressive falls in Wisconsin. Back in the 1990s, park personnel removed some dams on the Willow River, freeing the waters to again tumble over this three-tiered drop and produce rumbling echoes between rocky canyon walls. A bridge spans Willow River downstream and offers a great vantage point to view the falls. Willow Falls is accessible only by trail. Footpaths extend beyond the Willow River bridge and climb to the top of the gorge, where more panoramic vistas of the falls below and the land beyond await. More trails in the park criss-cross the 3,000 acres through prairies, past an old homestead, and through a surprisingly hilly oak forest. The swim beach on Little Falls Lake is a big draw during summer. The ultra-large beach has plenty of room to spread out your sunbathing setup on the grass. Picnic tables and a bathhouse complement the area.

The 172-acre Little Falls Lake is a no-gas-or-electric-motors impoundment, which keeps both the lake and the campground serene. Anglers in canoes and rowboats paddle the shoreline of Little Falls Lake for northern pike, largemouth and smallmouth bass, and panfish. Small sailboats are sometimes seen in the impoundment. The Willow River offers good stream-fishing for trout. Brown trout are mostly caught above the Willow Falls, along with a few smallmouth bass. More bass are caught below Little Falls Lake, along with native brook trout. The park also has a disc-golf course and nature center. Check out the naturalist programs, which are offered on summer weekends. Skilled rock climbers tackle walls along the Willow River gorge.

Nearby attractions include tubing the Apple River and visiting the Twin Cities Mall of America. Contact Float Rite at (715) 247-3453 for tubing information. Directions to the Mall of America are at the park entrance station. Proximity to the Twin Cities isn't a bad thing here at Willow River State Park.

To get there: From Exit 4 on I-94 near Hudson, take Highway 12 north for 1.8 miles to County Road U. Turn left on County Road U and follow it 0.3 mile, then keep forward on County Road A and follow it 1.5 miles to the park, on your left.

KEY INFORMATION

Willow River State Park
1034 County Road A
Hudson, WI 54016

Operated by: Wisconsin State Parks

Information: (715) 386-5931, www.wiparks.com, reservations (888) WIPARKS, www.reserveamerica.com

Open: Year-round, water and showers operating from last frost of spring to first frost of fall

Individual sites: 78

Each site has: Picnic table, fire ring, 25 sites also have electricity

Site assignment: By phone, internet, or first come, first served

Registration: At entrance station

Facilities: Hot showers, flush toilets, pit toilets, water spigots

Parking: At campsites only

Fee: Memorial Day weekend through Labor Day weekend Friday–Saturday $10 residents, $12 non-residents; summer weekdays and all days rest of year $8 residents, $10 non-residents; $3 extra for electricity

Elevation: 825 feet

Restrictions

  Pets—On leash only

  Fires—In fire rings only

  Alcoholic beverages—At campsites

  Vehicles—Two vehicles per site

  Other—21-day stay limit

NORTHWESTERN WISCONSIN

22. *AMNICON FALLS STATE PARK*

Superior

It is hard to believe how many times I drove past Amnicon Falls without stopping, but one day I decided to see just what this place might have to offer. I'm glad I did. Anyone traveling in northwest Wisconsin should devote a day to setting up camp in this fine campground and visiting the close-by falls in the unhurried manner of someone who knows they are staying for the night. And don't forget to bring your camera as well as your tent.

First established as a Douglas County park in the 1930s, Amnicon Falls grew in size over the years and was eventually taken over by the state in 1961. During this time, the park has been nicely developed, offering an adequate campground set on a hill. The campground is situated on a single loop, which starts just past the Thimbleberry Nature Trail. Evergreens such as white spruce and fir mix with aspens. Younger trees such as alder and maple along with underbrush provide decent campsite privacy. Much of the loop's center is grassy and serves as a play area for kids. Most of the campsites are shaded, though some may be open to noonday sun. Campsites #1–#6 are first come, first served. The rest of the sites are reservable. The first sites on the outside of the loop are on the edge of the river gorge.

Follow the loop around to reach shady campsite #8. Campsite #11 is well suited for

CAMPGROUND RATINGS

Beauty:	★★★
Site privacy:	★★★★
Site spaciousness:	★★★
Quiet:	★★★★
Security:	★★★★
Cleanliness/upkeep:	★★★★

The campground here makes for a great layover while you explore the numerous falls at this park.

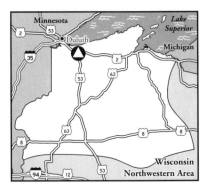

campers with lots of gear, but avoid campsite #14, as it is a bit sloped. Campsites #16 and #17 are two walk-in sites of special note. Campsite #16 is the closest, and campsite #17 is under a big red pine. The campsites beyond here are more open. Campsite #29 works well, and campsites #32 and #33 function as a group site. The river is audible from campsite #35, but the site is very open. Campsite #36 is encircled by brush for privacy seekers.

Amnicon Falls fills only one in three summer weekends. The park is a bit small for extended camping trips, but it's a great spot for a stopover or as part of a tour of the Wisconsin North Woods.

Waterfall-watching is the primary attraction here. There are three main waterfalls at Amnicon: Upper Falls, Lower Falls, and Snake Pit Falls. Numerous other unnamed rapids and cascades show off too, as the Amnicon River drops 180 feet in its nearly two-mile jaunt through the park. I was lucky enough to visit the park after a big mid-summer rain. The Amnicon was ripping and roaring and flowing strongly. The falls were quite a sight. Visitors admired the beauty and raw power of the water flow that was clearly audible up the hill at the campground. Now & Then Falls, located near Upper Falls, only runs at higher flows; it was pouring a wide veil of water over its ledge that day. Wading and rock-hopping along the river is a favorite pastime here during drier times; only a fool would've gotten in during my stay. The fishing is fair for musky and walleye, and the river has the only native population of muskellunge in Wisconsin.

The best way to see the main falls is by a short foot trail that crosses over to an island in mid-river. A rustic covered bridge crosses the Amnicon between Upper Falls and Lower Falls. From here, you can listen to the water echoing in the covered bridge. Follow the loop trail around the island perimeter. You have to peer down steeply to see the bottom of Snake Pit Falls. Little side trails spur from the main path as visitors strive to get the best camera angles. Steps have been carved into the rock just above Lower Falls. A short path leads to an open granite outcrop to view Lower Falls. Yet another trail leads up along the Amnicon to view unnamed cascades along the riverbank. The Thimbleberry Nature Trail heads downstream along the Amnicon River to a sandstone quarry, then loops back along the river escarpment. The accompanying nature-trail booklet will help you learn about this special slice of Wisconsin. I am glad to have learned about Amnicon Falls, especially after passing it by so many times.

To get there: From the junction of US 53 and US 2 south of Superior, head east on US 2 for 0.7 mile to County Road U. Turn left on County Road U, follow it for 0.2 mile, and turn left into the park.

KEY INFORMATION

Amnicon Falls State Park
6294 South State Road 35
Superior, WI 54880

Operated by: Wisconsin State Parks

Information: (715) 398-3000, www.wiparks.net, reservations (888) WIPARKS, www.reserveamerica.com

Open: Year-round, water spigots on May through October

Individual sites: 36

Each site has: Picnic table, fire ring

Site assignment: By phone, Internet, or first come, first served

Registration: At entrance station or at campground self-registration station

Facilities: Water spigots, pit toilets

Parking: At campsites and at walk-in parking area

Fee: Memorial Day weekend through Labor Day weekend Friday–Saturday $9 residents, $11 non-residents; summer weekdays and all days rest of year $7 residents, $9 non-residents

Elevation: 830 feet

Restrictions

  Pets—On leash only

  Fires—In fire rings only

  Alcoholic beverages—At campsites only

  Vehicles—Two vehicles per campsite

  Other—21-day stay limit

23. BIG BAY STATE PARK

Bayfield

The biggest of the Apostle Island Chain (and the only one not under the protection of the National Park), Madeline Island is also the only one inhabited year-round. During the winter, the island boasts a population of about 250; this swells to over 2,000 in the summer. To reach the island and the 2,500-acre Big Bay State Park, you must take a pay ferry, but the extra expense and trouble is worth it.

The campground has 60 sites but still exudes a sense of serenity. From Hagen Road, turn left to enter the park, and reach the first of two loops (on the right) which holds campsites #1–#30. Here a mixed pine forest reaches overhead, and oaks, maple, spruce, and brush grow beneath the pines. The sites on this loop are generally larger than on the other loop. Campsite #3 is recommended, as it is large and secluded. Campsite #9 is backed against evergreens. Campsites #15 and #21 are good, too. A short trail leads from near campsite #22 to Barrier Beach. Campsites #23–#25 are large and have good privacy. The end of the loop has campsites #26–#30. These are sizable and are closest to the modern shower building.

The second loop has a real mix of open and shaded campsites. Campsite #33 is well shaded. Tent campers should consider the walk-in campsites at #35–#41. Of these sites, #35–#39 are reservable. A gravel path makes a mini-loop to reach shady sites

CAMPGROUND RATINGS

Beauty:	★★★★
Site privacy:	★★★★
Site spaciousness:	★★★★
Quiet:	★★★★★
Security:	★★★★★
Cleanliness/upkeep:	★★★★★

Big Bay offers you a chance to camp in the famed Apostle Islands.

---

beneath spruce, birch, and maple. The second road loop continues. The sites on the inside of the loop are more open, whereas the sites on the outside of the loop are shaded and screened by evergreens. Make your reservations for odd-numbered campsites #47–#55. The last five campsites have a mix of sun and shade.

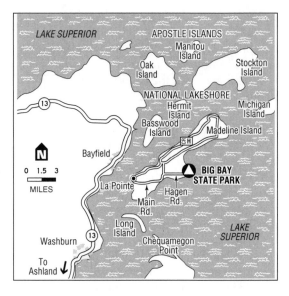

Only 9 of the 60 campsites are first come, first served. As summer warms here in the very north of Wisconsin, the campground fills. Sites are hard to come by without reservations anytime in July and August. Be sure to reserve in advance, or consider coming here in early June or September when last-minute sites are more easily had. Also, watch out for the raccoons here. They can be very pesky. Bears have been known to visit as well.

Campers like to pedal park roads and around Madeline Island, but bikes are not allowed on the seven total miles of park trails. The tan sands of Barrier Beach curves along Big Bay and makes for an excellent photography spot. Many hardy swimmers dip in Lake Superior here. Folks also surf-fish here or at other areas of the park's extensive shoreline for rainbow, lake, and brown trout. The lagoon behind Barrier Beach offers angling for pike. Canoes, paddleboats, and rowboats can be rented at Town Park, which also abuts the lagoon. Other parts of the shore feature craggy sandstone rocks, like the outcropping at the park picnic area. Waves crash against boulders that have fallen off the cliffs into the water.

Many campers like to hike the trails. Barrier Beach has a boardwalk that offers interpretive information along the shore of Lake Superior. The Lagoon

Ridge Trail stretches for 2.5 miles through the park's interior and connects to the Bay View Trail, which cruises along the shore for another 1.5 miles. The Point Trail also meanders along the edge of the lake.

Indigenous natives have inhabited Madeline Island, the largest of the Apostle Islands, for thousands of years before Europeans discovered it in the 1660s. Fur traders, missionaries, and fishermen followed. You can learn about the island's culture and life by taking an island bus tour, or check out the Madeline Island Museum in the village of La Pointe, the "town" on the island. La Pointe has stores and restaurants, too. You can rent mopeds or bicycles for wheeled explorations of Madeline Island. Various water-borne sight-seeing tours of the adjacent Apostle Island National Lakeshore are available in Bayfield; visit www.apostleisland.com for more information.

While the campground is open year-round, keep in mind that the ferry operates only from the spring ice break-up, generally late March or early April to freeze-up, usually in January. For a period of time, Madeline Island is accessible by snow road. If you do come then, campsites #26–#30 are kept open. You will be sure to get a campsite, but remember to bring lots of extra clothes!

To get there: From the intersection of US 2 and Highway 13 west of Ashland, follow Highway 13 north for 19.7 miles into Bayfield, until reaching the right turn to the Madeline Island Ferry. After debarking the ferry in La Pointe on Madeline Island, veer right, then turn left on Main Road. Keep forward for 6 miles. Main Road turns into Hagen Road at 4 miles, and the park will be on your left.

KEY INFORMATION

Big Bay State Park
P.O. Box 589
Bayfield, WI 54814

Operated by: Wisconsin State Parks

Information: (715) 747-6425, www.wiparks.net, reservations (888) WIPARKS, www.reserveamerica.com

Open: Year-round, showers and water on from mid-May through first full weekend in October

Individual sites: 60

Each site has: Picnic table, fire ring

Site assignment: By phone, Internet, or first come, first served

Registration: At contact station or self-registration

Facilities: Hot showers, flush toilets, vault toilets

Parking: At campsites and at walk-in parking areas

Fee: Memorial Day weekend through Labor Day weekend Friday–Saturday $10 residents, $12 non-residents; summer weekdays and all days rest of year $8 residents, $10 non-residents

Elevation: 625 feet

Restrictions

Pets—On leash only

Fires—In fire rings only

Alcoholic beverages—At campsites only

Vehicles—Two vehicles per site

Other—21-day stay limit

24. BIRCH GROVE

Washburn

Birch Grove Campground lies on an isthmus of land between two attractive North Woods lakes. This setup makes for twice the water, twice the fishing, and twice the beauty. The small size of the campground and its setting in a secluded parcel of the Chequamegon National Forest combine for a relaxed ambiance perfect for a getaway from the busy side of life. When I got to Birch Grove, the skies were dark, and the winds were cool. A few other campers were around, mostly huddled by campfires. The only sounds to be heard were winds pushing through the birch and aspen trees and birds galore that didn't seem to mind the chill, plus a chattering chipmunk determined to get a handout. Luckily, a hiking trail stretches around West Twin Lake, the other lake being East Twin Lake. I took off on the approximately one-mile loop trail and was fully heated up by the time that path returned to the campground.

I set up camp at site #13 and made my own fire. Later, the day warmed somewhat, and I fully enjoyed my experience at Birch Grove. Campsite #13 is not the only good site here. Most make for ideal tent sites. Paper birch trees, many of them with multiple trunks, grow abundantly on the land between the lakes. Red maple, red oaks, and spruce trees are common, too. Heavy vegetation thrives between the campsites. The campground is strung out along a road between the waters and lies a

CAMPGROUND RATINGS

Beauty:	★★★★
Site privacy:	★★★★★
Site spaciousness:	★★★★
Quiet:	★★★★★
Security:	★★★
Cleanliness/upkeep:	★★★

This campground lies between two small, scenic lakes.

bit closer to West Twin Lake than East Twin Lake. Pass the fee station and come to campsite #1, set on a hill above West Twin Lake. Campsite #2 lies across the gravel road from the boat ramp for East Twin Lake. Campsite #3 is close to East Twin and is heavily shaded. Campsites #5 and #7 are set back a bit from East Twin. After the road veers closer to West Twin Lake, you'll reach campsites #4, #6, and #8, which overlook West Twin and have short trails leading to the water's edge. Reach

the first of two pump wells and the short, small ramp leading into West Twin Lake. The shore beside the boat ramp has been stabilized with wood timbers, making for a grassy sitting area next to a tiny beach. Junior could take a dip here or shore-fish, while Mom and Dad watch the action from nearby benches.

Campsite #9 is large and set across from a set of vault toilets. Campsites #11, #12, and #13 lie along West Twin Lake. Reach a turnaround loop that has a pump well in its center. Campsite #14 is at the back of the loop and offers solitude but is less shaded. Campsites #15 and #16 also are isolated but don't offer lake views, since they are set a bit back from East Twin Lake.

The hiking trail around West Twin Lake meanders over wooded hills, where bracken ferns reach waist-high, then continues through younger, forested areas and along the shoreline. A short boardwalk leads into a small tamarack bog. The 16-acre West Twin Lake offers decent fishing for northern pike, large-mouth bass, and panfish. East Twin Lake is a little bigger at 22 acres and offers the same species as West Twin Lake. Both have completely undeveloped shorelines that make for pleasant watery outings.

Nearby Long Lake, passed on the way into Birch Grove, is renowned for its crystal-clear water. (East and West Twin Lake both have clear water, too.) At 36 acres, Long Lake has good fishing for largemouth bass. The boat ramp at Long Lake is carry-in. The picnic area has a swim beach and is very pretty. If you intend to swim at Long Lake or either of the Twin Lakes, then I hope the weather will be warmer for you than it was for me during my camping trip at Birch Grove.

To get there: From the intersection of US 2 and Highway 13 west of Ashland, drive north on Highway 13 for 5.6 miles to Wanabo Road. Turn left on Wanabo Road and follow it for 6 miles to Forest Road 435. Turn right on FR 435 and follow it 2.8 miles to the campground, on your left.

KEY INFORMATION

Birch Grove
P.O. Box 578, 113 Bayfield
 Street
Washburn, WI 54891

Operated by: U.S. Forest Service

Information: (715) 373-2667,
 www.fs.fed.us/r9/cnnf

Open: May through October

Individual sites: 16

Each site has: Picnic table, fire grate

Site assignment: First come, first served, no reservation

Registration: Self-registration on-site

Facilities: Pump wells, vault toilets

Parking: At campsites only

Fee: $10 per night

Elevation: 1,100 feet

Restrictions

Pets—On leash only

Fires—In fire rings only

Alcoholic beverages—At campsites only

Vehicles—None

Other—14-day stay limit

25. *BLACK LAKE*

Loretta

Whoever laid out Black Lake Campground made the most of the lakeside woods. Twenty-one of the 29 campsites abut this attractive lake in the North Woods, which is completely encircled by national forest property. The arrangement creates an appealing setting to pitch your tent, absorb nature, and maybe enjoy some outdoor recreation. However, a laid-back campground like this beckons you to snooze in the chair or take a little nap in the hammock as much as hiking down the trail.

Soon after the campground entrance, the lake comes into view just as you reach the Black Lake Picnic Area and the first boat launch. This is also the parking for campsites #27–#29, which are walk-in sites reached via the first portion of the Black Creek Trail. The campsite trail spurs right and leads to three top-notch camps beneath towering red pines. Each of these campsites offers a great view of Black Lake and a sense of remoteness unrivaled even at the rest of this remote campground. These sites are the best at Black Lake, and that is saying quite a lot.

Cross the lake outflow of Black Lake. This spot beneath a white pine is a favored fishing hole. Enter the main campground road, which is paved, to see a series of widely spaced campsites spur toward the lake. They are cut into woods of paper birch, red pine, and some spruce and aspen trees. Ferns and smaller trees form a

CAMPGROUND RATINGS

Beauty: ★★★★
Site privacy: ★★★★★
Site spaciousness: ★★★★
Quiet: ★★★★★
Security: ★★★
Cleanliness/upkeep: ★★★★

Most of the campsites here are lakefront.

thicket-like understory that allows maximum campsite privacy. The campsites away from the lake are even more thickly wooded and private but are used less.

A vault toilet lies past campsite #7. A pump well is next to campsite #13, which is very large. Many other sites are so large that they are open to the sun in the center. The sites become even more widely separated after #13. Campsites #16 and #17 are in a grove of paper birch. Campsite #19 is closest to the water. A short

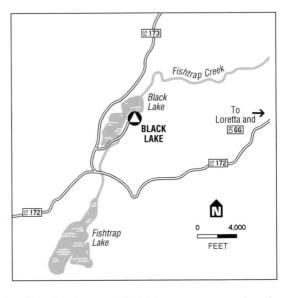

road to the campground boat landing lies beyond #19. The campground ends in a mini-loop. The first part of the mini-loop has no campsites, then lakeside sites resume with #20. Campsite #22 is highly recommended.

The reservable campsites at Black Lake are #1, #2, #6, #8, #10, #11, #13, #14, #15, #16, #18, #19, #20, #22, #24, #25, and #29. All but #11 and #14 are lakefront. Be advised that the Black Lake Trail runs between the campsites and the lake itself. Two pump wells serve the campground. The bathrooms here are the newer "SST" models. SST is short for "sweet smelling technology," an improvement over the hole-in-the-ground technology of old.

Black Lake covers 129 acres, and motors are allowed. Commonly sought fish species include muskellunge, largemouth bass, northern pike, and panfish. A swim beach lies along the lake, midway in the campground. A sloped grassy area dips into the water and leads to a small roped area in the lake.

The four-mile Black Lake Trail is a highlight of the area. It loops entirely around the lake, crossing Fishtrap Creek via bridge. Along the way are interpretive stops where you can learn about the logging history of the recovered woods. Pass through an old logging campsite, along a railroad grade, and by tree plantations from the 1930s. Much of Wisconsin's North Woods were cut over by the 1930s, after harvesting huge white pines and other trees. The federal government came in and bought these lands from timber companies, private landowners, and counties that had little use for tax-forfeited cut-over land. The U.S. Forest Service came in, planting thousands of trees with young men in the Great Depression–era Civilian Conservation Corps. The regenerated forests provide timber for harvest, food and cover for wildlife, protect watersheds from erosion, and make recreation areas such as Black Lake viable again. Just remember that when you snooze in the shade under that tall tree.

KEY INFORMATION

Black Lake

Highway 13 North, P.O. Box 126

Glidden, WI 54527

Operated by: U.S. Forest Service

Information: (715) 264-2511; www.fs.fed.us/r9/cnnf, reservations (877) 444-6777, www.reserveUSA.com

Open: May through October

Individual sites: 29

Each site has: Picnic table, fire ring, a few also have upright grill

Site assignment: By phone, Internet or first come, first served

Registration: Self-registration on-site

Facilities: Pump well, vault toilet

Parking: At campsites and at walk-in campsite parking

Fee: $10 per night

Elevation: 1,400 feet

Restrictions

Pets—On leash only

Fires—In fire rings only

Alcoholic beverages—At campsites only

Vehicles—None

Other—14-day stay limit

To get there: From Loretta, drive north on County Road GG for 8 miles to Forest Road 172. Turn left on FR 172 and follow it for 5.6 miles. Stay straight for 0.1 mile further, now on FR 173, then turn right onto paved FR 1666 into the campground.

26. BOIS BRULE

Brule

Canoers and kayakers develop a certain reverent tone when they talk about paddling the Bois Brule River. I don't know if it is the history, scenery, trout fishing, rapids, or what, but a trip on the Bois Brule is a near-religious experience for many Badger State floating aficionados. Bois Brule Campground is conveniently located midway along the river, offering float trips encompassing different characters of the river amid the 42,000-acre Brule River State Forest.

This river, called the "River of Presidents" from the many American leaders who have cast lines here (from Grant to Eisenhower), first saw the Chippewa tribe make their way up the chilly waters from Lake Superior, then portage to the St. Croix River and on into the Mississippi River drainage. Voyageurs and fur traders followed the Chippewa. Later, summer residences, including Cedar Island Estate, were built along the Brule. Still later, Nebagamon Lumber Company donated Bois Brule land to the state, which along with the riverside landowners, have attempted to keep this spring-fed watershed beautiful.

Bois Brule Campground has many stellar campsites, as well as some that are merely desirable. Enter the campground and come to campsite #1, a walk-in site shaded by white pines and balsams. Campsite #2 offers a secluded drive-up campsite, while campsites #3–#5 rest on a flat shaded by

CAMPGROUND RATINGS

Beauty:	★★★★
Site privacy:	★★★
Site spaciousness:	★★★★
Quiet:	★★★★
Security:	★★★★
Cleanliness/upkeep:	★★★★

Tent camp next to one of Wisconsin's best—and coldest— canoeing rivers.

towering red pines. While these lack privacy now, Forest Service personnel have planted evergreens that will separate the sites in time. The campground road splits, and large boulders keep cars where they should be. The sites along the right road lie on the edge of the escarpment above Bois Brule River. Near this road are three excellent walk-in tent sites, #7–#9. Drop down steps to the heavily shaded and wooded river plain. These next three sites stretch along the river and are worth tot-

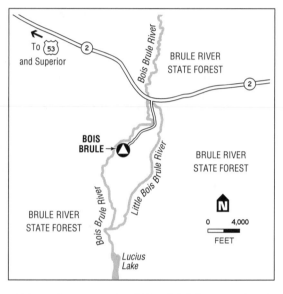

ing gear up and down the steps. I stayed at campsite #10, which has much privacy vegetation. The campground opens up again with sites #11–#14 under pines. Campsites #15 and #16 are closest to the canoe landing and picnic area.

The left campground road holds sites #17–#22. These sites are generally open under the pines and lack an understory. Most are large, so bring the big tent. The final campsite, #23, sits by itself, offering maximum privacy and shade.

Water can be had at the artesian well by the park headquarters garage, just a bit down Ranger Road. Vault toilets are near any site in the campground, which fills nearly every summer weekend. I advise making a special effort and coming during the week, when the campground and river are serene.

Most anyone can paddle the upper 26 miles of the river, which drop at a rate of 3.5 feet per mile, though there are some named rapids. Then comes a stretch of 12 miles dropping at 17 feet per mile, much of it just below Copper Range Campground, including Mays Ledges, which has been known to dump a paddler or two. The last part of the river levels out before reaching Lake Superior. Luckily, Brule River Canoe Rental is located a mere mile distant from the campground. They offer canoes, kayaks, and shuttle services covering the entire river; call them at (715) 372-4983.

Hikers have options here, too. The Stoney Hill Nature Trail runs 1.7 miles just across from Bois Brule Campground. You can enjoy a view of the landscape from an old fire tower site. Hikers can also travel 16 miles of the North Country Trail here. The Historic Portage Trail in the forest's southwest corner follows the two-mile portage route connecting the Bois Brule to Upper St. Croix Lake. Many angler parking areas are located along the Brule, especially the lower river. Coldwater species range from trout to salmon. A picnic area is located at the mouth of the Brule, where you can overlook Lake Superior from a bluff, and even take a swim if you dare. A long sandy beach stretches along the big lake. After your first visit, you may be stretching out your tent-camping adventure in the Brule River State Forest.

To get there: From the intersection of US 53 and Highway 2 south of Superior, drive east on Highway 2 for 16 miles to the town of Brule. Turn right on Ranger Road, just beyond the bridge over the Bois Brule River, and keep forward on Ranger Road for 1 mile to reach the campground, on your right.

KEY INFORMATION

Bois Brule
6250 South Ranger Road
Brule, WI 54820

Operated by: Wisconsin Department of Natural Resources

Information: (715) 372-4866, www.wiparks.net

Open: Year-round, water available May through October

Individual sites: 23

Each site has: Picnic table, fire ring, wood bench

Site assignment: First come, first served, no reservation

Registration: Self-registration, on-site

Facilities: Pump well, vault toilets

Parking: At campsites and at walk-in parking area

Fee: $7 per night residents, $9 per night non-residents

Elevation: 1,000 feet

Restrictions

Pets—On maximum 8-foot leash

Fires—In fire rings only

Alcoholic beverages—At campsites only

Vehicles—Two vehicles per site

Other—One family or 6 unrelated adults per site

27. BRUNET ISLAND STATE PARK

Cornell

The Chippewa River is an historic waterway, used for travel by Wisconsin's first peoples long before voyageurs, loggers, and settlers arrived in Chippewa Valley. One fellow, a Frenchman named Jean Brunet, stands out among the later history makers of this region. Brunet came to the United States from France in 1828 and settled in Chippewa Falls, where he established the first sawmill in the area. He later became a state legislator representing Chippewa Falls. But civilized life was too much for Jean, and he pushed farther up the Chippewa River valley, settling near this present-day park at a falls on the Chippewa. He operated a ferry and trading post here until he died in 1877. Today, Brunet Island State Park bears his name, and the rustic island exhibits the spirit of this pioneer. Today you can camp here and enjoy even more non-island land on the banks of the Chippewa River.

There are two campgrounds to choose from here, but campers will want to avoid pitching their tents in the South Campground. The 24 sites found here have electrical hookups, making it an RV haven. However, this campground has the only shower building at Brunet Island, so campers may not want to avoid it altogether. The North Campground is much more to a tent camper's liking. Set partly along the Chippewa River and partly along a couple of lagoons off the river, this

CAMPGROUND RATINGS

Beauty:	★★★
Site privacy:	★★
Site spaciousness:	★★★
Quiet:	★★★
Security:	★★★★
Cleanliness/upkeep:	★★★★

Camp on an island in the Chippewa River.

loop holds campsites #25–#69. A hardwood forest mixed with white pine and hemlock stands overhead, but the very high deer population keeps any understory within easy reach eaten away, obliterating all understory and privacy in the campground. The first set of sites are #25–#43. Campsites on both sides of the road overlook water, with sites on the left-hand side of the loop directly on the Chippewa River. Bridge the outlet of a lagoon and reach the second set of sites

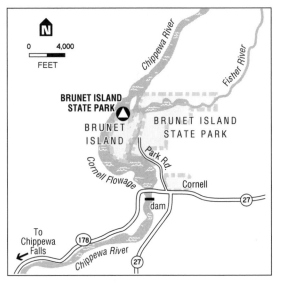

between two lagoons of the Chippewa. These sites are more heavily wooded than the first set. A small mini-loop at the end has more shaded sites. Recommended reservable campsites include #33, #42, #44, #46, #47, #48, #52, and #64. Do not take #65, as it is small and flood-prone.

Brunet Island campers are mostly locals and families from about a 40-mile radius, so it tends to fill on summer weekends. Reservations are highly recommended. Insects can be bothersome at times. Call ahead for the latest bug update before you make your reservation.

With all this water around, it is no wonder that boating and canoeing are popular activities here. Motor boaters are mostly fishermen, as the Chippewa and adjacent Fisher rivers are too rocky for recreational boating. Anglers can find some good fishing for muskie, walleye, smallmouth bass, and catfish. Spring and fall are good for panfish. Canoes and kayaks can be rented in nearby Cornell. The islands and back bays of area make for good wildlife-watching and fishing spots. The shoreline of the Chippewa River is undeveloped for three miles upriver and one mile up the Fisher River. The current here is generally moderate, as the Chippewa is dammed not too far downstream. A fishing pier is located near the South Campground and in the lagoon at the center of the North Campground. A large picnic area and swim beach are located on the south end of the island.

Over seven miles of hiking trails course across Brunet Island and the adjoining mainland. Old-growth hemlock trees tower over the Jean Brunet Nature Trail and along parts of the Timber Trail. The Nordic Trail makes a 2.8-mile loop on the "mainland." Bikers often pedal the paved park roads. A one-mile paved bike trail connects to the 20-mile Old Abe State Trail. This trail was named for an eagle used in the Civil War as a mascot for troops from Wisconsin. This rail trail extents south for 20 miles to near Lake Wissota State Park (campground 16 in this guidebook).

To get there: From Chippewa Falls, take Highway 178 north for 21 miles to Highway 64. Keep forward on Highway 64 east and follow it over the Chippewa River into Cornell, turning left on Park Road after 1 mile. Follow Park Road for 1 mile into the park.

KEY INFORMATION

Brunet Island State Park
23125 255th Street
Cornell, WI 54732

Operated by: Wisconsin State Parks

Information: (715) 239-6888, www.wiparks.net, reservations (888) WIPARKS, www.reserveamerica.com

Open: Year-round, water on from last frost of spring to first frost of fall

Individual sites: 69

Each site has: Picnic table, fire ring, 24 also have electricity

Site assignment: By phone, Internet, or first come, first served

Registration: At entrance station

Facilities: Hot showers, flush toilets, pit toilets, water spigots

Parking: At campsites only

Fee: Memorial Day weekend through Labor Day weekend Friday–Saturday $9 residents, $11 non-residents; summer weekdays and all days rest of year $7 residents, $9 non-residents; $3 electricity

Elevation: 1,025 feet

Restrictions

Pets—On leash only

Fires—In fire rings only

Alcoholic beverages—At campsites only

Vehicles—Two vehicles per campsite

Other—21-day stay limit

28. COPPER FALLS STATE PARK

Mellen

This park's namesake is just one element of the beauty found at this Wisconsin jewel. The Bad River and its feeder branches gain water from lakes and streams to the south, then begin cutting through gorge-ous scenery that includes not only Copper Falls, but also Brown-stone Falls and other cascades and ledges amid craggy, colorful rock formations and thick forests. The camping doesn't quite match the incredible scenery, but it will pass muster for most tent campers.

Copper Falls actually has two camping areas. The better of the two, the South Campground, has sites #34–#56. Pass a modern shower building, then reach the first five-site mini-loop. A dense hardwood forest shades these campsites, which are somewhat pinched in, but they do have dense swaths of greenery between them. The second mini-loop also has five camp-sites and backs up against a hill. The third mini-loop holds 12 campsites. Pass five shaded sites, then reach the four walk-in sites at #49–#52. A trail leads uphill to a level bench where these desirable sites are located under hardwoods. A cart aids campers in toting their gear. The last few sites on this loop, #53–#56, are larger than the rest in the South Campground.

The North Campground is strung out along a side road. While these sites are a little larger than those in the South Campground, they are more open to overhead

CAMPGROUND RATINGS

Beauty:	★★★
Site privacy:	★★★★
Site spaciousness:	★★★
Quiet:	★★★★
Security:	★★★★
Cleanliness/upkeep:	★★★★

Three waterfalls are only part of the natural beauty here.

sun. Evergreens and small trees screen the average-sized campsites from one another. Campsites #1–#13 are electric and draw in the hard-sided tents, a.k.a. RVs. The road climbs a bit and splits. The right road leads to campsites #16–#29, which are open to the sun over-head, too. The left-road sites, #30–33, are more shaded and secluded. Campsite #33 is the most isolated in the entire campground. All but four sites are reservable, including all the walk-in sites. Definitely make reser-

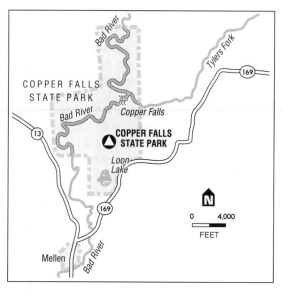

vations, as this campground can fill daily between late June and late August.

Copper Falls is a hiker's park. The best way to see the beauty around here is by foot. The Nature Trail is the primary attraction. It starts at the large and pretty park picnic area. Before you hit the trail, check out the historic and pic-turesque log building at the trailhead, built by the Civilian Conservation Corps in the 1930s. This building houses a concession stand in the summer. They offer ice cream, cold drinks, and light lunches. Cross a bridge over Bad River just upstream of its entrance into the gorge. To the left, you can climb to an observation tower and gain a perspective on the countryside. The trail to the right leads to Copper Falls and views into the ragged, craggy rocks and frothing water of the gorge. Cross a second bridge to reach the Devils Gate, a rocky area through which the Bad River cuts. Brownstone Falls lies at the mouth of Tyler's Fork River where it drops into Bad River. The third bridge leads back to the picnic area. The whole gorge is alive with a rich forest that contrasts with the ancient red-brown rock of the gorge, once unsuccessfully mined for copper.

The North Country National Scenic Trail runs directly through the North Campground. Also, on its five-mile trek through Copper Falls, the North Country Trail descends Bad River Gorge to the north and past Loon Lake to the south. Hikers can also walk the 2.5-mile Red Granite Falls Trail, which passes yet another scenic waterfall. Hikers can join mountain bikers on two other loops, one of which passes Murphy Lake.

Over eight miles of river run through the park. Bad and Tyler's Fork rivers offer challenging fishing for rainbow, brown, and brook trout. Lake anglers can try their hand at Loon Lake, a no-motor venue offering largemouth bass, northern pike, and panfish. If you want to dunk yourself instead of a line, head for the sandy swim beach at Loon Lake. Swimming is prohibited in the Bad River due to the sharp rocks and fast water. However, exploration on the park trails is encouraged at this protected jewel of a park.

To get there: From Mellen, head north on Highway 13 for 0.5 mile to Highway 169. Turn right on Highway 169 and follow it 1.6 miles to the park, on your left.

KEY INFORMATION

Copper Falls State Park
Rural Route 1, Box 17AA
Mellen, WI 54546

Operated by: Wisconsin State Parks

Information: (715) 274-5123, www.wiparks.net, reservations (888) WIPARKS, www.reserveamerica.com

Open: Year-round

Individual sites: 55

Each site has: Picnic table, fire grate, 13 have electricity

Site assignment: By phone, Internet, or first come, first served

Registration: At campground entrance station

Facilities: Hot showers, flush toilets, vault toilets, water spigot

Parking: At campsites and a walk-in camper parking area

Fee: Memorial Day weekend through Labor Day weekend Friday–Saturday $10 resident, $12 non-residents; summer weekdays and all days rest of year $8 residents, $10 non-residents; $3 extra for electricity

Elevation: 1,100 feet

Restrictions

Pets—On leash only

Fires—In fire rings only

Alcoholic beverages—At campsites only

Vehicles—Two vehicles per site

Other—21-day stay limit

29. DAY LAKE

Clam Lake

The beautiful 640-acre lake that the campground sits on serves as a haven for wildlife. Waterfowl, especially loons, congregate on the lake's many floating islands. But the first you will notice is the very large campground. Under most circumstances, a campground this large would hold twice the number of campsites here at Day Lake, but those responsible for developing the campground gave each site more than ample room. And a myriad of outdoor activities are quite convenient. Boating, fishing, swimming, and hiking are just feet away, so pack your tent, bring your watercraft and fishing pole, and be prepared to have a good time.

Day Lake Campground is broken into six large loops with no more than ten campsites per loop. Overhead, tall red pines, jack pines, paper birch, and sugar maple sway with gentle breezes. A thick understory of ferns, brush, and small trees such as alder screen campsites from one another. Overall, the sites are as far apart as you are going to see in any drive-up campground. The campground as a whole is neat and well kept. Surprisingly, Day Lake doesn't often fill on weekends. I nabbed a first come, first served campsite on July 4th! But to eliminate worries, about half the campsites are reservable.

Each loop is reached via a spur road leading left from the main road. The first loop, Jack Pine Circle, houses campsites

CAMPGROUND RATINGS

Beauty:	★★★★★
Site privacy:	★★★★★
Site spaciousness:	★★★★★
Quiet:	★★★★
Security:	★★★
Cleanliness/upkeep:	★★★★

Campsite beauty is second only to natural beauty here at Day Lake.

#1–#10. Jack pines dominate the tree cover. Campsites #7–#9 face Day Lake and are reservable. The next loop, Heron Circle, is set away from the water but offers amble space and privacy. The sites here, #11–#17, lie on the outside of the loop, and except for #17, can all be reserved.

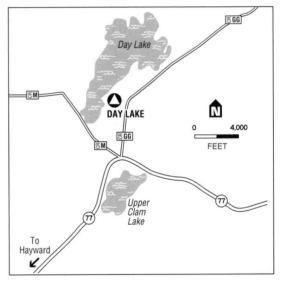

The next spur road leads to Paper Birch and Red Pine Circle. Paper Birch is paved and has sites suitable for RVs, few of which ever show up. A couple of the all-access sites have paved pads. Campsites #18–#22 are toward the lake. Some of the sites are so large they are open to the noon sun overhead. The Red Pine Circle has even larger sites at #29–#39. Try reserving sites #29 and #30 if you want a lot of room.

The Blueberry Circle has only six campsites, #40–45. All are first come, first served and are the least used in the entire campground. The loop is a bit away from the lake, but the sites are all desirable. The potentially buggy brush and tree marsh lying near campsites #41 and #42 must scare campers away. However, campsite #42 offers the most solitude in the entire campground. Musky Bay Circle, with sites #46–#52, is the final loop. It may have the most widely dispersed sites of them all. Campsites #48–#49 are toward the lake and are reservable. Each loop has a bathroom and pump wells conveniently located in the center and connected by woodsy paths to the loops.

Day Lake was formed in 1968, when the West Fork of the Chippewa River was dammed. The impoundment created many islands. If you notice some of these islands moving, you aren't seeing things. These masses of vegetation with the occasional small tree are drifting bogs; they provide ideal nesting habitat for loons, which are frequently seen and heard on Day Lake. Muskellunge, largemouth bass, and panfish lie beneath the waters.

Side trails connect the campground to several mini-piers for fishing or docking your boat as well as the interpretive nature trail that runs along the lake, connecting the campground to a picnic area near the dam. Informal shore-fishing spots have been established just off the nature trail. A longer L-shaped fishing pier lies near the Paper Birch Loop.

Kids will enjoy the large, grassy play area near Jack Pine Circle. Here, kids can play on the playground or throw horseshoes while their parents sit on nearby benches. If a swim is desired, there is also a campground swim beach nearby. A sandy waterfront near the picnic area leads to a second roped-off swim beach, where visitors will find yet another fishing pier. Check out the little island by the Day Lake Dam, connected to the mainland by a small wood bridge. Supplies can be had at the small store in nearby Clam Lake. The hamlet also has a few eateries. Get all the food and supplies you want—with these large campsites, you will have plenty of room.

To get there: From Clam Lake, head west on County Road M for 100 yards, then turn right (north) on County Road GG. Keep forward on GG for 0.8 mile to the campground, on your left.

KEY INFORMATION

Day Lake
Highway 13 North, P.O. Box 126
Glidden, WI 54527

Operated by: U.S. Forest Service

Information: (715) 264-2511; www.fs.fed.us/r9/cnnf, reservations (877) 444-6777, www.reserveUSA.com

Open: May through October

Individual sites: 52

Each site has: Picnic table, fire ring

Site assignment: By phone, Internet, or first come, first served

Registration: Self-registration, on-site

Facilities: Pump wells, vault toilets

Parking: At campsites only

Fee: $12 per night

Elevation: 1,460 feet

Restrictions

Pets—On leash only

Fires—In fire rings only

Alcoholic beverages—At campsites only

Vehicles—None

Other—14-day stay limit

30. INTERSTATE STATE PARK

St. Croix Falls

One look at the rock formations here, the "Dalles of the St. Croix," and you will see why this became Wisconsin's first state park. Urbanization has crept up on the area, so if you are looking for a completely rustic backwoods experience, read no further. However, if you want to enjoy some good canoeing on the St. Croix River, hiking amid the Dalles, and biking on the Gandy Dancer State Trail, then come here and appreciate this place for what it is, and be grateful that supply runs will never be easier.

Each campground area has its advantages and drawbacks. The North Campground has larger, more widespread sites, some of which are quite pleasant. However, the camp is very close to Highway 8, which connects Wisconsin and Minnesota, and you can clearly hear auto traffic (even more so than on your average suburban street). You won't hear as much traffic in the South Campground, but the sites tend to be small and a little too close together. They also are situated next to a swampy area beside the St. Croix River, so the bugs will be more bothersome here. Actually, both are tolerable and the drawbacks can be avoided with some judicious site picking or visiting during the week or off-season. The mosquitoes just have to be lived with here.

To reach sites #1–#40 in the North Campground from Highway 35, turn onto

CAMPGROUND RATINGS

Beauty: ★★★
Site privacy: ★★
Site spaciousness: ★★
Quiet: ★
Security: ★★★
Cleanliness/upkeep: ★★★

Check out the rock formations on the St. Croix River at Wisconsin's oldest state park.

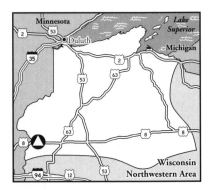

Highway 8 toward Minnesota, then turn right into the campground. Come to an intersection and follow the loop right. The beginning of the loop has several sites with just enough trees to keep you from getting completely sunburned, and they are the closest to Highway 8. As the loop circles around, it becomes more heavily wooded with nice campsites among the hardwoods and white pines. A spur road leading to the Department of Natural Resources fish hatchery con-

tains the three best campsites in the loop, #23–#25. All are walk-in tent sites. The loop continues around to come along the St. Croix River. The sites here are a bit cramped. Campsite #30 overlooks the St. Croix. A second dead-end road spurs off to the right with sites #37–#40. Campsite #39 and #40 overlook the river but are very close to Highway 8. Recommended reservable campsites are #19, #23, #24, #25, and #37.

The South Campground is free of noise, except maybe from your nearby neighbor. The narrow loop is heavily wooded. The sites are small to average in size, so bring the little tent. These sites would be fine, save for their proximity to one another. Recommended reservable campsites include #41, #60, #61, #65, #67, and #68. Generally speaking, reserve a site on the outside of the loop, and definitely reserve ahead of time at either campground during the summer season.

If you come here, you have to walk the trails above the St. Croix River—they are among the finest in Wisconsin. The Pothole Trail overlooks the river, the rocky bluffs studded with majestic white pines, and the trail passes by the large water- and rock-carved holes that give the trail its name. This is a popular place for rock climbers. The trail passes just above the St. Croix River, but don't be tempted to jump in: Cliff jumping into the St. Croix River is expressly forbidden. The Summit Rock Trail leads to another overlook where you can see the "Old Man of the Dalles," a clearly visible outline of a human face. Echo Canyon Trail cuts through a rock garden amid white pines and mossy ground. The River Bluff Trail borders precipitous cliffs that will make you dizzy. The Eagle Peak Trail heads from the South Campground to an overlook.

The no-motor Lake of the Dalles has a large swim beach and beach house, plus angling for northern pike, walleye, crappie, and panfish. The St. Croix River offers paddling among the bluffs and good fishing for smallmouth bass and walleye. Hikers and bikers may want to check out a portion of the nearby Gandy Dancer State Trail. This 98-mile rail trail starts in St. Croix Falls and extends north to Superior. Quest Canoe Rental, located just outside the park, rents bikes and boats. They also provide shuttles for water or land travel on the St. Croix or the Gandy Dancer Trail.

Interstate State Park is one of nine units of Wisconsin's Ice Age Reserve. Take a little while to visit the park's Ice Age Interpretive Center and learn more about what shaped the area and so much of Wisconsin here at the Badger State's first state park.

To get there: From St. Croix Falls, take Highway 35 south 1 mile to the park, on your right.

KEY INFORMATION

Interstate State Park
P.O. Box 703
St. Croix Falls, WI 54024

Operated by: Wisconsin State Parks

Information: (715) 483-3747, www.wiparks.net, reservations (888) WIPARKS, www.reserveamerica.com

Open: South Campground April through December; North Campground May through October, water and showers on May 15 through October 15

Individual sites: 85

Each site has: Picnic table, fire ring

Site assignment: By phone, Internet, or first come, first served

Registration: At entrance station

Facilities: Hot showers, flush toilets, pit toilets, water spigots

Parking: At campsites only

Fee: Wisconsin residents $8 per night Sunday–Thursday, $10 per night Friday, Saturday; non-residents $10 per night Sunday–Thursday, $12 per night Friday, Saturday

Elevation: 700 feet

Restrictions

Pets—On leash only

Fires—In fire rings only

Alcoholic beverages—At campsites only

Vehicles—2 vehicles per site

Other—21-day stay limit

31. LAKE OF THE PINES

Hawkins

The Flambeau River is a remote watercourse flowing through a state forest of 90,000 acres, where bears, wolves, and other wildlife abound. I found proof of this on the nature trail at Lake of the Pines campground—fresh bear scat! Don't think that deterred me from staying here overnight. Quite the contrary, it only reinforced my opinion that this was a great place to camp; you are really getting back to nature when a bear or two has enough room to roam. And Lake of the Pines Campground is an ideally located base camp for canoeing both forks of the Flambeau in addition to other forest pursuits.

Lake of the Pines is the headwater for Connors Creek, which flows into the North Fork Flambeau River. Lake of the Pines Road dead-ends into the campground, which has two loops. The lower loop has eight campsites resting beneath a hardwood forest of sugar maple, birch, basswood, and a few spruce trees. Thick brush grows between most of these widespread sites all located on the outside of the loop. The road climbs a small hill to the upper loop. These sites are well shaded but are closer together than the lower loop, offering only average campsite privacy. The forested setting is just as pretty as the lower loop. The sites outside the loop are on the edge of a slope that drops off to Lake of the Pines. The loop swings away from the water and passes larger sites.

CAMPGROUND RATINGS

Beauty:	★★★★
Site privacy:	★★★
Site spaciousness:	★★★
Quiet:	★★★★
Security:	★★★
Cleanliness/upkeep:	★★★★

This campground lies near the Flambeau River, one of the state's wildest canoeing destinations.

These sites back up to a thick forest that makes for an attractive setting. A pump well and vault toilets are provided for each loop. Since this campground fills only on holiday weekends, most sites will be readily available on your average summer weekend.

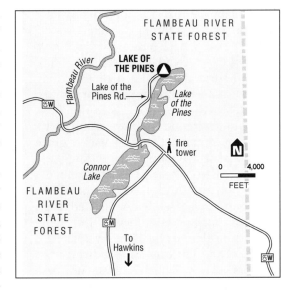

Canoeing is the number-one draw to Flambeau River State Forest. Over 60 miles of water can be paddled on the South and North Forks of the Flambeau River. State forest land protects its banks and offers a truly wild setting. Boat landings are adequately spaced along the rivers. The South Fork is rougher and can be too low to run in summer. However, when spring comes, get ready for some good class II–III rapids. You may want to consider portaging around Little Falls Rapid, a class V challenge.

The North Fork is more commonly paddled and has more reliable water. Its uppermost run extends for 12 miles from Nine Mile Creek to Oxbo Landing. The next day trip heads from Oxbo Landing to County Road W, where the forest headquarters is located. This is considered some of the wildest river in the forest, yet it offers fairly gentle water with no named rapids. The next trip, from County W to Camp 41 Road, has the Porcupine Rapids, a three-pitched shoal. The action picks up below Camp 41 with two sets of rapids just before the confluence of the South and North Forks. Six more named rapids can be found along the Flambeau before it exits into Big Falls Flowage in Rusk County.

Most paddlers bring a fishing pole to angle for the musky, walleye, and smallmouth bass that roam the waters. For a more convenient experience, try

Lake of the Pines. A boat landing is conveniently located at the campground. Lake of the Pines is noted for its walleye, bass, pike, and crappie fishing. Bass Lake is close if you want a wilderness fishing experience. No motors are allowed, and accessing the lake requires a 0.4-mile boat carry. Try for largemouth bass and bluegill there.

A small swim beach is located on Lake of the Pines via a short path between campsites #13 and #14 on the upper loop. This neat little hideaway offers a grassy shore and small buoys in the water. If you are looking for something bigger, head just a short distance to Connors Lake Picnic Area. It has over 300 feet of beachfront, complemented with picnic tables, shade trees, and a shelter.

Landlubbers will want to check out the Flambeau Hills Trail System, very near Lake of the Pines. Hikers and bikers are welcome to use the 14 miles of interconnected paths that double as winter ski trails. And don't forget the nature trail that loops out of the campground. You might also keep an ear out for one of the wolf packs that roam Flambeau River State Forest.

KEY INFORMATION

Lake of the Pines
W1613 County Road W
Winter, WI 54896

Operated by: Wisconsin Department of Natural Resources

Information: (715) 332-5271, www.wiparks.net

Open: Year-round

Individual sites: 30

Each site has: Picnic table, fire ring, log bench

Site assignment: First come, first served, no reservation

Registration: Self-registration on-site

Facilities: Pump well, vault toilets

Parking: At campsites only

Fee: $7 per night Wisconsin residents, $9 per night non-residents

Elevation: 1,425 feet

Restrictions

Pets—On leash only

Fires—In fire rings only

Alcoholic beverages—At campsites only

Vehicles—Two vehicles per site

Other—21-day stay limit

To get there: From the junction with US 8 in Hawkins, take County Road M north for 18 miles to County Road W. Turn left on County Road W. Follow County Road W for 1 mile to Lake of the Pines Road. Turn right on Lake of the Pines Road and follow it for 1.6 miles to dead-end into the campground.

32. LAKE THREE/BEAVER LAKE

Mellen

After hearing about the view from St. Peters Dome, I knew it was a "must-see." But where to stay? The two nearby campgrounds, Lake Three and Beaver Lake, both deserved to be included in this book, but since they were so close to one another, I have lumped them together here. Both offer small, secluded, and quiet campgrounds and quality lakeside tent camping. And there are plenty of hiking, boating, and fishing opportunities nearby. No matter which one you pick, you will come out a winner.

The ten campsites at Beaver Lake are strung out on a small loop beside the water. There are some first come, first served campsites, but sites #4, #5, #7, #9, and #10 can be reserved. A forest of maple, basswood, aspen, birches, and evergreens shade this campground and provides mostly good campsite privacy. The first three campsites lie away from the lake but near the pump well and vault toilet. Campsite #2 is a small, tent-only unit. The loop curves around past a marshy down-hill and below the camp to reach campsite #4. This large and attractive site overlooks Beaver Lake. Campsites #5, #7, and #8 all have good lake views with short water-access trails. Campsite #7 has the best lake view of them all. Campsites #6, #9, and #10 are inside the loop.

Lake Three Campground has eight sites, all first come, first served. Campsite #1 is

CAMPGROUND RATINGS

Beauty:	★★★★
Site privacy:	★★★★
Site spaciousness:	★★★
Quiet:	★★★★★
Security:	★★★
Cleanliness/upkeep:	★★★★

Both these campgrounds lie in the shadow of St. Peters Dome.

inside the loop but is well screened with spruce and fir trees. Maples tower overhead. Campsite #2 is large and set away from the road. Campsite #3 may be the best of all; it is large and closest to the lake. Continuing on, you'll reach an area of shaded but open campsites. Further along the loop is campsite #4; located inside the loop, this small site is shaded and has open ground. Campsites #5 and #7 are close to the lake but have little campsite privacy. Campsites #6 and #8 are

large but are also limited on privacy. The campground pump well is down near the boat landing, which doubles as a swim area. The vault toilet is in the campground loop.

Short access trails from each campground connect to the three-mile North Country Trail, which connects the two areas. The access trail at Lake Three also leads down to the lake dam, where campers often tie up their boats. West of Beaver Lake is the Marengo Non-motorized Area, through which the North Country Trail also runs. The Brunsweiler River, a potential trout stream, is two miles east from Lake Three on the North Country Trail.

St. Peters Dome is a mandatory destination for hikers. I hit the trail in the cool of the morning, first stopping at Morgan Falls, a 60-foot narrow cascade slicing between ancient rocks. The path then led past an old homesite—the rock chimney and well were still discernible. A few ups and downs led to the final climb, and the northbound view lay before me. From the rock bluff, Morgan Creek and the forest lay in the foreground. Scattered farms with their tell-tale silos lay in the distance. And, to the right, 20 miles distant, were the waters of Lake Superior. The view was well worth the two-mile hike to the top. To reach the dome, continue north on Forest Road 187 past Lake Three Campground. After 0.5 mile, turn left on Forest Road 199 and stay with it for 5.5 miles to reach the signed trailhead on your right.

Lakes are directly beside both campgrounds. The 35-acre Beaver Lake sports trout, panfish, and catfish. A boat landing is 0.5 mile distant from the campground. Lake Three is 72 acres in size and holds largemouth bass and panfish. The boat ramp here is just off the campground road. A short trail leads to the grassy dam area on Lake Three, and it's a fun place for kids to toss in a line for panfish or watch the bats come out at night from a bat box on the dam levee.

Picking a campground in the shadow of St. Peters Dome is a tough choice. Neither is bound to fill except for holiday weekends. You could just take the hike to the top of the dome, then flip a coin. Either way, you will come out a winner.

To get there: From the junction with Highway 13 in Mellen, drive west on County Road GG for 8 miles to Forest Road 187. Turn right on FR 187, Mineral Lake Road, and follow it for 3 miles to Pine Stump Corner. To reach Beaver Lake, keep forward, now on Forest Road 198 for 2 miles and it will be on your right. To reach Lake Three, turn right at Pine Stump Corner and follow Forest Road 187 for 1 mile further, and it will be on your right.

KEY INFORMATION

Lake Three/Beaver Lake Highway 13 North, P.O. Box 126 Glidden, WI 54527

Operated by: U.S. Forest Service

Information: (715) 264-2511; www.fs.fed.us/r9/cnnf, reservations (877) 444-6777, www.reserveUSA.com

Open: May through October

Individual sites: Lake Three 8, Beaver Lake 10

Each site has: Picnic table, fire ring

Site assignment: By phone, Internet, or first come, first served

Registration: Self-registration, on-site

Facilities: Pump well, vault toilets

Parking: At campsites only

Fee: $10 per night

Elevation: 1,415 feet

Restrictions

Pets—On leash only

Fires—In fire rings only

Alcoholic beverages—At campsites only

Vehicles—None

Other—14-day stay limit

33. *PATTISON STATE PARK*

Superior

Big Manitou Falls is the centerpiece of this park. Superlatively speaking, it is the highest waterfall in the state and certainly one of its most photographed. Not only do you get a view of the falls from the many overlooks, but vistas also open up to the north and down the canyon of the Black River, which rushes to meet the Nemadji River on its way to Lake Superior. Back in the late 1800s, Martin Pattison took part in logging the Black River watershed and saw the beauty of the falls, as well as its upstream cousin, Little Manitou Falls. Later in life he became a wealthy man, and upon hearing of a plan to dam the Black River and submerge the falls, Pattison bought 660 acres of land along the river, thus saving the falls. He donated this land to the state of Wisconsin in 1920. The land formed the nucleus of the scenic state park. During the 1930s, the Civilian Conservation Corps made the park more visitor-friendly with their handiwork. A campground, added later, completes the picture. Today, Pattison is a worthwhile tent-camping destination.

At first, I wasn't crazy about the campground, as it is a little too close to the day-use facilities. However, after staying here, the convenience of having Interfalls Lake, the swim beach, Big Manitou Falls, and the park's trail system so close at hand proved to be a plus. There is one drawback, however: Highway 35 and County Road B are

CAMPGROUND RATINGS

Beauty:	★★★
Site privacy:	★★★
Site spaciousness:	★★★
Quiet:	★★
Security:	★★★
Cleanliness/upkeep:	★★★

Pattison is home to Wisconsin's highest waterfall.

well within earshot. Tent campers that disdain auto noise might head elsewhere. The campground is laid out in two loops, an outer loop and an inner loop. Most of the campsites have pull-through parking. The forest is a mix of North Country evergreens such as balsam, spruce and white cedar. Aspens, white birch, maple, and a few oaks round out the woods. The forest grows thick between the camp-sites, but most are open to the sky overhead, letting in the mid-day sun to shine on the grassy campsite floors.

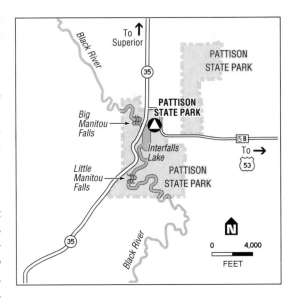

Campsites #1–#34 can be found on the outer loop, portions of which swing close to County B. Most sites are large and private, and while the loop starts near the day-use are, it quickly curves away from here. The first six sites are non-reservable. The best of these is #3. Four of the last five sites have electric-ity. Recommended reservable sites on this loop include #9, #16, #22, and #31. The inner loop holds campsites #35–#59. More of the sites are electric in this loop, but there are plenty of good non-electric sites. Often, sites on an inside loop can be small and have no privacy, but this loop is even more thickly wooded than the outer loop. Recommended reservable sites on this loop are #42, #43, and #52.

Pattison is popular during the summer and will fill on warm weekends. Make your reservations early. There are many double campsites here—if none of the recommended reservable sites are available, check to make sure you are not getting one half of a double site.

With such easy access, viewing Big Manitou Falls is the first order of business. Several vantage points grant good views of this 165-foot cataract. I took a few pictures for my scrapbook. On the way from the campground, you will pass the swim beach, located on Interfalls Lake. The Civilian Conservation Corps developed this 300-foot wide beach, bathhouse, and the adjacent structures. Head inside the nature center and admire the rustic lodge-like wood building, as well as the informative displays that reveal the park's geology, logging, and mining history. Interpretive nature programs are held most evenings during the summer.

Other parts of the park can be accessed by trail. The Logging Camp Trail makes a 4.7-mile loop through the park's south side and along Black River. The Little Falls Trail heads to Little Manitou Falls, a double falls dropping over a rock outcrop. On your return trip, take the bridge over Black River and return via the Beaver Slide Nature Trail. After exploring the park, you will understand why Martin Pattison put up his own money to preserve this natural resource.

To get there: From Superior, head south on Highway 35 for 13 miles to reach the park, on your left.

KEY INFORMATION

Pattison State Park
6294 State Road 35
Superior, WI 54880

Operated by: Wisconsin State Parks

Information: (715) 399-3111, www.wiparks.net, reservations (888) WIPARKS, www.reserveamerica.com

Open: Year-round, water on from Memorial Day weekend through September

Individual sites: 59

Each site has: Picnic table, fire ring, bench, 18 also have electricity

Site assignment: By phone, Internet, or first come, first served

Registration: At visitor center

Facilities: Hot showers, flush toilets, pit toilets, water spigots

Parking: At campsites only

Fee: Memorial Day weekend through Labor Day weekend Friday–Saturday $10 residents, $12 non-residents; summer weekdays and all days rest of year $8 residents, $10 non-residents; $3 extra for electricity

Elevation: 830 feet

Restrictions

Pets—On leash only

Fires—In fire rings only

Alcoholic beverages—At campsites only

Vehicles—Two vehicles per site

Other—No generators may be operated in park

34 . *PERCH LAKE*
Drummond

CAMPGROUND RATINGS

Beauty:	★★★★
Site privacy:	★★★★
Site spaciousness:	★★★★
Quiet:	★★★
Security:	★★★
Cleanliness/upkeep:	★★★

Explore the Rainbow Lake Wilderness from this campground.

Perch Lake is a fine destination in its own right. The 70-acre lake is scenic, quiet, and encircled by nothing but nature. The campground is divided into two quality loops. But what makes this campground special is its proximity to the Rainbow Lake Wilderness. This preserve lies just across the road from the campground. Numerous hiking trails lead to pristine lakes where you can fish and explore the wild side of the North Woods.

The two loops of Perch Lake Campground are not connected but are near one another. The North Loop contains sites #1–#10. All the campsites in the North Loop are near the water. Pass the small boat ramp and fee station to reach a forest of red pine, birch, fir, and some white pine that shade the campsites. Campsite #1 is up a bit of a hill; it overlooks the lake and is just steps away from the water, like the other campsites. Campsite #3 is larger. Pass a pump well, then come to shady campsite #4. Thickets of younger evergreens screen the campsites from one another, as does distance. The tree cover is less dense toward Perch Lake, allowing water views. Campsite #8 is very large, yet is close to the water. The road curves away from the water a bit as you approach campsite #9, which is also large. Campsite #10 is farthest from the water and the other campsites. A trail leads from this camp to the lake.

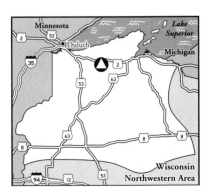

The South Loop holds campsites #11–#21 and is set in a hardwood forest with lush grass, ferns, and small trees underneath the maples, oaks, and birches. Enter this lesser-used loop and arrive at the small Campsite #19. Like most of the campsites here, it is well shaded. Swing around the loop and pass sites #20 and #21. They are small but secluded. Campsites #17 and #18 are near the fee station and are a bit larger, but they're also very shaded, with moss near the picnic tables. Campsites #11–

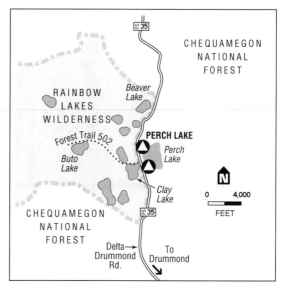

#16 are the largest in the loop and are used more often. They are up a bit of a hill and have many oaks and some pines. Perch Lake is visible below the hill. Campsites #15 and #16 are closest to the lake and are the most popular. Each loop has a pump well and vault toilets. The North Loop is better, but in case it is full, sites on the South Loop should be available in this first come, first served campground.

Perch Lake is over 70 acres in size. Most anglers paddle a canoe or row a small boat around the water in search of largemouth bass, panfish, and trout. The deepest part of Perch Lake is over 70 feet down It averages 19 feet deep, which keeps the water cool enough for trout. Numerous other lakes with small-boat access are just a short drive from Perch Lake. Most notable is Star Lake, a 234-acre no-motor lake. Star Lake has good fishing for musky, largemouth bass, and panfish. Consult your national forest map to access these other lakes.

Have you ever wanted to hike to a pristine lake in the back of beyond to cast a line, admire the scenery, or listen to the sounds of nothing but nature?

Visit the Rainbow Lake Wilderness, which is 6,600 acres in size. A six-mile section of the North Country National Scenic Trail crosses the wilderness. Forest Trail 502 leaves from across the South Loop of Perch Lake Campground and heads west to intersect the North Country Trail. Along the way it passes Clay Lake, a 31-acre lake with largemouth bass and panfish. Bufo Lake lies near the junction of the North Country Trail and Forest Trail 502. A scenic lake of 21 acres, Bufo also has largemouth bass and panfish. Beaver Lake is a short walk from a trail access just a bit up Forest Highway 35. It offers trout fishing. The other lakes and ponds are also good trout-fishing venues. Here at Perch Lake, you will be able to access water and its recreation opportunities from the campground, your car, or by foot.

To get there: From the junction of US 63 and Delta Drummond Road (Forest Highway 35), just west of Drummond, drive north on FH 35 for 5.5 miles to the campground, on your right.

KEY INFORMATION

Perch Lake
P.O. Box 578, 113 Bayfield Street
Washburn, WI 54891

Operated by: U.S. Forest Service

Information: (715) 373-2667, www.fs.fed.us/r9/cnnf

Open: May through October

Individual sites: 16

Each site has: Picnic table, fire grate

Site assignment: First come, first served, no reservation

Registration: Self-registration on-site

Facilities: Pump well, vault toilets

Parking: At campsites only

Fee: $10 per night

Elevation: 1,240 feet

Restrictions

Pets—On leash only

Fires—In fire rings only

Alcoholic beverages—At campsites only

Vehicles—None

Other—14-day stay limit

35. *SPEARHEAD POINT*
Westboro

This campground is situated on appropriately named Spearhead Point, a narrow peninsula jutting into Mondeaux Flowage, itself a scenic impoundment of the Mondeaux River in Taylor County. This narrow slice of land allows the campground to be nearly surrounded by water, making it a popular campground for boaters and anglers. The added mini-piers at most of the campsites make it even more attractive. More than water makes this campground appealing. The blufftop forest shades and screens campsites that look over Mondeaux Flowage. Furthermore, the whole Mondeaux Flowage Recreation Area offers fishing, swimming, and hiking opportunities.

You may just want to hang around this campground. Problem is, eventually you will be drawn to the water, especially if you have a pier extending from your campsite to the lake. Here's the deal: campsites #1, #3, #4, #7, #8, #11, #12, #13, #14, #15, #16, #17, and #18 all have these piers. A spur trail leads from the above sites down steps to the water's edge, where a small floating dock makes for easy water access and individual boat docking. You do pay extra for the campsites with piers, as they are designated "premium" sites, and they tend to go first. However, all campsites in the #1–#15 range are reservable, whether they are "premium" spots or not.

CAMPGROUND RATINGS

Beauty:	★★★★
Site privacy:	★★★★
Site spaciousness:	★★★
Quiet:	★★★
Security:	★★★★
Cleanliness/upkeep:	★★★★

Thirteen of the campsites here have their own individual mini-pier.

A thick hardwood forest of sugar maple, birch, and basswood, complemented with a few evergreens, grows on Spearhead Point. Pass the Ice Age Trail, which circles the northern half of Mondeaux Flowage, and reach campsites #25–#27, located on the "shaft" of the spearhead. These are among the largest of the campsites here, which are average-sized overall. Enter the main campground loop. Smaller spur loops to the right lead to several premium sites, which stand a good 30 feet

or more above the water. Campsite #4 is out on the edge of the peninsula. Campsite #8 is very well screened. Pass an attractive shelter building handy for rainy days, as it was during my visit.

Reach another spur loop toward the end of the spearhead containing sites #11–#15; here you'll find nothing but lakeside premium sites. Campsite #14 is a little too open. Return to the main loop and pass sites #16–#18; all three widely separated campsites are premium sites. Beyond a side road leading to the campground boat landing are four standard campsites that are nice but lack their own piers.

Most campers come here for the water activities. And why not, with the multitude of water accesses? Mondeaux Flowage offers fishing for musky, pike, largemouth bass, crappie, and panfish. You can fish from your pier, too, but most folks take their boat out on the 400-acre lake, created back in the 1930s by the Civilian Conservation Corps. A nice swim beach is located at the Mondeaux Picnic Area. A grassy field borders the buoyed swim area. Picnic tables and a playground complement the beach, as does a snack bar with food, beverages and ice. Paddleboats and canoes can also be rented here.

Hikers can enjoy the Ice Age Trail as it follows the northern half of Mondeaux Flowage on its 42-mile trek through the Medford District of the Chequamegon National Forest. A quick hike on the Ice Age Trail could lead from the Mondeaux Picnic Area back to Spearhead Point Campground. The Aldo Leopold Commemorative Trail makes a 1.2-mile loop just across from the Mondeaux Picnic Area. This path memorializing one of Wisconsin's great naturalists offers a vista. Another trail of interest is the Chippewa Lobe Interpretive Trail, located west of Mondeaux Flowage. This seven-mile interpretive loop path spurs off the Ice Age Trail, passing interesting glacial features in a primitive no-motor area. To reach this path, drive south from the campground on FR 106, then head west on FR 102, then south on FR 108. The Ice Age Trail crosses FR 108 and shortly offers access to the Chippewa Lobe Interpretive Trail. Chances are, however, that with all the water around you at Spearhead Point, you won't be spending much time on the land.

To get there: From Highway 64/13 in Medford, drive north on 13 for 15.5 miles to County Road D. Turn left on County Road D and follow it 6.5 miles to Forest Road 104. Turn left on FR 104 and follow it 1.1 miles to Forest Road 106. Keep on FR 106 for 1.6 miles to reach the campground, on your left.

KEY INFORMATION

Spearhead Point
850 North 8th, Highway 13
Medford, WI 54451

Operated by: U.S. Forest Service

Information: (715) 748-4875, www.fs.fed.us/r9/cnnf, reservations (877) 444-6777, www.reserveusa.com

Open: May through October

Individual sites: 27

Each site has: Picnic table, fire ring, some sites have small dock at water's edge

Site assignment: By phone, Internet, or first come, first served

Registration: Self-registration on-site

Facilities: Pump well, vault toilets

Parking: At campsites only

Fee: $10 per night, $12 per night for premium sites

Elevation: 1,400 feet

Restrictions

Pets—On leash only

Fires—In fire rings only

Alcoholic beverages—At campsites only

Vehicles—None

Other—14-day stay limit

36. ST. CROIX

Grantsburg

It is hard to believe a campground this nice and near so many natural resources is so little used. Set in Governor Knowles State Forest adjacent to the St. Croix Wild and Scenic River, this campground offers first rate canoeing and hiking from a campground that most would love to be their backyard. I stayed here on a weekday after an overnight canoe trip on the St. Croix River and had the whole campground to myself—in July! St. Croix Campground could also serve as pre-trip stopover spot, or as a base camp for day trips on the St. Croix. However, Governor Knowles State Forest stands tall as a destination in its own right, with over 50 miles of hiking trails, wildlife viewing, and fishing opportunities. This forest parallels the St. Croix River for 55 miles, yet never exceeds two miles in width. It has an important role in protecting the St. Croix watershed.

St. Croix Campground at Governor Knowles State Forest was developed in 2000. Forest service personnel did a fine job in laying it out. The park road climbs onto an escarpment above the confluence of the Wood River and the St. Croix River. This high-ground location cuts down on insects more prevalent along the banks of the St. Croix. The campground's beautiful forest setting is immediately evident. Overhead are tall oaks and white pines, complemented by ash, maple, jack pine, and a few aspen. A thick understory of

CAMPGROUND RATINGS

Beauty:	★★★★★
Site privacy:	★★★★★
Site spaciousness:	★★★★★
Quiet:	★★★
Security:	★★★
Cleanliness/upkeep:	★★★★★

This is the most underutilized forest and campground in the Wisconsin state forest system.

ferns and smaller trees enhances the scene.

The paved campground road leads past widely dispersed campsites that are quite large. Eleven of the 30 sites are on the inside of the loop. Campsite #1 exemplifies the average campground site here: a wide grassy area around a gravel auto pad encircled by tall trees, yet open to noon sun overhead due to its large size. It is surprisingly far to the next campsite.

Drop down a bit of a hill and come to more lush sites

with ramparts of ferns bordering the sites. Some of these campsites have wooden benches in front of fire rings cut into the hillside. Climb a bit and come to drier sites. Jack pines and white pines become more prevalent. Just after campsite #14, the Wood River Interpretive Trail leaves right and returns after site #20. The already well-separated sites spread apart even further after site #24. Three water spigots serve this campground, and there are open sites on weekends (including holiday weekends). Modern vault toilets are accessed via six short trails leading into the loop.

Canoeing the St. Croix River is the primary activity around these parts. The river deserves its wild and scenic status. Lush banks of grass and thick trees line the clear water teeming with smallmouth bass and other fish. Slender islands break up the shallow sandy river bottom. The swift current speeds up even more on the occasional riffles and shoals. The wildlife along this river will amaze. I saw bald eagles, osprey, a porcupine, ducks, and more deer than people. A canoe landing is located within walking distance of the campground. A short trip would be five miles from the campground canoe landing to Stevens Creek Landing, located on the Minnesota side of the river. It is nine miles down to County O Landing in Wisconsin. Upstream trips can end at the campground landing. Consider putting a whole day in and make the 13-mile float from Nelson's Landing to the campground. This section has many riffles and shoals. Before you come, be sure to visit the St. Croix National Scenic Riverway website at www.nps.gov/sacn and learn more about potential float trips. Numerous outfitters operate along the river; however, Wild River Outfitters is conveniently located near St. Croix Campground. They offer all lengths of trips and shuttles. For more information, visit www.wildriverpaddling.com.

Don't forget about hiking here at Governor Knowles State Forest and vicinity. The Wood River Interpretive Trail offers a one-mile leg-stretcher with views of the Wood River and information about the flora and fauna of the area. A spur trail connects the campground with the forest picnic area. Two long trails extend through the forest, each running about 22 miles; these are popular with backpackers. Just north of the campground, at Highway 70 Landing, is the Sandrock Cliffs Trail, which makes a narrow five-mile loop along the St. Croix River and the escarpment above it. The St. Croix Trail extends in both directions from the Marshland Visitor Center just across Highway 70 in Minnesota. And after a night or two at St. Croix Campground, you may decide to extend your stay in this underutilized Wisconsin resource.

> **To get there:** From Grantsburg, drive west on Highway 70 for 4.5 miles to a left turn into a marked road wayside. Turn left again into the campground.

KEY INFORMATION

St. Croix
P.O. Box 367
Grantsburg, WI 54840

Operated by: Wisconsin Department of Natural Resources

Information: (715) 463-2898

Open: May 1 through October 15

Individual sites: 31

Each site has: Picnic table, fire ring

Site assignment: First come, first served, no reservation

Registration: Self-registration on-site

Facilities: Water spigots, vault toilets

Parking: At campsites only

Fee: Wisconsin residents $7 per night Sunday–Thursday, $9 per night Friday–Saturday; non-residents $9 Sunday–Thursday, $11 per night Friday–Saturday

Elevation: 840 feet

Restrictions

Pets–On leash only

Fires—In fire rings only

Alcoholic beverages—At campsites only

Vehicles—None

Other—21-day stay limit

NORTHEASTERN WISCONSIN

37. *BAGLEY RAPIDS*

Mountain

If you look at a map of the Nicolet National Forest, you will see many private inholdings, denoted in white, amidst the holdings owned by the U.S. Forest Service. While scouring campgrounds in Wisconsin, I was certainly glad that the Bagley Rapids Campground along the North Branch Oconto River was "in the green." This destination at the southern end of the Nicolet lies on the North Branch of the Oconto River, a scenic watercourse that originates in lake-studded lands around the hamlet of Wabeno. From Wabeno, the North Branch of the Oconto twists, turns, and falls southward, pausing repeatedly to drop over granite rocks. In other places the river becomes blocked by fallen timber, forming dark hideaways for the trout that lurk in its waters.

Bagley Rapids Campground is located in what many consider the most impressive stretch of this river. The ledge-type rapids crash and boil over a rocky rampart that provides symphonic music for campers who choose to pitch a tent nearby. And you are very likely to get a site here—the campground is large enough such that all the sites aren't constantly taken, but it's not so big you feel like you are in a tent suburb. First come, first served means take your chances, but apart from the summer holidays, you should be able to get a campsite at 6 p.m. on Friday, if not noon on Saturday, even during high summer.

CAMPGROUND RATINGS

Beauty:	★★★★
Site privacy:	★★★
Site spaciousness:	★★★
Quiet:	★★★★
Security:	★★★
Cleanliness/upkeep:	★★★

The scenic North Branch Oconto River is just steps away from this campground.

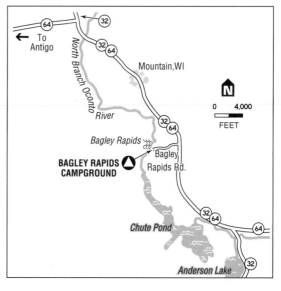

To reach the campground, drive through a leafy green cathedral. Overhead is a mix of North Woods trees as well as species more comfortable in southern climates. One spot will have dark hemlock, spruce, or fir, another will have hickories and oaks, and still another will reveal aspen, white pine, or paper birch. The campground has two loops stretched along the noisy river. Strategically placed boulders keep cars parked in their spurs and add a rocky touch to each campsite. Metal campsite fire rings have been placed atop circular rock platforms. Vegetation is thick between the campsites. Trees growing in the middle of the camps keep shady sites even shadier. Fourteen of the 30 sites rest along the river. These sites are the first to go, while the sites on the back of the loop offer more privacy. A little trail reaches the water from nearly every waterside site. Wherever you lay your head, the North Branch Oconto is loud enough to resonate throughout the campground.

Anglers have developed an informal trail system that stretches along the banks of the river and into the campsites. Though these trails travel along the main shoreline, the North Branch of the Oconto defies simple bank-fishing. Here and there, the Oconto splits around islands, making covering all the streamside water from the bank next to impossible. Casual fishermen won't likely bother with waders and such, but if you really want to fish this river, bring your felt-soled fishing shoes anytime of year and waders during spring. Otherwise, you can admire the scenery from the shore, or just take a little dip in the pools between fast-moving river rapids.

Just south of Bagley Rapids, the North Branch of the Oconto River flows into Chute Pond, a 417-acre impoundment. This island-dotted lake has muskie, pike, walleye, large mouth bass, and panfish in its waters. A boat ramp is conveniently located south of Bagley Rapids. Skilled paddlers will be seen zipping down the North Fork in spring or at times of higher water. The most popular trip, a nine-mile run, starts on Forest Road 2104 above Mountain. Most rapids are class II. Loon Rapids is 2.4 miles downriver, then paddlers pass the Old Krammer Dam site, where big boulders lie in the North Branch Oconto. The last two miles are placid before reaching Bagley Rapids, which are often too rocky to be run, except at high water. End at the campground or take out at the Chute Pond boat ramp. This river run adds fishing possibilities for rainbow, brown, and brook trout. Also, Forest Service roads and other roads cross the Oconto and offer fishing access points. Consult a Forest Service map, which should be ordered before arrival. Supplies can be had back in Mountain or just a bit north in Lakewood. Then you can head back to Bagley Rapids and be "in the green."

To get there: From Mountain, drive south on Highway 32 for 2 miles to Bagley Rapids Road. Turn right on Bagley Rapids Road and follow it 2 miles to the campground.

KEY INFORMATION

Bagley Rapids
15085 State Road 32
Lakewood, WI 54138

Operated by: U.S. Forest Service

Information: (715) 276-6333, www.fs.fed.us/r9/cnnf

Open: May through October

Individual sites: 30

Each site has: Picnic table, fire grate

Site assignment: First come, first served, no reservation

Registration: Self-registration on-site

Facilities: Pump well, vault toilet

Parking: At campsites only

Fee: $10 per night

Elevation: 900 feet

Restrictions

Pets—On leash only

Fires—In fire rings only

Alcoholic beverages—At campsites only

Vehicles—Three vehicles per site

Other—14-day stay limit

3 8 . *B E A R   L A K E*

Wabeno

Isn't life great when we are faced with a "win-win" choice? Bear Lake Campground offers three distinct camping options: walk-in camping, lakeside camping, or blufftop camping. Each option offers watery vistas and easy access to the campground's namesake, Bear Lake. Of course, after you pick your campsite, you will have to decide whether to fish, swim, canoe, hike, bird-watch, or just relax in the hammock. Oh, life's dilemmas!

First, you must make your campsite decision. Enter Bear Lake Recreation Area and pass the road leading left down to the Bear Lake boat landing. Ahead, the campground road splits. The road to the left leads to campsites #21–#27. Campsite #21 is small, open, and probably the least used in the campground, while campsite #22 is large, well shaded, and is used by larger groups. The other five sites are walk-in sites, accessed by a short trail that passes by the campground swim beach. Parking is available at the small auto turnaround. These walk-in sites are situated on a peninsula that juts into Bear Lake, and all have direct lake access via short foot trails. Campsite #23 is on a cove of the lake and is a bit open. Campsite #24 is more shaded. Campsite #25 overlooks the main body of Bear Lake. Campsite #26 is just a few steps from the water. Campsite #27 stands at the tip of the peninsula and is the most popular site. These campsites have

CAMPGROUND RATINGS

Beauty:	★★★★
Site privacy:	★★★★★
Site spaciousness:	★★★
Quiet:	★★★★★
Security:	★★★
Cleanliness/upkeep:	★★★

Walk-in campsites add even more lakeside overnighting options here.

access to a vault toilet also used for the nearby picnic area.

The remaining 22 sites, 9 of which are on bluffs near the lake, lie along a road running parallel to the shoreline of Bear Lake. The mixed forest of hardwoods and many conifers grows dense, especially between campsites, which are average in size and have mostly gravel and dirt for their floors. Campsites #5 and #6 have trails leading to the water. The blufftop camp-sites begin past site #9.

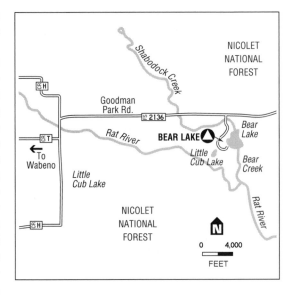

Campsite #12 is of special note, with steps leading up from the parking spur to a secluded hilltop site. Campsite #13 has maximum solitude away from the lake, and campsite #15 has an awesome blufftop view of the lake. Keep those binoculars handy for loon-watching—the birds were visible and calling during my visit. The shoreline curves away, and lake views become scarce past site #17, but campsites #18–#20 feature good solitude, both in distance from one another and from the thick vegetation between campsites. A foot trail runs along the shore below the bluffside campsites. Two water spigots and vault toilets serve the campground.

Adventurous anglers and explorers can check out five-acre Little Cub Lake, where they can fish for trout. The trail to Little Cub Lake starts on the loop road curving away from the campground. A parking area and trail sign mark the spot. Little Cub Lake is 27 feet at its deepest. If you want to fish nearer to camp, choose 68-acre Bear Lake. It has excellent panfish and northern pike opportunities, and largemouth bass are found in good numbers, too. Bear Lake has a 10-horsepower motor limit, though it is hard to see the need for a motor here. Bear Lake also has one of the best swim beaches in the Nicolet National Forest. A large, sandy shore is framed by wooden berms, while buoys float in the copper-colored water. Grass flourishes away from the beach.

Two hiking trails require a short drive to reach their trailheads. Continue east beyond the campground on Forest Road 2136 (Goodman Park Road) and travel 1.3 miles to the Halley Creek Bird Trail, created in concert with the Wisconsin Audubon Society. This path makes a mile-long loop that passes through varied bird habitats. To reach the Michigan Rapids Trail, continue east on FR 2136 just a bit beyond the Halley Creek Trail, then turn left on Forest Road 2134 (Michigan Rapids Road). The trailhead is just south of the bridge on the Peshtigo River. This trail makes a two-mile loop along the Peshtigo. Check out the rock formations and islands on the river. The Peshtigo is also good for canoeing and trout fishing. A six-mile paddle starts near the Michigan Rapids Trail and heads down to the Burton Wells Bridge, which can be reached by following FR 2136 east beyond Michigan Rapids Road. You may have to portage Ralton's Rip Rapids, a class III endeavor. The Nicolet National Forest map comes in handy here—a quick look will show how close all these "win-win" destinations are.

To get there: From Wabeno, head north on Highway 32 for 6 miles to County Road T. Turn right on County Road T and go 3 miles to County Road H. Turn left on H and drive 0.5 mile, then turn right on Forest Road 2136 (Goodman Park Road). Follow Goodman Park Road 4 miles to Forest Road 3770. Turn right on FR 3770 and reach the campground in 0.3 mile, on your left.

KEY INFORMATION

Bear Lake
4978 Highway 8 and 32
Laona, WI 54541

Operated by: U.S. Forest Service

Information: (715) 674-4481, www.fs.fed.us/r9/cnnf

Open: May through November

Individual sites: 32

Each site has: Picnic table, fire ring

Site assignment: First come, first served, no reservation

Registration: Self-registration on-site

Facilities: Pump well, vault toilets

Parking: At campsites only

Fee: $10 per night

Elevation: 1,400 feet

Restrictions

  Pets—On leash only

  Fires—In fire rings only

  Alcoholic beverages—At campsites and at walk-in parking area

  Vehicles—Two vehicles per site

  Other—14-day stay limit

39. *GOODMAN PARK*

Wabeno

The Civilian Conservation Corps originally developed Goodman Park in the
1930s. Their handiwork added a rustic
touch to an already scenic location. Strong
Falls loudly crashes among big boulders as
the Peshtigo River makes its way downstream to Green Bay. It is along this scenic
swath of the Peshtigo that the CCC built
beautiful log structures by the river that
complement the richly wooded river valley. And the camping here is first rate, especially if you like the sound of rushing water
as your evening lullaby.

This county park is one of the best in the
state. Covering 240 acres, the locale is
culled from the greater Marinette County
Forest, which covers over 220,000 acres.
The county forest was established after
lands were forfeited in lieu of taxes. Loggers had cut over this part of the state from
the 1880s through the 1920s, taking the
fantastic stands of white pine so prevalent
then. Later, they came back for hardwoods. Farmers eventually moved in from
southern Wisconsin, often buying property site unseen. The soil and terrain were
not conducive to farming, and the land
quickly played out. Farmers gave up and
left. Marinette County took over the abandoned farmland and began restoring and
cultivating the land for what it grew best—
trees. Today, the timber industry brings
revenue and jobs to Marinette County,
which in turn set aside many parks in the

CAMPGROUND RATINGS

Beauty:	★★★★
Site privacy:	★★★
Site spaciousness:	★★★★★
Quiet:	★★★★★
Security:	★★★
Cleanliness/upkeep:	★★★

*Enjoy the view of Strong Falls
from a picturesque river bridge.*

special spots of their forest. Marinette County is also the waterfall capital of the state, and while Strong Falls may not be the biggest or the tallest falls, the cascade, surrounding scenery, and the quiet, out-of-the-way campground add up to a great yet often unheralded tent-camping destination.

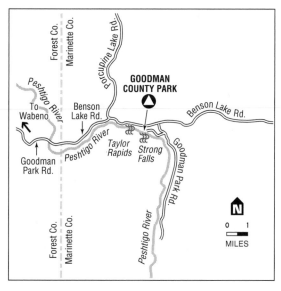

Pass through the main part of the park and resist the temptation to stop until you have selected your campsite. Enter a loop on high, level ground above the Peshtigo River, which is clearly audible. The pump well is near the fee station. Campsite #1 lies between a widespread oak and a line of red pines. Campsites #2 and #4 are on the inside of the loop in an open, grassy area with a few aspens in the middle. Campsite #3 is large and open, too. Here, the loop passes beneath enormous red pines with a mixed understory of spruce and hardwoods, and the campground completely changes character. Campsites #5 and #6 are backed into the tall pines, with red needles covering the ground. Campsite #7 is inside the loop and private. Campsite #8 is L-shaped and private, too. A pair of vault toilets are on the inside of the loop.

The loop eventually curves along the river to the best campsites. These are all large sites with red pines growing in and around them, and there is enough greenery between the sites for decent privacy. Trails lead from most campsites down to the river. I stayed in site #12 and had the whole place to myself on a nice July weekday, though there were many day visitors at the falls area.

Once you grab a campsite, head down to Strong Falls. Boulders stand defiant in the copper-colored water. Wide rock slabs border the river. A grassy flat has shade trees and picnic table along the water. Two rustic lodge buildings and a gazebo border the Peshtigo River. Other charming log structures rest away from the river, including a cabin that can be rented by the night. An arched wooden bridge crosses the Peshtigo and leads to an island where water dances between rocks on the far side. A board-walk connects to the second bridge to the far bank. Informal paths head along the river and rocks. People like to get sun on the rocks, fish for trout and panfish in pools between the numerous rapids, or just relax by the gazebo. And relaxing may just be the best thing to do at this fine county park.

To get there: From Wabeno, head north on Highway 32 for 6 miles to County Road T. Turn right on County Road T and follow it 3 miles to County Road H. Turn left on H and follow it 0.5 mile, then turn right on Forest Road 2136 (Goodman Park Road). Follow Goodman Park Road 15 miles to Goodman Park Road yet again. (That's not a misprint. The first Goodman Park Road turns into Benson Lake Road upon entering Marinette County.) Turn right on Goodman Park Road for the second time, and follow it 0.5 mile to Goodman County Park, on your right.

KEY INFORMATION

Goodman Park
Parks Office, Courthouse
1926 Hall Avenue
Marinette, WI 54143

Operated by: Marinette County

Information: (715) 732-7530

Open: April 15 through deer season

Individual sites: 15

Each site has: Picnic table, in-ground fire ring

Site assignment: First come, first served, no reservation

Registration: Self-registration on site

Facilities: Pump well, vault toilet

Parking: At campsites only

Fee: $10 per night

Elevation: 1,230 feet

Restrictions

Pets—On leash only

Fires—In fire rings only

Alcoholic beverages—No consumption of alcoholic beverages between 1 a.m. and 4 a.m.

Vehicles—Only 2 vehicles per site

Other—Pack it in, pack it out.

40. LAURA LAKE

Laona

The Nicolet National Forest brochure describes Laura Lake this way: "If you could create a perfect campground what would it include? For setting, maybe it should lie between two beautiful lakes. Of course, the lakes would be clear, with good fishing and excellent swimming. There would need to be a trail circling one of those beautiful lakes for scenic walks. And naturally, there would be no development on either lake. Sound perfect? Don't bother creating it. It already exists at Laura Lake."

That's quite a claim, but Laura Lake fully lives up to the Forest Service's billing. It was a long drive getting there, and I was hoping for the best while pulling in, remembering how other highly touted campgrounds had turned out to be duds. But as I pitched my Eureka! tent at campsite #10, I was ecstatic at what I saw. I knew I had found a winner in the great North Woods of Laura Lake. But, campsite #10 is not the only winner here. All the sites are winners. The campground is divided into three sections. The first campground road houses sites #1–#15, though they appear in reverse order as you enter. Nine of these sites are stretched along Laura Lake. Overhead is a beautiful mix of maples, paper birch, yellow birch, basswood, a few oaks, and evergreens—hemlock, spruce, and balsam. Ferns, grass, and small trees provide ample privacy between the well-separated campsites that are a bit back from the

CAMPGROUND RATINGS

Beauty:	★★★★★
Site privacy:	★★★★
Site spaciousness:	★★★★★
Quiet:	★★★★★
Security:	★★★★
Cleanliness/upkeep:	★★★★

This is a gem of the Nicolet National Forest.

water. However, the water can be easily accessed from your camp. The sites away from the water are even more private and are used less often. A pump well lies at the end of the loop near the small boat launch on Laura Lake.

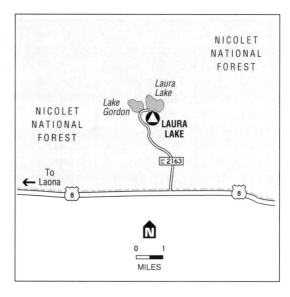

Campsites #16–#26 are stretched along the next campground road. The lakeside sites sit atop a hill. Campers park and take steps down to some of the sites, also located in very attractive woods. Again, the sites away from the water are more private. Campsite #25 is set in the woods away from the water and everyone else. A pump well is located at the beginning of the road. The third area lies at the end of the dead end and houses campsites #27–#41. The first few of these are the farthest from the lake but are also widely separated from each other. Campsites #37, #38, and #39 are lakeside.

Vault toilets are conveniently situated throughout the long and narrow campground. Laura Lake often fills on weekends, but this place is special enough to justify a little effort to get here during the week and hold your site down. A closer look at Laura Lake will reveal the crystal-clear water promised by the Forest Service. Furthermore, the lake is completely encircled by national forest land, making for a natural landscape. The 110-acre lake is an "electric motors only" lake, adding to the pristine experience. Largemouth bass, smallmouth bass, and panfish can be caught from Laura Lake. The 50-acre Gordon Lake, just a walk away, also has a boat ramp. Gordon Lake also has largemouth bass, smallmouth bass, and panfish in good numbers. The swim beach here is scenic enough to match the surroundings. A grassy lawn rises from the sand and is complemented with picnic tables. Nearby woods offer shade for those who don't want to be in the water.

The final piece to the puzzle is the Laura Lake Trail. This footpath officially begins near the turn to the Laura Lake boat ramp. It passes the isthmus of land between Gordon Lake and Laura Lake, then works around to near the shore of Laura Lake, keeping within sight of the water. A short spur trail leads north to Bog Lake. A contemplation bench marks the halfway point. Watch for osprey or loons on the lake. Chances are you will already have heard a loon by the time you take to the trail. The Forest Service came through on this trail as they did on their campground description, but don't believe *everything* you read.

KEY INFORMATION

Laura Lake
4978 Highway 8 and 32
Laona, WI 54541

Operated by: U.S. Forest Service

Information: (715) 674-4481, www.fs.fed.us/r9/cnnf

Open: May 1 through October 15

Individual sites: 41

Each site has: Picnic table, fire grate

Site assignment: First come, first served, no reservation

Registration: Self-registration on-site

Facilities: Pump well, vault toilets

Parking: At campsites only

Fee: $10 per night

Elevation: 1,500 feet

Restrictions

Pets—On leash only

Fires—In fire rings only

Alcoholic beverages—At campsites only

Vehicles—Two vehicles per site

Other—14-day stay limit

To get there: From the junction of US 8 and Highway 32 in Laona, head north on US 8 for 15.2 miles to Forest Road 2163. Turn left on FR 2163 and follow it 5 miles to dead end at the campground.

41. LAUTERMAN LAKE/ PERCH LAKE

Cavour

Campers who place a very high value on campsite privacy will love these two destinations. Lauterman Lake and Perch Lake have been turned into walk-in camping areas that take some effort to get to (anywhere from 200 yards to a mile walk), but they are the most rustic campsites in this entire guidebook.

Before you come here, call ahead and ask to be sent maps for Perch Lake and Lauterman Lake walk-in campground and surrounding trails. You can also inquire about getting an annual parking pass or use the pay station at Perch Lake to get your daily parking permit. There is no actual fee for the camping, just for the parking. The five campsites on Lauterman Lake are laid out on a 3.1-mile loop trail, though some of the sites offer shorter ways in. To reach the loop trail, do not take the Beginners Loop Trail, which leaves directly from the parking area. Instead, take the Lauterman Trail, located across the road from the parking area. Continue on the Lauterman Trail until you reach a junction. For units #1–#3, follow the trail indicating "Best Direction," which leads right. (Walk left to reach units #4 and #5.) Circle around and come to the trail leading left to unit #1, which is perched on a grassy hill with limited shade. A side trail leads a short distance to Highway 70. You could walk to the site from the parking area, find the campsite, then drop your

CAMPGROUND RATINGS

Beauty:	★★★★★
Site privacy:	★★★★★
Site spaciousness:	★★★★★
Quiet:	★★★★
Security:	★★★
Cleanliness/upkeep:	★★★★

All the campsites on these two lakes are walk-in!

gear near Highway 70 via car (making for a shorter carry), but the proximity of Highway 70 is the downside of this site. The trail continues and splits. The uphill route leads to unit #2 and is on a shaded knob with a trail leading down to the water. You can reach unit #3 by continuing down the trail, but most people use Forest Road 2553, one road west of the Lauterman parking area. From here, a 200-yard trail leads up to a beautiful, level site under hardwoods and above the

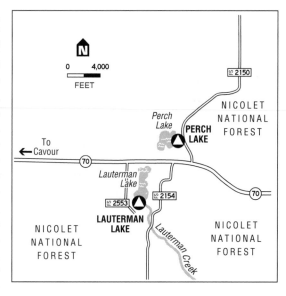

lake. This is the most popular site on Lauterman Lake.

To reach sites #4–#5, turn left at the junction mentioned above. Campsite #4 is on the south end of the lake near a shelter built for cross-country skiers. The shelter could come in handy during a rain. Campsite #5 is the least used, as the lake is a little more difficult to reach from there.

The five campsites on Perch Lake are laid out on a 1.3-mile loop trail that encircles the lake. Leave the Perch Lake parking area and climb over a hill. Turn right on the loop (left for unit #5) and soon come to unit #1. It is well shaded and near the canoe launch, making for quick and easy water access. Campers heading to other sites could paddle their gear across the lake to ease gear toting. Unit #2 is on a point. Unit #3 is perched on a hill and is the least popular, being too open and far above the lake. Unit #4 is close to the water and is shaded by big maples. Don't be surprised if you hear loons. They nest on Perch Lake. Unit #5 is close to the lake in a mix of sun and shade. It has easy water access to a gravel shore and would be ideal for canoes. Fishing canoers and shore anglers can vie for northern pike, bass, and bluegill on this

51-acre lake. At 44 acres, Lauterman Lake offers fishing for muskie, bass, and panfish.

Lauterman Lake Campground never fills, and Perch Lake Campground very rarely fills. Come here anytime for a great getaway. If you are here visiting Whisker Lake Wilderness, try to come in spring or fall—the trails will be less overgrown. The Lauterman trail system, which includes the Perch Lake Loop Trail and many others, is mown and/or otherwise well maintained. The Lauterman National Recreation Trail is nine miles long; it and many other connecting paths are depicted on the Forest Service's Lauterman Lake National Recreation Trail map. Mountain bikers and hikers will enjoy the undulating, mostly forested path that also crosses boardwalks over wetlands. A trail connects Lauterman Lake to Perch Lake. The 2.8-mile Porky Trail loops from the shelter near Lauterman unit #4. The Chipmunk Trail leads beyond the Porky Trail all the way to the Pine River. The trailhead for Whisker Lake Wilderness is 0.6 mile north of the Perch Lake parking area. Here, you can head for Riley Lake and Riley Creek for some backwoods trout fishing.

KEY INFORMATION

Lauterman Lake/Perch Lake HC1, Box 83, State Highway 70 and US 2 Florence, WI 54121

Operated by: U.S. Forest Service

Information: (715) 528-4464, www.fs.fed.us/r9/cnnf

Open: Year-round

Individual sites: Lauterman Lake 5, Perch Lake 5

Each site has: Picnic table, fire ring, most have vault toilet

Site assignment: First come, first served, no reservation

Registration: No registration

Facilities: None

Parking: At Lauterman Lake and Perch Lake walk-in parking areas

Fee: $3 daily parking fee required

Elevation: 1,450 feet

Restrictions

  Pets—On leash only

  Fires—In fire rings only

  Alcoholic beverages—At campsites only

  Vehicles—None

  Other—14-day stay limit

To get there: From Cavour, head north on Highway 139 for 21 miles to Highway 70. Turn right (east) on Highway 70, and follow it for 8.2 miles to Forest Road 2154. Turn right on FR 2154, and the Lauterman Lake parking area is on your left. To reach Perch Lake, keep forward on Highway 70 for 0.3 mile beyond FR 2154, and turn left on Forest Road 2150. Follow FR 2150 for 0.5 mile to reach the Perch Lake parking area, on your left.

42. *LOST LAKE*

Cavour

Lost Lake got its name for having no visible inflow or outlet to the body of water. The water in this lake has nowhere to go, and thus it is "lost." Tall white pines, hemlocks, and other evergreens border the deep, cool lake, which is fed by underground springs, making a good place even better. Many of these trees are old growth. A hiking trail runs in their shadows. At Lost Lake, you can camp in a fine shoreline setting and enjoy these natural assets and others concentrated in the area.

The campsites are strung along a road running atop a low rise by the lake. Most campsites are well shaded. The sites abutting the lake dip toward the water. Not all are perfectly level. Sixteen of the 27 campsites face Lost Lake. Campsite #1 is narrow, open, grassy, and is usually the last to be taken. A forest of maple, aspen, birch, and a few evergreens begins just past this site. Campsite #7 is large and inside the loop. Beyond here, many campsites bordering the lake are two-tiered—the parking area is on one level and the tent site, picnic table, and fire ring are just a short walk below. These two-tiered sites are mostly large and close to the lake with short paths meeting a hiking trail that runs parallel to the shoreline between the water and the campsites. The hardwood leaves overhead are so dense in places that only grass, ferns, and small trees grow beneath them. This attractive look does compromise campsite pri-

CAMPGROUND RATINGS

Beauty:	★★★★
Site privacy:	★★★
Site spaciousness:	★★★★
Quiet:	★★★★
Security:	★★★
Cleanliness/upkeep:	★★★

Old-growth trees border this spring-fed lake.

vacy, however. The camp-
sites become more widely
spaced after campsite #16.
After the access road turns
away from Lost Lake, the
campsites get even larger.
Basswood and maples shade
the last five campsites nearly
every minute of the day. Lost
Lake generally fills only on
holiday weekends, but the
lakeside sites are scooped up
by mid-Saturday on every
weekend. Vault toilets and
water sources are immedi-
ately available in the campground.

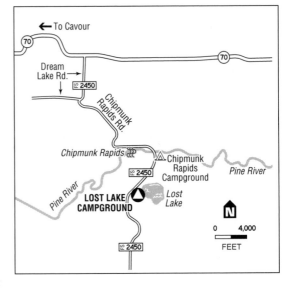

A fine picnic area lies next
to the boat landing under some hemlocks. No gas or electric motors are
allowed on this serene lake. Anglers can vie for trout, bass, and panfish. A
sandy swim beach is located on the shore of Lost Lake about midway along
the campground. Buoys delineate the swim area. The Pine River lies just north
of Lost Lake and offers stream fishing for native brook trout. Access is at Chipmunk Rapids Campground—a fine place to tent, but it has only six sites.
Chipmunk Rapids also has an artesian well with the finest drinking water in
northeast Wisconsin. You ought to check it out. The Pine River, a Wisconsin
Wild River, can also be canoed. A good six-mile run can be made from the
bridge at Highway 139 down to Chipmunk Rapids Campground. The river
gets tougher downstream of Chipmunk Rapids, and portages are required.
Check water flow before undertaking this paddle in later summer.

The land-based recreation at Lost Lake offers some of the best hiking in the
Nicolet National Forest. The Assessors Trail leaves from near the end of the
campground and makes a one-mile loop beneath those impressive old-
growth white pines and hemlocks. Of special note is the Assessors Pine, a tree

preserved at the behest of a taxman. Learn the full story on this not-to-be-missed interpretive path. I was very impressed with the Ridge Trail, which makes a 3.8-mile loop from the campground. First, it heads over to Chipmunk Rapids, then along the Pine River, where you can gain glimpses of the rocky stream. The trail then turns away from the river on a narrow, spindly ridgeline that drops off nearly vertically for quite a distance. The path then descends from the ridge and returns to Lost Lake amid more of those beautiful hemlocks. White rectangles mark the trail, making sure you won't get lost at Lost Lake.

To get there: From Cavour, head north on Highway 139 for 21 miles to Highway 70. Turn right (east) on Highway 70 and follow it for 3.6 miles to Forest Road 2450 (Dream Lake Road). Follow FR 2450 and keep forward (the name changes to Chipmunk Rapids Road) for 6 miles to the campground, on your left.

KEY INFORMATION

Lost Lake

HC1, Box 83, State Highway 70 and US 2

Florence, WI 54121

Operated by: U.S. Forest Service

Information: (715) 528-4464, www.fs.fed.us/r9/cnnf

Open: May through October

Individual sites: 27

Each site has: Picnic table, fire ring

Site assignment: First come, first served, no reservation

Registration: Self-registration on-site

Facilities: Water spigot, pump well, vault toilets

Parking: At campsites only

Fee: $10 per night

Elevation: 1,525 feet

Restrictions

 Pets—On leash only

 Fires—In fire rings only

 Alcoholic beverages—At campsites only

 Vehicles—Two vehicles per site

 Other—21-day stay limit

43. LUNA LAKE/ WHITE DEER LAKE

Eagle River

Mother Nature was working overtime in this neck of the Wisconsin woods. The two lakes adjacent to this campground, White Deer Lake and Luna Lake, are among the prettiest in the state, and that is saying a lot. They both have ultra-clear water, undeveloped shorelines of varied forest types, and some hilly terrain that adds vertical variation to the landscape. Speaking of hills, the campground here is set atop a hill that has campsites overlooking each lake. From your perch, you will want to see more of the water below. And exploring White Deer Lake and Luna Lake is easy, with boat launches and hiking trails—some of the finest around—circling both of them.

Pass the road leading left and downhill to the swim beach on White Deer Lake before entering the campground. A road to the left leads to a circular loop holding campsites #1–#9. A rich forest of cherry, spruce, fir, and maple thrives on a hill. Campsite #2 is a bilevel site, with steps leading to a tent pad. Descend a bit and reach sites overlooking White Deer Lake. The sites with red-banded posts (sites #5 and #7) have the lake view and the higher price. Steep trails lead down to the water. Campsites #6 and #9 are inside the loop but are heavily shaded. Spindly understory trees grow so tightly that it's hard to walk among them, making for good campsite privacy.

CAMPGROUND RATINGS

Beauty:	★★★★★
Site privacy:	★★★★
Site spaciousness:	★★★★
Quiet:	★★★★★
Security:	★★★
Cleanliness/upkeep:	★★★★

Two scenic lakes are available here for your enjoyment.

The second loop is long and narrow, stretched along the strip of land between the two lakes. Campsites #12 and #14 are very close to Luna Lake but have limited views because of the dense forest. A huge yellow birch grows behind campsite #14. Stately hemlocks circled my campsite at #16; these trees are prevalent throughout the area. Campsites #17 and #19 are hilltop sites looking out on Luna Lake. The loop curves around to the left, and the sites on the outside of the loop now overlook

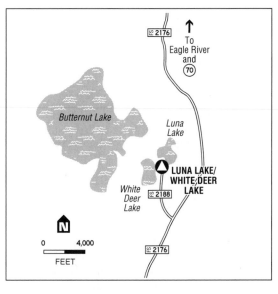

White Deer Lake. Some of these sites are a bit sloped but are still among the first to be scooped up. Two large, level sites, #25 and #26, are inside the loop. Rocks and red pines become more prevalent near campsite #27, which is a pull-beside site. Campsites #28 and #29 are on their own road bisecting the oblong loop. Most of the last eight campsites are lakeview sites. They are fairly large and well separated, offering great privacy aided by the hilly nature of the campground. Campsite #37 is shaded by a large maple in the middle. Surprisingly, this gem of a campground fills only erratically, but sites are usually open on non-holiday weekends. Get here fairly early on Friday, and you should get a site with no problem.

The no-motor lakes offer such attractive paddling and exploring opportunities that you may not even care if the fish aren't biting. Both lakes have largemouth and smallmouth bass and panfish. White Deer Lake is purported to have trout, too, and at 62 acres and a maximum depth of 45 feet, they could indeed be in there somewhere. Luna Lake is 67 acres in size. You may want to get a lay of the land and lakes before you toss in a line. The Luna-White Deer

Trail makes a four-mile figure-eight loop around both lakes, and it can be shortened to a pair of two-mile hikes for quicker getaways. Both loops traverse sun-splashed sandy shores, beneath tall red pines on steep hillsides, through hardwood forests with grass and ferns galore, under dark hemlock thickets, and across wetlands via wooden bridges. The portion along Luna Lake also passes two rustic campsites across from the campground. Part of the Hidden Lakes Trail system, the Luna-White Deer Trail connects ambitious hikers with the 13-mile Hidden Lakes Trail loop that heads over to Franklin Lake Campground and into remote backcountry areas. Major trail intersections are signed. Make time on your camping adventure to at least hike around Luna Lake or White Deer Lake if you aren't up to the Hidden Lakes Loop.

The swim beach has a good natural setting. A little trail leads to this grassy locale shaded by pines. Wooden berms circle a developed sand beach, and secured buoys delineate a swimming area that's about as clear as you'll find in the state. After a visit here, you also will be clear about how hard Mother Nature worked on this slice of the Nicolet National Forest.

To get there: From the intersection of US 45 and Highway 70 on the east end of Eagle River, near the Eagle River Ranger Station, take Highway 70 east for 14 miles to Forest Road 2176. Turn right on FR 2176 and follow it for 6 miles to Forest Road 2188. Turn right on FR 2188 and follow it 0.8 mile to the campground.

KEY INFORMATION

Luna Lake/White Deer Lake
P.O Box 1809, 4364 Wall Street
Eagle River, WI 54521

Operated by: U.S. Forest Service

Information: (715) 479-2827, www.fs.fed.us/r9/cnnf

Open: May through third weekend in October

Individual sites: 37

Each site has: Picnic table, fire grate

Site assignment: First come, first served, no reservation

Registration: Self-registration on-site

Facilities: Pump wells, vault toilets

Parking: At campsites only

Fee: $10 per night, $12 per night for lakeview sites

Elevation: 1,700 feet

Restrictions

  Pets—On leash only

  Fires—In fire rings only

  Alcoholic beverages—At campsites only

  Vehicles—Maximum three vehicles per site

  Other—14-day stay limit

44. NORTH TROUT LAKE

Woodruff

Trout Lake is big—3,816 acres in size to be exact. And out of all that shoreline, Northern Highland-American Legion State Forest personnel may have picked the prettiest spot of all to develop North Trout Lake Campground. Here, the shoreline rises high up a hill covered in mixed pines. Campsites are situated both down near the lake and atop a high bluff that gives a commanding view of this fish-filled lake. So grab your tent (and maybe some binoculars) and head on up to Trout Lake.

The campground makes a big loop divided in the middle. Pass the wood shed, and three walk-in tent campsites are in a pine-dotted flat to your left. These large campsites offer good lake views and access but have limited privacy due to minimal understory. Enter the campground loop. Campsites #1–#4 are also in a piney flat with excellent lake views, but again have limited privacy. Pine needles carpet the ground. Climb a steep hill and come to some neat blufftop sites, 100 or more feet above the lake. The pines are thick here, and so is the understory vegetation, creating good campsite privacy yet offering vistas between the tall tree trunks. Even-numbered campsites #6–#14 overlook the lake from outside the loop. The odd-numbered inside-loop campsites are shaded and fine, but they don't offer the blufftop vistas the even-numbered sites do. Reach the parking area for North Trout

CAMPGROUND RATINGS

Beauty: ★★★★
Site privacy: ★★★
Site spaciousness: ★★★★
Quiet: ★★★
Security: ★★★★
Cleanliness/upkeep: ★★★

Shady camping atop a piney bluff awaits visitors to this big lake.

Lake's walk-in tent camp-sites. A foot trail leads steeply off the bluff down to a second flat where the walk-in sites, #15–#19, lie beside Trout Lake. Pines shade these sites. The sites are a bit close together for walk-in sites, but I would be proud to pitch my tent at any one of them. Campsite #19 is the most secluded and is set away from the lake. Campsite #20 is a drive-up site all by itself. The road cutting through the loop houses very shady sites, #21–#31, that work

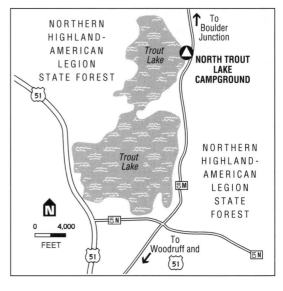

especially well for privacy seekers. The sites are quite widespread for being in the middle of a loop (save for campsites #30 and #31, which are too close together). The outside of the loop holds campsites #32–#45. Pass the North Trout Nature Trail and reach campsite #32. Evergreens add a scenic touch to the shady campsites here. Two pairs of campsites are double sites for larger groups. The last four sites are off the bluff in a piney flat. The sites are nice but lack privacy and are a little close to the action. They do offer quick access to the water.

It is not all about water here at Trout Lake. The North Trout Nature Trail leaves directly from the campground. The path makes a one-mile loop around a mature black spruce–tamarack bog and along North Trout Lake. But that is not the only trail around here. A paved bike trail leads north, roughly paralleling County Road M, to the town of Boulder Junction. That way you can leave your car at the campground for those supply runs. The paved bike trail also leads south to Crystal Lake Campground and Saynor, over by Plum Lake. If you make it to Saynor, you will be plum tired.

Trout Lake obviously harbors its namesake, as it is 117 feet at its deepest. Besides trout, Trout Lake offers muskellunge, northern pike, walleye, bass, and panfish for anglers. A boat landing is conveniently close to the campground, as is a water-access area. This spot near the boat landing has a nice swim beach. A grassy area, partly shaded, offers a spot to relax and take in the scenery and action. Boats are often tooling around Trout Lake for recreation and to fish. And they have plenty of water to cover, considering the acreage of Trout Lake.

To get there: From the intersection of US 51 and Highway 47 in Woodruff, take US 51 north for 6.2 miles to County Road M. Turn right on County Road M and travel 6.8 miles to the campground, on your left.

KEY INFORMATION

North Trout Lake
4125 CTH M
Boulder Junction, WI 54512

Operated by: Wisconsin Department of Natural Resources

Information: (715) 385-2727, www.wiparks.net

Open: Opens and closes with snow conditions, pump well open Memorial Day weekend through Labor Day weekend

Individual sites: 48

Each site has: Picnic table, fire ring

Site assignment: First come, first served, no reservation

Registration: Attendant will come by and register you

Facilities: Pump wells, vault toilets

Parking: At campsites only

Fee: Memorial Day weekend through Labor Day weekend, $9 per night residents, $11 per night non-residents, summer weekdays and all days rest of year $7 residents, $9 non-residents

Elevation: 1,625 feet

Restrictions

Pets—On leash only

Fires—In fire rings only

Alcoholic beverages—At campsites only

Vehicles—None

Other—21-day stay limit

45. *POTAWATOMI STATE PARK*

Sturgeon Bay

The Door County peninsula, the "thumb" of land extending northeast from Green Bay, is a popular summer tourist destination. The natural beauty of the peninsula, with its central ridge dropping to steep slopes and cliffs overlooking Lake Michigan, was what originally drew people to this location. Now, all sorts of tourist offerings beckon. However, much of the beauty remains, especially at Potawatomi State Park. This scenic swath preserves over two miles of shoreline along Sturgeon Bay, which opens into Green Bay on Lake Michigan. Here, you can camp in a pretty forest and enjoy many recreational activities in the park as well as those attractions of Door County beyond the park's borders.

The Potawatomi State Park campground, known as Daisy Field, is broken into two units—a south unit and a north unit. Both are located on a bluff above Sturgeon Bay, where an interesting agglomeration of trees grows overhead—cedar, basswood, maple, paper birch, beech, and some scattered oaks and aspens. It all adds up to an appealing setting. To reach the campground, continue through the park's entrance, go past the bathhouse, then turn right to enter the South Unit. Because of the nice scenery and lack of nearby roads, the South Unit is the better of the two areas. Follow the road counterclockwise, passing by the electric sites, which tend to

CAMPGROUND RATINGS

Beauty:	★★★★
Site privacy:	★★★
Site spaciousness:	★★★
Quiet:	★★★
Security:	★★★
Cleanliness/upkeep:	★★★★

Access the tourist sites of Door County from this less-busy park that is a fine destination unto itself.

pack in the big rigs. Before you wonder if you made a mistake coming here, continue around, past a cross road leading left to more electric sites, and you'll come to the good part. Here, even-numbered sites on the outside of the loop, #32–#54, are backed against a rock escarpment. This rock wall is partially covered with moss and adds a scenic touch to the sites. As the loop curves left, reach the outside sites #54–#66, which have partial views of Sturgeon Bay. The sites on

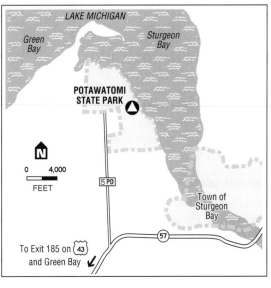

the inside of this loop are generally more wooded and shaded, especially by hemlock trees. At this point, a cross road provides access to sites #67–#80, which are heavily wooded with a thick understory adding campsite privacy. Continue around the loop to return to the electric sites at the very end of the South Unit.

While the North Unit is set in an attractive forest, the two nearby park roads make this the least desirable of the two units. These campsites are well separated and more level. The shade is good, but the understory is lacking in some areas. The even-numbered sites, #82–#124, are non-reservable. Avoid even-numbered sites #84–#102; they are too close to Shore Road. The odd-numbered sites through #85–#103 will work. The opposite is true for the rest of the loop: Avoid sites #105–#125 and go for #106–#124. But I would first try for sites in the South Unit.

Potawatomi is adequately served by a common bathhouse with water spigots and vault toilets throughout the campground. However, the water here has an iron-ish taste you may find unpleasant, so consider bringing your own drinking water. Most of the sites are reservable, so grab a site and come on up. Potawatomi will fill on summer weekends starting in late June and will stay full through mid-August.

Bring your bicycle here. The park has eight miles of paved park roads great for scenic pedaling in addition to the campground roads. It also has a four-mile off-road bike trail. Hikers can choose from six miles of hiking-only paths that wander along the cedar-lined lakeshore. There are views of the lake and up-close looks at the woodlands on the inner peninsula. The Tower Trail leads to an observation tower, also accessible by bike or auto, that offers far-reaching vistas into Green Bay and beyond. The Hemlock Trail makes a loop in the south end of the park.

Potawatomi has its own boat launch, complete with a dock and fish-cleaning station. You can shore-fish along the bay for brown trout, walleye, pike, and bass. If you don't have your own boat, canoes are for rent at the park, as are bikes. The park even rents fishing gear!

Swimming is discouraged at the park, but the nearby town of Sturgeon Bay has public beaches. The town is also the northeast terminus for the 30-mile Ahnapee State Trail—a multi-use path winding along the Ahnapee River that flows into Lake Michigan and on to Casco. For detailed information, visit www.sturgeonbay.net, then head up to enjoy the "thumb" of Wisconsin in Door County.

To get there: From Exit 185 on I-43 near Green Bay, take Highway 57 north for 37 miles to County Road PD. Turn left on County Road PD and follow it 2.5 miles to the park, on your right.

KEY INFORMATION

Potawatomi State Park
3740, County Road PD
Sturgeon Bay, WI 54235

Operated by: Wisconsin State Parks

Information: (920) 746-2890, www.wiparks.net, reservations (888) WIPARKS, www.reserveamerica.com

Open: Year-round, bathhouse and spigots open May through October

Individual sites: 125

Each site has: Picnic table, fire grate, wood bench, 25 sites also have electricity

Site assignment: By phone, Internet, or first come, first served

Registration: At entrance station

Facilities: Hot showers, flush toilets, pit toilets, water spigots, camp store, telephone

Parking: At campsites only

Fee: Memorial Day weekend through Labor Day weekend, $10 per night residents, $12 per night non-residents, summer weekdays and all days rest of year $8 residents, $10 non-residents

Elevation: 700 feet

Restrictions

Pets—On leash only

Fires—In fire rings only

Alcoholic beverages—At campsites only

Vehicles—None

Other—21-day stay limit

46. ROCK ISLAND STATE PARK

Sturgeon Bay

S ome claim that the best of the best in tent camping is on Rock Island, known as Wisconsin's "furthest northeast point." Located two ferry rides northeast of the tip of the Door Peninsula, a tent-camping trip to this island park may leave you nodding your head in agreement. Once the home of a wealthy inventor, Chester H. Thordarson, Rock Island comprises 900 acres of history and nature where beaches, bluffs, and woodlands contrast with the relics of voyageurs, settlers, and parts of Thordarson's estate. The campground here lives up to its heady surroundings.

Campers visiting here live on "ferry time." All who visit here are at the mercy of the ferryboat schedule. Be sure to bring all your gear and food (there are no stores on the island) and come ready to walk, since no cars or bikes are allowed. You will have to tote your gear anywhere from 200 yards to a half-mile. I recommend staying at least two nights given all the effort it takes to reach Rock Island.

Get off the second ferry, walk past buildings left over from the Thordarson Estate, and pass the water spigot for the campground. Walk between impressive rock walls. Ahead, three trails lead to various parts of the campground. "Michigan Avenue" leads toward sites #1–#12. Pass pit toilets and a changing station at the end of Michigan Avenue. A big dune separates you from the Lake Michigan on the south-

CAMPGROUND RATINGS

Beauty:	★★★★★
Site privacy:	★★★★★
Site spaciousness:	★★★★
Quiet:	★★★★★
Security:	★★★★★
Cleanliness/upkeep:	★★★★

It takes a lot of effort to reach Rock Island, but the effort is worth it.

west shore of Rock Island. Campsites #1–#3 are in cedar, sugar maple, and oak woods just inland from a sandy shoreline. Campsites #4–#7 are a bit back from the water near an old cemetery. All these sites are near an old Potawatomi Indian village and a building site of the voyageur LaSalle. Campsites #9, #11, and #13 are just on the back side of the dune in a mix of sun and shade.

A grassy trail leads into thick cedar woods atop a bluff. Campsites #15–#19 are on the edge of the bluff offering a stunning view of Lake Michigan. Campsites #20 and #22 are a bit back from the water. Campsite #21 offers lake views. Next comes a line of campsites, #23–#29, directly beside the water toward Washington Island. This line offers great sites in a mix of sun and shade on the edge of a rock beach.

The third trail leads inland toward heavily wooded, well-separated sites, #30–#35, offering maximum solitude. These sites are large and fine, and while they are the last ones taken, they provide shelter when the weather is cool and windy. By the way, a stone shelter building with a fireplace inside lies near the campground for bad-weather days. Six vault toilets are spread throughout the campground. All campsites can be reserved from Memorial Day to Labor Day. Rock Island will fill on Memorial Day weekend, on the last two weekends of July, and most days in August. Chilly winds blowing off Lake Michigan keep campers away early in the season. Consider coming in September.

The sand and rock beaches are a big draw at Rock Island State Park. No wonder—they offer picture-postcard scenery. The trail system explores some of the human and natural history of the island. Everyone likes to take the mile walk to the Potawatomi Lighthouse. Built in 1836, it is the oldest lighthouse in Wisconsin. The 5.2-mile Thordarson Loop Trail continues beyond the lighthouse around the perimeter of the island to the old fishing village (the first settlement in Door County), where water tower and settler house foundations can still be seen. The Algonquin Nature Loop Trail details the flora and lake history of the island. Check out the rock carvings on the bluffs just below the campground. The Viking Hall stands over a beautiful stone boathouse, part of the Thordarson Estate. In here, you can check out artifacts from the days of the Potawatomi tribe to a more recent past, including old photos and some of Thordarson's original Icelandic carved-oak furniture.

Some campers shore-fish for smallmouth bass and perch, but what campers like most about Rock Island is living on ferry time. You come and go with the ferries, so just relax and leave your worries on the mainland. Just remember to bring your tent—and everything else you will need for camping on this island getaway.

To get there: From Sturgeon Bay, head north on Highway 42 for 46 miles to its end. Here, you must take a pay ferry to reach Washington Island. From Washington Island, drive north on Lobdells Point Road for 1.7 miles to Main Road. Turn left on Main Road and follow it 2.6 miles to Jackson Harbor Road. Turn right on Jackson Harbor Road and follow it 3.6 miles to the Rock Island Ferry. Campers must park in the state park lot, just north of the passenger-only pay ferry.

KEY INFORMATION

Rock Island State Park
Route 1, Box 118A
Washington Island, WI 54246

Operated by: Wisconsin State Parks

Information: Summer: (920) 847-2235; off season: (920) 847-3256, www.wiparks.net, reservations (888) WIPARKS, www.reserveamerica.com

Open: Year-round—Private ferry services run only from May 24 to Oct 14

Individual sites: 35

Each site has: Picnic table, fire ring

Site assignment: By phone, Internet, or first come, first served

Registration: At visitor center

Facilities: Hot showers, flush toilets, pit toilets, water spigots, pay phone

Parking: At campsites only

Fee: Memorial Day weekend through Labor Day weekend Friday and Saturday $10 residents, $12 non-residents; summer weekdays and all days rest of year $8 residents, $10 non-residents

Elevation: 600 feet

Restrictions

Pets—On leash only

Fires—In fire rings only

Alcoholic beverages—At campsites only

Vehicles—No vehicles or bicycles allowed in park

Other—21-day stay-limit, 6 people per campsite

47. SANDY BEACH LAKE

Woodruff

Northern Highland-American Legion State Forest was established in 1925 to protect the headwaters of many Wisconsin rivers. This area has the most abundant and closely concentrated group of lakes in the state. From this agglomeration of over 900 lakes flow the Wisconsin, Flambeau and Manitowish riverways. One such protected headwater lake is Sandy Beach Lake, which feeds the Flambeau River. After seeing Sandy Beach Lake, you may think it was protected for its scenic beauty alone. Spruce, fir, pine, and white birch ring the shoreline of this undeveloped lake, and its dark waters contrast with the tan sand for which the lake was named. Being distant from the North Country tourist towns keeps it a quiet tent-camping destination in this vast, 222,000-acre state forest.

The campground sits on a level parcel of thick forest land adjacent to Sandy Beach Lake. The first set of campsites in the loop, #1–#13, are situated away from the lake. A dense forest of paper birch, spruce, fir, maple, and hemlocks shades from above. The woods are even thicker between the campsites than they are over them, making for great campsite privacy. Campsite #11 has a pair of shady spruce trees in the middle of the campsite. Campsite #12 is the only sunny campsite here. The loop curves around and reaches the three walk-in tent campsites, #14–#16, two of which are directly lakeside. Campsite #14 is

CAMPGROUND RATINGS

Beauty:	★★★★
Site privacy:	★★★★
Site spaciousness:	★★★
Quiet:	★★★★
Security:	★★★★
Cleanliness/upkeep:	★★★★

The campground at this good swimming lake rarely fills.

away from the lake. Just past the walk-in sites are the coveted lakeside sites. The lakeside sites are large, accommodating a tent, bug-screen shelter, and a small boat, and many red pines provide shade. There are seven drive-up lakeside sites. Two other sites are close to the lake, but lush woods obscure the water view. The sites on the inside of the loop are smaller but will do, though I would just as soon camp in the more private sites at the beginning of the loop, #1–#11, if a lakeside site was not available.

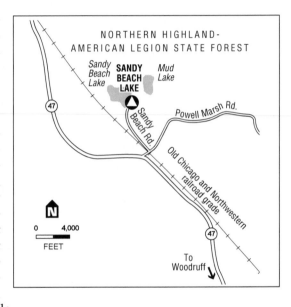

A campground host lives on-site for your convenience and safety. Two water spigots and three vault toilets serve the campground. Sandy Beach Lake fills only on holiday weekends and sometimes not even then. Be advised that the mosquitoes can be troublesome early in the camping season.

The lakeside sites are perfect for beach lovers, who can enjoy the sandy waters directly from their campsite. Campers without lakefront sites can walk a short distance to the water access and picnic area, where a grassy flat pocked with pines overlooks a developed swim beach with deep water buoys. Though the dark-water lake is only 111 acres, gas motors are allowed. Anglers can vie for muskellunge, pike, walleye, largemouth bass, and panfish. Many campers leave their boats directly in front of the campsite. Others use the boat launch located near the campground entrance. The launch also has a small dock. A trail located in pines near the swim beach parking area will lead anglers to Mud Lake, where they can fish for bass in a wild setting. Another fishing option is on the Manitowish River, located just north of Sandy Beach

Lake near US 51. It also offers good canoeing and fishing opportunities.

Wildlife-watching is easy here with Powell Marsh State Wildlife Area just a few miles distant. Turn left out of Sandy Beach Road and follow Powell Marsh Road a few miles to a cleared overlook on your right. The wildlife area offers great views of this home for sandhill cranes and other bird life. Explorers will want to hike the dikes in this open watery country. Hikers can also trek the cross-country ski trails located just a short distance from Sandy Beach Road on Powell Marsh Road. Bicyclers can tool around the paved campground road and the road to the swim beach or follow the old Chicago and Northwestern railroad grade near the campground. (You passed over it on the way in, at the junction of Sandy Beach Road and Powell Marsh Road.) Pedal north to Mercer or south to the La du Flambeau Indian Reservation. This trail is popular with snowmobiles in the winter. With the attractiveness of Sandy Beach Lake, I think the campground should be more popular with campers in summer.

To get there: From the intersection of US 51 and Highway 47 in Woodruff, head north on Highway 47 for 23.6 miles, passing through Lac du Flambeau on the way to Powell Marsh Road. Turn right on Powell Marsh Road and follow it 0.2 mile to Sandy Beach Road. Turn left on Sandy Beach Road and follow it for 1 mile to reach the campground, on your right.

KEY INFORMATION

Sandy Beach Lake
4125 CTH M
Boulder Junction, WI 54512

Operated by: Wisconsin Department of Natural Resources

Information: (715) 385-2727, www.wiparks.net

Open: Wednesday before Memorial Day through Labor Day weekend

Individual sites: 33

Each site has: Picnic table, fire ring

Site assignment: First come, first served, no reservation

Registration: Campground host will register you

Facilities: Pump wells, vault toilets

Parking: At campsites only

Fee: $7 per night residents, $9 per night non-residents

Elevation: 1,600 feet

Restrictions

 Pets—On leash only

 Fires—In fire rings only

 Alcoholic beverages—At campsites only

 Vehicles—None

 Other—21-day stay limit

48. STARRETT LAKE

Woodruff

No gas motors are allowed at Starrett Lake—at least on your boat. This rule sets the tone for this campground: peace and quiet come first. The land encircling Starrett Lake is owned by the Northern Highland-American Legion State Forest, further making the lake a natural respite. Busy roads are far from earshot. The campground, mostly set in a towering pine forest with secluded campsites, adds to the overall serenity of this North Woods getaway.

The campground lies along the shores of Starrett Lake. Enter the camping area from North Muskellunge Road, and dead ahead you'll see the boat landing, a pump well, and the beach access area. Head left and come to two small loops. Red pines and jack pines grow high overhead, and maples, oaks, and young trees reach partway up the pines, screening most campers from one another. Pass by campsites #1, #2, and #4, situated beside the lake access area, then campsites #5 and #6. All five sites are coveted lakefront campsites. Reach the walk-in tent-site parking area, where a short path leads downhill to walk-in sites #9–#11, also on the lake. Campsite #10 is beneath a huge white pine. Campsite #11 is a little too open to the sun. Return to the main drive-up campsites and continue to site #12, resting all by itself. Take the other loop in this section of the campground, and curve around and reach widely separated sites with piney floors

CAMPGROUND RATINGS

Beauty:	★★★★
Site privacy:	★★★★
Site spaciousness:	★★★
Quiet:	★★★★★
Security:	★★★
Cleanliness/upkeep:	★★★★

*Tent camp beneath the pines
on quiet Starrett Lake.*

away from the lake. The brush is thick between sites. I enjoyed campsite #19. Campsite #23 is banked against a hill and offers a nice dose of solitude.

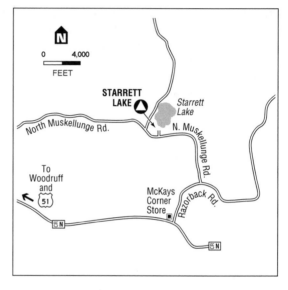

To reach the other half of the campground, head right from the main entrance and reach three walk-in tent sites (campsites #31–#33). While these sites are usually the first to go, they may be a little too close to the lake action for some, as the boat ramp and water-access area are nearby. All three sites are large and shady, however. Keep driving to the loop to find other sites that are more typical of what campers expect of walk-in sites. Enter the final loop. More hardwoods grow in this hilly area. Campsites #34–#37 are the least used and have much shade and privacy. Campsite #36 is in its own little world. Campsite #38 rests atop a hill. Campsite #39 overlooks the lake from its vantage point. The loop drops toward the lake and reaches sites #40, #42, and #44, each one big and facing toward Starrett Lake. The sites on the inside of this loop are used less.

Families and other campers return year after year to Starrett Lake. The campground usually fills on summer holiday weekends, but it often has open slots on other summer weekends. Friday arrivals are very likely to grab a site; I stayed here on a Friday in July, and many sites remained open. The facilities, including three pump wells and three bathrooms, are spread evenly throughout the camping area. Hot showers are available for a fee down the road at McKay's Corner Store, where treats like ice cream and a few hokey souvenirs are available. Mountain bikers will be happy to learn about the Razorback Ridges trail system. Developed and maintained by the Staynor-Star Lake

Lions, the single- and double-track paths make numerous loops of varied difficulties. The trail system starts behind McKay's Corner Store. A map is available at the trailhead, and a donation is requested to help maintain the paths.

Water recreation is the name of the game here, but leave that gas motor behind. Consider bringing your canoe or a rowboat to explore the 66-acre Starrett Lake. Self-propelled craft can easily cover the water surface, and anglers will find northern pike, walleye, and panfish in decent numbers. Largemouth bass are abundant, while smallmouth bass live here in lesser numbers. Campers can leave their boats by the small dock at the landing, while lakefront campers pull their boats up to their site. The cove also has a beach area. Kids can be found horsing around in the lake, while adults float on rafts. A second water-access area lies across the cove near campsites #31–#33. One thing you won't hear (or smell) on the water is a gas motor—at least from a boat.

To get there: From the intersection of US 51 and Highway 47 in Woodruff, head north on US 51 for 6.2 miles to County Road M. Turn right on County Road M and follow it 2.7 miles to County Road N. Turn right on County Road N and follow it 4.9 miles to Razorback Road, near McKay's Corner Store. Turn left on Razorback Road and follow it 1 mile to North Muskellunge Road. Turn left on North Muskellunge Road and follow it 1.8 miles to the campground, on your right.

KEY INFORMATION

Starrett Lake
4125 CTH M
Boulder Junction, WI 54512

Operated by: Wisconsin Department of Natural Resources

Information: (715) 385-2727, www.wiparks.net

Open: Wednesday before Memorial Day through Labor Day weekend

Individual sites: 46

Each site has: Picnic table, fire ring

Site assignment: First come, first served, no reservation

Registration: Attendant will come by and register you

Facilities: Pump wells, vault toilets

Parking: At campsites only

Fee: $7 per night residents, $9 per night non-residents

Elevation: 1,650 feet

Restrictions

  Pets—On leash only

  Fires—In fire rings only

  Alcoholic beverages—At campsites only

  Vehicles—None

  Other—21-day stay limit

49. TWELVE FOOT FALLS PARK

Dunbar

Forget the roar of automobiles—the only roar you'll hear at this out-of-the-way campground is from its namesake waterfall. Marinette County, where this park is located, touts itself as the waterfall capital of Wisconsin. I have to agree. No less than 14 major named falls drop in the watersheds of this forest land, and five of these waterfalls, including Twelve Foot Falls, are in close proximity to this campground.

You won't see any RVs here; campers with holding tanks—camping code for RVs—are prohibited! The campground has two distinct areas, each offering different settings. Pass a pump well to reach the first camping area on the left, located on a small loop on an elevated flat covered in red pines. Some undergrowth separates these large and level campsites, and except for #5, all are located on the outside of the loop. At every site you will notice some unusual fire rings. They are circular and metal—that is nothing extraordinary—but they are placed into the ground so the lip of the fire ring is at ground level. Campsite #1 is large and set back from the road. Pass the next two campsites before reaching a short trail to a pair of vault toilets, one for each sex. Come to another short path leading to a site where you can purchase firewood. The loop continues around to campsite #4, large and set off by itself. Campsite #5 is the only undesirable site in the whole campground. The final two

CAMPGROUND RATINGS

Beauty:	★★★★
Site privacy:	★★★★
Site spaciousness:	★★★★
Quiet:	★★★★★
Security:	★★★
Cleanliness/upkeep:	★★★★

This waterfall-side campground is rustic and secluded.

sites, #6 and #7, are well shaded in the pines with the help of few oak trees.

To reach the second part of the campground, continue along main road, which drops off the escarpment into a day-use area. Twelve Foot Falls comes into view. Look for a narrow, gravel road leading right to the lower campground, less than 100 feet from the North Fork Pike River. The roar of Twelve Foot Falls is louder down here. This small loop is dominated by evergreens

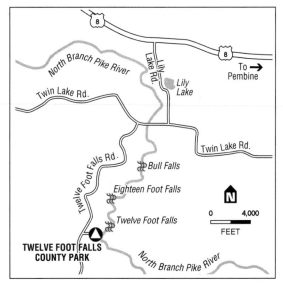

growing thickly together. Campsite #8 is the most popular in the park, since it is closest to the falls. The loop continues around to reach campsite #10, which has a side trail leading directly to the river. Campsite #12, the last, is all alone. A pair of vault toilets for each sex is located on the hill away from the river.

The first order of business is to take the trails to the falls. The trail to the right as you face the falls goes a short distance to a rock outcrop. Here you'll see the North Fork Pike River as it pours over a granite ledge into a large, swirling pool in its quest to meet the Menominee River to the east. To your right, the river again gathers steam and rushes around an island, working toward more waterfalls downstream. Across the water Twelve Foot Falls—dark copper water of the North Fork Pike River—spills over a gray granite rampart in a frame of trees. The outcrop on which you stand makes for a great place to fish and a good place to drown—don't swim below the falls! The trail leading left as you face Twelve Foot Falls bridges a stream and works around to the head of the falls, where you can stand close to the rushing water and overlook the waterfall's pool. Informal trails continue both upriver and downriver for trout and pike fishing possibilities and to view a smaller falls just downriver.

Falls viewing and fishing are the two obvious campside activities. Twelve Foot Falls isn't one of those places where all the fun is laid out for you. You have to create your own action. If you are smart enough not to swim in the falls pool but still want to take a dip, head to Lily Lake. You passed it on the way in. This quiet lake has a roped-off swim beach with a convenient changing station. You can also execute a falls viewing tour of Marinette County. Make sure and call the Marinette County parks office for an official highway map of the county or get one at the ranger station in Pembine. The map shows all the falls. You passed the side road to Eighteen Foot Falls on the way in. Horseshoe Falls is just a few miles distant from Twelve Foot Falls, as are Carney Rapids and Four Foot Falls. Then you can return to Twelve Foot Falls and be sung to sleep by its white noise.

To get there: From the intersection of US 8 and US 141 near Pembine, head west on US 8 for 8 miles to Lily Lake Road. Turn left on Lily Lake Road and follow it 1.6 miles to Twin Lakes Road. Turn right on Twin Lakes Road and follow it 0.4 mile to Twelve Foot Falls Road. Turn left on Twelve Foot Falls Road and follow it 2.7 miles to the campground, on your left.

KEY INFORMATION

Twelve Foot Falls Park
Parks Office, Courthouse, 1926 Hall Avenue
Marinette, WI 54143

Operated by: Marinette County

Information: (715) 732-7530

Open: April 15 through deer season

Individual sites: 12

Each site has: Picnic table, in-ground fire ring

Site assignment: First come, first served, no reservation

Registration: Self-registration on site

Facilities: Pump well, vault toilet

Parking: At campsites only

Fee: $10 per night

Elevation: 1,000 feet

Restrictions

Pets—On leash only

Fires—In fire rings only

Alcoholic beverages—No consumption of alcoholic beverages between 1 a.m. and 4 a.m.

Vehicles—Only 2 vehicles per site

Other—Pack it in, pack it out

50. TWIN LAKES

Fifield

Maybe it was the cobalt-blue skies and the sunshine of the beautiful day, but Twin Lakes Campground shone during my camping trip there. The mixed forest of pines, evergreens and hardwoods were deep green, the bark of paper birches glowing white. Twin Lake reflected the forest across the placid waters. I set up camp, promising to wet a line later, and headed just across Forest Road 142 to the Round Lake Non-motorized Area. Here, a network of trails beckoned, open to both hikers and bikers.

This campground is a true-blue winner. Campers that discover Twin Lakes end up returning year after year. Twin Lake is off to your left as you pass the boat launch and enter the campground, set on a brow overlooking Twin Lake. The campground road divides the camping area into two distinct groups. The sites to the left of the campground road—those that overlook the lake—are large, open in the center, and surrounded by tall trees such as red pine, maple, and birch that obscure all but the noonday sun. Spruce, fir, and brush grow between and among the campsites, which all have views of Twin Lake. Evergreen needles, gravel, and grass lie at the campsite floor. Campsite #17 is large and overlooks the lake. The most coveted site is #8, which lies all by itself at the end of a small auto turnaround.

CAMPGROUND RATINGS

Beauty:	★★★★★
Site privacy:	★★★★★
Site spaciousness:	★★★★
Quiet:	★★★★★
Security:	★★★
Cleanliness/upkeep:	★★★★

Twin Lakes is very appealing, and so is the adjacent Round Lake Non-motorized Area.

The sites to the right of the road are smaller and are heavily shaded by evergreens and hardwoods. They look literally cut out of the forest. Heavy vegetation screens the sites, many of which are far back from the paved campground road. Campsites #1 and #2 exemplify these characteristics to the maximum. A grassy path runs behind many of the campsites here, and some are reservable (sites #5–#11). Of these, the more secluded sites include #5–#7. The water pump here is

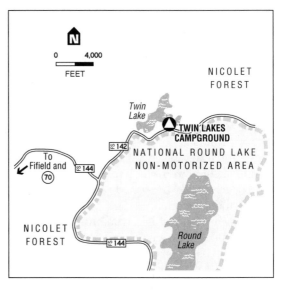

solar powered, so all you have to do is turn the faucet to get good aqua.

Twin Lake offers good fishing for largemouth bass on its 19 acres. Also sought are crappie, perch, and panfish. A short path near campsite #8 leads down to a small non-fishable lake. In my opinion, this unnamed small lake doesn't resemble Twin Lake. Two other lakes within short driving distance are Emily Lake and Wabasso Lake. Emily Lake, which has a fine campground of its own, has northern pike and panfish in its 26 acres. Wabasso Lake is bigger, and has bass, northern pike, and panfish.

The 3,600-acre Round Lake Non-motorized Area is detailed in a color map at the campground kiosk, or you can call ahead and ask for a map beforehand. The area is reached by foot from the trail just across from the campground road entrance. You can enjoy hiking or biking past prime waterfowl habitats, open fields, and thick woods, or take a trail to Round Lake. A nice but narrow gravel beach lines the north shore of Round Lake. Old-growth hemlocks shade the forest floor between Round Lake and Tucker Lake. Little metal maps on signs can be found at each trail intersection. I saw a fisher, beavers, and many birds on my hike. Bikers should be aware that the trails are grassy, and the grass can get high in summer.

Round Lake is the origin of the Flambeau River. An historic logging dam on Round Lake, built in 1878, has been restored; it is located on the way to Twin Lakes Campground. Back in the 1800s, Round Lake was filled with felled white pine logs, the dam gates were lowered, and off the logs went, destined for mills on the Chippewa and Mississippi rivers. Restoration of the dam was finished in 1997. An interpretive trail crosses the dam and circles around the South Fork Flambeau River. You could hike to the dam from Twin Lakes Campground, but consider driving and save your hikes from the campground for the non-motorized area. Round Lake has a boat launch and fishing opportunities, too. Give yourself an opportunity to visit Twin Lakes and all it has to offer.

To get there: From the intersection of Highway 13 and Highway 70 in Fifield, drive east for 16.5 miles to Forest Road 144. Turn left on FR 144 and follow it for 5.9 miles to Forest Road 142. Turn right on FR 142 and follow it 2.3 miles to the campground, on your left.

KEY INFORMATION

Twin Lakes
1170 4th Avenue South
Park Falls, WI 54552

Operated by: U.S. Forest Service

Information: (715) 762-2461, www.fs.fed.us/r9/cnnf, reservations (877) 444-6777, www.reserveusa.com

Open: May through October

Individual sites: 17

Each site has: Picnic table, fire grate

Site assignment: First come, first served and by reservation

Registration: Self-registration on-site

Facilities: Water spigot, vault toilet

Parking: At campsites only

Fee: $10 per night

Elevation: 1,600 feet

Restrictions

Pets—On leash only

Fires—In fire rings only

Alcoholic beverages—At campsites only

Vehicles—None

Other—14-day stay limit

APPENDICES

APPENDIX A
Camping Equipment Checklist

Except for the large and bulky items on this list, I keep a plastic storage container full of the essentials for car camping so they're ready to go when I am. I make a last-minute check of the inventory, resupply anything that's low or missing, and away I go!

Cooking Utensils
Bottle opener
Bottles of salt, pepper, spices, sugar,
  cooking oil, and maple syrup in
  waterproof, spill-proof containers
Can opener
Cups, plastic or tin
Dish soap (biodegradable), sponge,
  and towel
Flatware
Food of your choice
Frying pan
Fuel for stove
Lighter, matches in waterproof
  container
Plates
Pocketknife
Pot with lid
Stove
Tin foil
Wooden spoon

First Aid Kit
Band-Aids
First aid cream
Gauze pads
Aspirin
Insect repellent
Moleskin
Snakebite kit
Sunscreen/chapstick
Tape, waterproof adhesive

Sleeping Gear
Pillow
Sleeping bag
Sleeping pad, inflatable or insulated
Tent with ground tarp and rainfly

Miscellaneous
Bath soap (biodegradable), washcloth,
  and towel
Camp chair
Candles
Cooler
Deck of cards
Fire starter
Flashlight with fresh batteries
Lantern
Maps (road, topographic, trails, etc.)
Paper towels
Plastic zip-top bags
Sunglasses
Toilet paper
Water bottle
Wool blanket

Optional
Barbecue grill
Binoculars
Field guides on bird, plant, and
  wildlife identification
Fishing rod and tackle
GPS

APPENDIX B
Information

Chequamegon-Nicolet National Forest
68 South Stevens Street
Rhinelander, WI 54501
(715) 362-1300
www.fs.fed.us/r9/cnnf

Wisconsin Department of Tourism
(800) 432-8747
www.travelwisconsin.com

Wisconsin State Parks, Forests and Recreation Areas
Department of Natural Resources
Bureau of Parks and Recreation
P.O. Box 7921
Madison, WI 53707
(608) 266-2181
www.wiparks.net

INDEX

ABOUT THE AUTHOR

Johnny Molloy is an outdoor writer based in Nashville, Tennessee. A native Tennessean, he was born in Memphis and moved to Knoxville in 1980 to attend the University of Tennessee. It is in Knoxville where he developed his love of the natural world that has since become the primary focus his life.

It all started on a backpacking foray into the Great Smoky Mountains National Park. That first trip, though a disaster, unleashed an innate love of the outdoors that has led to his averaging over 100 nights in the wild per year since 1982, backpacking and canoe camping throughout our country and abroad. Specifically, he has spent over 650 nights in the Smokies alone, where he cultivated his woodsmanship and expertise on those lofty mountains.

In 1987, after graduating from the University of Tennessee with a degree in economics, he continued to spend an ever-increasing time in the natural places, becoming more skilled in a variety of environments. Friends enjoyed his adventure stories; one even suggested he write a book. Soon he was parlaying his love of the outdoors into an occupation. The results of his efforts are books covering his home state of Tennessee and much of the United States from Florida to Wisconsin to Colorado. Molloy has also written numerous magazine articles for magazines such as *Backpacker* and *Sea Kayaker*. He has also has written for websites such as gorp.com. He continues to write to this day and travel extensively to all four corners of the United States, pursuing a variety of outdoor interests and activities.

into thin hips. McAdams recognized the look and then studied the face, clean shaven and with astonishing green eyes.

"You're the ball player, yes?" she said.

"Uh, yes ma'am."

"I've seen you during the games, the ones with the Cuban Giants that Mr. Flagler displayed out back."

"Yes ma'am," he said again, with no less humility at being recognized.

"If I'm not mistaken, you played third base, yes?"

"Yes ma'am."

"And pitched one game?"

"Yes ma'am."

The baseball games, always played by Negro teams, were organized by the hotel during the winter months and were a favorite among the guests. McAdams had become quite enraptured during the first season that the Royal Poinciana was opened. The Cuban Giants were an especially entertaining team with a group of athletically talented men who seemed unbeatable. Most of the hotel guests knew of course that relatively none of the players were actually from Cuba but played under assumed names so they would be allowed to participate in venues where Negroes were not allowed.

"I believe I saw you hit a home run against a Mr. Sachel Paige," she said, recalling a game from one of those earlier seasons.

"Yes ma'am. Uh, but Mizz Fleury, ma'am, she really needs to see you ma'am," he said, taking a step back as if to draw her out of the room by creating a vacuum.

"Oh, of course," McAdams said, gathering herself. "Right away, Mr. Santos. If you could wait in the lobby, sir. I will be right there."

McAdams dressed in her most conservative black skirt and a ruffled blouse that buttoned high on her neck. She supposed the clothes she selected were in response to the fact that she had been in such a mode of undress when Mr. Santos was just outside her apartment door. She rolled her hair and tucked it up under a straw hat and went downstairs.

Santos was just near the entryway. She went directly to him and again he drew her outside by backing his large, muscular body away. Not seeing Miss Fleury, she looked questioningly into the black man's eyes.

"She's in the laundry, ma'am," he answered the unasked question. "She's holding someone there and can't come herself, but she needs you."

CHAPTER EIGHT

MARJORY McADAMS LEFT THE ROYAL POINCIANA and walked the distance back to the Breakers alone. The heat of midday reached only into the high seventies with the ocean breeze rising. She strode briskly. Those who nodded and smiled their greetings as they passed would have been instead turning their eyes away if they could see the visions she was conjuring in her head: the fire-seared trousers of a dead man, his shirt melted into his charred skin, his body lumped onto the crude lean-to floor like a roll of soft dough settling flaccid without the shape of formed muscle and air-filled lung, and the flame-scarred face with the obscenity of rolled bills protruding from the mouth and that one single eye that had turned a milky white as if the fluid inside had actually boiled. McAdams shivered in the heat, breathed deeply, and extended her stride. She tried again to reconstruct the face as it appeared when the man was alive. And what of the watch? Had Pearson or any of the others noticed that exquisite silver pocket watch the dead man was wearing on a chain attached to his vest? She had seen it. Certainly Pearson would not have missed it.

She spoke only briefly to staff at the Breakers and made her way to her suite, which was oceanfront and on the third floor, which she preferred despite the stairs. The maid was finishing with the bed and was gathering linens. McAdams searched the young woman's face as she had the other workers, looking for pain or some sign of loss.

"Hello, Armie, are you all right?" McAdams said.

"Ma'am?" the girl said.

"I'm sorry, your name is Armie, yes?"

"Yes, ma'am."

"Are you. Excuse me, were you, living in the Styx, Armie, and how did your family fare in the fire?"

"Uh, yes ma'am, I was in the Styx, ma'am, but I ain't got family with me, ma'am."

The girl was younger than McAdams but many of the locals and even women from other parts of the state and beyond followed the work that the trains and resorts had opened for them.

"Do you have someplace to stay, Armie? Someone to stay with?"

"Oh, yes ma'am. Mizz Fleury, she say she already found us a roomin' house on the other side of the lake, ma'am. We gone stay in a big place over near the church on Mr. Flagler's order hisself," the girl said, her chin and voice rising with the use of the man's name as if she was talking of a proud uncle. "Mizz Fleury say Mr. Flagler gone build us our own places in West Palm an ride us to the island ever day for work."

"How nice," McAdams said, but the tone of her voice set the girl to lower her eyes and turn to gather the linens and leave. McAdams did not doubt the rumor. Flagler was noted for innumerable projects he had built along his burgeoning railway. But she had been around wealthy, powerful and paternal men enough to know that there was always a price for their philanthropy. When the girl offered to bring in fresh water for her basin McAdams declined and let her leave.

Alone in the suite McAdams again washed the grit and salt sheen of humidity and sweat off her face and then removed her blouse and did the same for her arms with a sea sponge her father had given her as a present from a place in Florida called Key West. She removed her skirt and sat on the edge of the bed and washed down her legs as well. When she was finished she pulled a sitting room chair over to the double French doors to the balcony and then opened them to the beach and ocean. A salt breeze was blowing in, sweeping back the sheerings of the curtains. She sat and crossed her ankles on a European ottoman, and with the wind brushing the silk of her camisole and her bared legs, she dreamed she was flying.

She was a child in a tree, most likely one of the huge oaks at the family's vacation home in Connecticut. She'd been allowed to climb there, the rules for young ladies and societal appearances be damned in the summertime, said

her mother. In the dream she was high in the upper branches and a mist under her, obscuring the ground below. She felt frightened and gloriou, same time, the wind in her face, the gauze below and an odd smell of the air though she knew they were nowhere near Nantucket, which w only place she'd been to smell the sea. She stepped out farther on the standing up but keeping her balance by grasping the thin branches just a The exhilarating feeling of simply stepping off, spreading her arms and so over the familiar grounds of their summer getaway was glowing in her head. that glimmer of ultimate danger kept her feet in place. She raised her nose to wind and closed her eyes. The freedom of soaring, or the fear of death? Deci my dear. You could fly for seconds or for miles. You could fall screaming fifty feet, or soar forever. She stepped off. The air in her lungs caught in h throat as she went out and down. She was falling, but at the same time hearing knock at the door, someone assaulting the wood, the noise snapping her awak in midflight.

Marjory's eyes shot open and her hand went immediately to her chest. The knocking was real and shook her awake and she lurched forward, seeing the empty blue sky before her at first and then the horizon, the ocean, the beach, the railing, and finally the floor beneath her.

"My Lord!" she said and caught her breath, closed her eyes and touched her face. Now she distinctly heard the knocking at the door, stood and realized her state of undress. In reaction she brought her spread palms up in a butterfly pattern to cover her exposed breasts.

"Uh, coming!" she called out. "One moment please, I'm not decent!"

When she had draped herself in a housecoat and slipped her shoes back on, she finally went to the front door of the suite and opened it. Before her stood a tall black man, his hat in his hands, the brim pinched between the tips of extremely long and strong fingers. There was a sheen of sweat on his face and he was dressed in the manner of a bellman.

"Yes?" McAdams said, still out of sorts from her dream but her head clearing by the second.

"Excuse me, Miss McAdams. I'm very sorry, ma'am, to disturb you, ma'am. My name is Santos, Carlos Santos. I come to fetch you for Mizz Fleury, ma'am. She needs you to come meet her, please and it's in a hurry, ma'am."

His voice was urgent, his eyes also. McAdams stepped back and took a second accounting. He was a muscular man, one could tell by the squared shoulders, the stretch of fabric over his arms and the V-shape of his chest tapering down

There was no panic in the man's voice but an urgency that started Marjory's own blood to step up its pace in her chest. This Santos was obviously keeping his voice low and out of earshot of others, and the conspiratorial feel made her even more excited.

"Where?" she simply said.

"The laundry, ma'am."

"Let's go then."

Santos motioned to the Afromobile parked at the base of the stairs. Before Santos had the chance to help, she climbed up into the seat. He swung his leg up over the saddle and with powerful strokes set the vehicle moving quickly north down the raked stone path in the direction of the electric plant.

Santos got them to the laundry in minutes and came to a stop at the front door of the long wooden structure. McAdams had been to the building before because she'd been intrigued that, unlike the hotels she was familiar with in the north, the laundries at the hotels in Florida were not located in the basement. There were no basements in Florida. The water table was simply too high and one could not dig down far before striking water, her father had explained. The next best location was near the electric plant where the commercial style steam laundry machines and the huge, flat mangles for pressing the sheets and table cloths could be easily powered and still kept out of sight of the guests.

Marjory hopped out of the carriage before Santos could assist, but she did allow him to open the door to the laundry for her to pass. When she stepped into the building she was hit by a wave of heated, wet air and a cacophony of noise that had only been a low rumble from the outside. Here in the midst of the machinery, hissing steam pipes, rotating rolling pins, and the snap of fabric being shaken and folded, it was an assault on the ear.

Marjory adjusted her eyes to the darkness, there only being a dull wash of sunlight leaking through the windows near the roofline. Before her were a dozen or more Negro women moving as if to a complicated dance from washing to drying to pressing to stacking the innumerable loads of laundry. Santos finally led her to the back of the open work room to a small office with a door where they could talk without shouting. Inside was Miss Ida, standing uncharacteristically still when there was work all around her. Her left arm was crooked at her waist, her right elbow was settled in one palm and her other hand wedged into her brow, a sign of worry or of deep thought, or of defeat. It was difficult to judge. Sitting in a straight-backed chair in the corner was the woman called Shantice who had found the body of the white man behind her shack.

The young woman's feet where pulled up so that her heels rested on the edge of the seat and her skirt was wrapped around her legs. She was bent at the waist, her head rested on her knees and she was weeping.

McAdams looked first at Miss Ida and then at the childlike figure in the corner and said nothing. The muffled noise in the big room settled like a cocoon around them.

"They's word out that Sheriff Cox gone arrest this poor girl for the killing of that white man," Miss Ida said, breaking the silence. Her voice was more tired than Marjory had ever heard it, like it held a century of hard and weary trouble.

"The sheriff went out to her house and inspected the body. The boys out there who was trying to salvage some of they own possessions watched after him. They said he walked around a bit and done kicked some burnt up trash around Mizz Shantice's place and dug around with a stick where her eating place used to be. They say he poked into some ash and found a ol' carvin' knife that was black from the fire and held it up and stared at it like it was Jesus' golden chalice itself and then put it in a bag of his.

"Lanie Booker's boy said the sheriff done smiled an said, 'We got ourselves a murder weapon' an then told the rest of 'em to wrap up the body and put it in the wagon. Then he asked the boys where Mizz Shantice was at an they said she was workin' at the hotel. While the sheriff was loadin' that man one of the boys come runnin' to me."

When Ida May was finished with her report she looked up into Marjory's eyes and the expression may have been, although it was foreign to the woman's nature, a plead. "It ain't right, Miss McAdams," she said. "You know this ain't right."

"Right?" Marjory said, gathering herself. "Why it's...it's quite unacceptable." She looked around at Santos as if he would join her and therefore embolden her reaction of astonishment and disbelief.

"Why...why we were all standing there ourselves. This slip of a girl could no more kill and drag a man of that size across this room. And with a knife? Good Lord! She would have of had to be standing on a chair to put a knife into such a man's throat and you saw the wound yourself, Mizz Ida."

The girl called Shantice started to rock on the chair, a keening sound coming from her throat.

"Oh, I am so very sorry," Marjory said moving over to put her hip against the young woman and pressing the girl's head into her own skirts. "You weren't there at all, were you?"

"I was at the fair, ma'am," the girl said, avoiding Marjory's inquisitive gaze. "Mizz Ida. I swear I was at the fair and I ain't never seen that man before I seen him a layin' there all burnt up."

Marjory looked to Miss Ida with a "see there" look on her face.

"Surely there are witnesses to that," she said. "Folks who accompanied her to the fair?"

Miss Fleury dropped her hand to her lonely elbow, crossing both arms.

"Logic nor witnesses don't make no difference in this, Miss McAdams," she said. "The only thing we need is a way to get this girl off the island and headed back to Georgia country before the sheriff comes an finds her or I'm afraid there'll be a hangin'.

"A white man has been found dead in nigger town and that's the only truth they gone need. That's the way it's always been and that's the way this will be too.

"If you can help us get Mizz Shantice here across the lake without being seen, ma'am, that's all I'm askin'. If you can't, then I am truly sorry for bringin' you into it."

This time it was Marjory's turn to be taken aback by the housekeeper's graphic language. She yawped once, her mouth opening in a circle, and then closing with a perceptible pop. She was not naïve about matters of discrimination and race. Her father had been open about discussing the Reconstructed South and the advent and demise of slavery whenever she had asked. Her penchant for crossing societal boundaries and neighborhoods in New York City had given her a firsthand look at how different classes were used and often abused at the hands of power. She was also familiar with the sheriff's heavy-handedness and the tacit approval given him by Mr. Flagler and his lieutenants, including her father. The small town of West Palm Beach on the inland side of Lake Worth was booming with the train bringing in supplies and in return shipping out thousands of pounds of tomatoes and pineapples and a dozen other warm-weather vegetables and fruit up to the cold northeast. As the rail workers moved south down the line, they were soon followed by carpenters and masons and construction workers the from North and even the Southern States searching for opportunity. And not just to work at Flagler's huge hotel projects but to lay the foundations for towns like Juno, Lemon City and Miami itself. With so many people in so short a time carrying so many dreams to fulfill, it was inevitable that tempers would flair, jealousy and greed would hitch a ride, and something would break. Why, an item in *The Gazetteer* last June reported that the first train car load of keg beer had arrived in town and it wasn't but two months later that Sam S. Lewis—who was awaiting trial for killing the tax collectors J. F. Highsmith and George Davis in Lemon City—was broken out of the jail in Juno by a lynch mob and then hung from a telegraph pole, his body riddled with bullets. The jailer himself was killed by the mob when he was mistaken for the colored deputy sheriff come to stop them. Marjory couldn't say for certain, but she often considered that the arrival of copious amounts of beer and men behaving in animalistic ways were somehow connected.

At the behest of Mr. Flagler, Sheriff Cox had begun to clamp down on the lawlessness of not just the inevitable drifters but also the workers, railroad men out for a night or carpenters out to relax after a day of swinging hammers. There would be no such bad behavior for Mr. Flagler's rich guest to witness or even hear of in his Eden. The idea of making an arrest and bringing to a quick and quiet close an actual homicide on the island itself would be of paramount interest, and the quicker it was done the quicker would come the praise and reward.

Miss Fluery's request for help might pit Marjory against the sheriff, a challenge she rather warmed to, but would also give her opportunity to ask young Shantice questions in a more, shall we say, conducive surrounding.

"Can you keep her someplace in hiding, Mizz Ida?" Marjory said, looking into the eyes of housekeeper and then to Mr. Santos, who was still standing at the door as if at guard.

"Yes, ma'am," Fluery said, "We do know how to hide our own. For a time anyways. Can't say how long though. That would depend on how hard Sheriff Cox gets to lookin' an how mad he get when he can't find her."

Again Marjory took a few minutes to chart a course of action in her head.

"I frankly don't think it would do well to keep her on the island overnight," she said. "The sheriff will surely have someone watching the walking bridge to the mainland, and at some point he will begin threatening or simply paying off anyone he can for information as to her whereabouts.

"Can you row a boat, Mr. Santos?"

"Yes, ma'am."

"Well, sir, I can secure one. If we meet up near the old dredge wharf north of the golf course at say, nine o'clock this evening, I believe you and Mizz Shantice may row across the lake unseen.

"Can you alert someone on the other side to meet them and take Mizz Shantice in for a couple of days, Mizz Ida? At least long enough for me to consult my father and find a way to calm and control the sheriff?"

"We know folks on the mainland, ma'am. Folks who we can trust, yes."

"All right then, dear," Marjory said to Shantice in an odd sing-song voice, as if she were talking to a child and not a young woman and a noted prostitute.

"Don't you worry a bit, we'll see that you'll be safe, dear, and that the truth will be told. You may indeed be back working by the weekend. Now wouldn't that be fine?"

Shantice had stopped her tears and keening during the discussion but had yet to raise her face to the others. She looked up now to Miss Ida, perhaps wondering which of her professions she might again be working, but the baleful expression on the housekeeper's face gave her a defining clue.

"I will find her some clothing for traveling," Miss Ida finally said, speaking perhaps to herself as much as the others in the room. "Some young men's clothes. We do not want to bring no trouble to our town friends."

She turned specifically to Marjory. "We often dressed girls on the old underground railway in men's clothes so's not to draw attention to them."

"Fine then," Marjory said. "It's settled. If you will take me back to the hotel, Mr. Santos, I will prepare to meet you tonight at the wharf."

Santos opened the office door and allowed McAdams to pass out into the heat and steam and noise of the work room. A large Negro athlete and a young, high-society white woman moved through a place where neither of them belonged and not a single face lifted to note their passage.

CHAPTER NINE

ON THE PATHWAY BACK, MARJORY REDIRECTED Mr. Santos to the Royal Poinciana instead of the Breakers. A plan was forming in her head and she would need accomplices if it had any chance of succeeding. Not that any of those whom she pulled in on the enterprise would have any idea of their involvement. It would be best that way. A bit cruel perhaps, but best.

When Santos cycled up to the rear entrance of the hotel, this time Marjory allowed him to help her out of the carriage seat and then paid him a dollar for appearances. "Nine o'clock," she whispered. "The boat shall be there, pulled up into the brush just north of the wharf."

Santos accepted the money, held her eyes for a moment and said: "Thank you, Miss McAdams. And I do believe that Mizz Ida thanks you to, just in case you didn't hear her say so."

Inside the hotel Marjory strolled across the ornate lobby with the air of a girl with nothing but leisure to direct her. She nodded to a familiar couple, spoke a greeting to a passing valet and found the nearest powder room where she fixed her hair, her cheeks and her mouth and became presentable to the society that would now surround her. She thought of her dead mother, the lessons passed down at an early age and the decisions she had made on her own: which lessons to follow, which to disregard and which to simply give the illusion of following depending on what company one was in. She had loved her mother dearly, but since her death Marjory had in many ways defied her strict views of comportment in a young ladies' world. She saw it as payback for leaving her all alone to fend for herself. What she was about to do would have made her dearly departed mother blanch in front of proper company. But Marjory liked to think that in private she would have said, "Atta girl, M," using the nickname that was only employed when they were alone together.

"Live one life, M," her mother had rasped as she lay on her death bed. "And make it yours."

Marjory returned to the lobby and wrote a note at the front desk, then folded it into an envelope. On the front she wrote in a fine, boarding school script "Mrs. Roseann Birch" and found her way to the Birch's fifth floor corner suite. Her knock at the door was answered by a maid.

"Good afternoon, Abby," McAdams said, recognizing the young woman who always traveled with the family. "Is Mrs. Birch in?"

"Why yes, Miss McAdams. Ma'am is taking her refreshment on the side portico," Abby said with a raised "if you know what I mean" eyebrow that she would only have used with someone like Marjory, who had become close to her employer in the time since Marjory had lost her own mother. "I will find out if she's taking visitors, Miss McAdams."

Marjory was used to the exquisite appointments that her friend always made to the living space when she arrived from New York at the beginning of the season. Despite her sometimes boisterous character in public and displays of athletic prowess before her male counterparts, the woman had a delicate eye for artwork and her husband was rich enough to concede to her passions.

McAdams was drawn as always to a framed mass of gold, reds and purples titled "Japanese Bridge, Water Lilies Pond" by a French impressionist whose name Marjory could never recall. She started slightly when Abby returned and called her name.

"Ma'am would like very much to see you, Miss McAdams," she said, indicating the way with an open palm.

Roseann Birch was stretched out on an odd-looking wooden chair, the seat and backrest of which was angled in the rear to such a degree as to make the buxom woman look as though she were tipping backward.

"You can't believe how comfortable it is till you sit in it, honey, which might be awhile," Birch said with an amiable gruffness unusual to any other woman of her station. "My husband got it as a present from a friend in Westport, New York, up in the Adirondacks. Hell of an ugly thing but my, when you lean back and get your feet up, it's a wonder."

Birch's feet were indeed up, ankles crossed on the cover of a thick leather-bound book which was itself placed atop an expensive-looking ottoman. The crystal goblet in her hand was half-filled with what Marjory guessed was a chardonnay and she looked over the rim with a satisfied but still sharp glint in her eyes.

"Sit down, sweet Marjory, and we shall swap some gossip, and though I will not stoop to adding to the delinquency of a minor, I can get Abby to bring you an apple juice or even a small sherry if you like?"

Marjory pulled a wrought-iron patio chair over the slate patio decking and sat at Birch's right hand.

"Nothing for me, ma'am," she said. "I really wasn't planning to stay long, but did want to see if I could join you at your table for dinner tonight. My father is not due until tomorrow and I'm quite tired of dining alone."

Birch looked over the rim of her glass again, studying Marjory as she assessed the request. She took a deep draught of the wine. "Bullshit."

Even Marjory, who had known this undoubtedly frank and spicy woman for some time, felt her eyes go wide at the profanity.

"OK. OK. I apologize dear. That may have been uncalled for, but we'll see," Birch said, setting her glass aside. "And what else are you requesting, sweetheart, knowing that you are always, always, always welcome at our table and that you don't have to ask. Hmm? Any other guests you think might make the evening interesting? Like maybe the fire inspector? Or maybe that cast iron kettle of a sheriff from the other side of the lake?"

Marjory was caught unawares. She knew Roseann Birch was more plugged in to the workings of the island than any of the other guests and, in some cases, more than management itself. Her advantage was a woman's amiability to chatter while carrying on through the day and her understanding that such talk was not limited only to the upper-class women. Abby, and every housekeeper, maid, laundress, kitchen sweep and handmaiden were her allies in word-of-mouth communication. She was as open to them as any member of her high-class sisterhood, and during her time in the hotel she had turned them from wary to willing in sharing with her the stories of their world. At first they did it for her generous tips, then for her entertainment and finally for their own hunger to know more about the other side, a woman's place in a society far different from their own. Birch had won over all except Ida May Fleury, who respectfully maintained the wall of separation between the whites who hired and the Negroes who did the work.

"Oh come now, dear," Birch said in reaction to the look of surprise on McAdams's face. "Word has been spreading like chicken feed all day about the fire in the Styx and now that bowling ball of a man Sheriff Cox is strutting around the coop like the mad hatter himself."

She took a sip of wine and leaned over and in a conspiratorial whisper that was totally unnecessary on her own patio: "I've even heard there might have been a dead body involved."

Marjory took a moment, knowing that she had to stoke her friend's curiosity without revealing too much. She would have to protect herself and her plan as much as protect Birch from some embarrassing questions should the effort go awry.

"I smelled the smoke myself, Mrs. Birch. It raised me out of my bed, and I've heard talk that the entire community where the workers lived was consumed by the blaze."

She let that soak in, but could tell by Birch's face that it was too little news.

"I've also heard tell, like you, that there was a death involved. Word at the Breakers is that it was the body of a white man that was found."

It was like finding a new aperitif. Birch's face lit, her eyes widened, she may have actually licked her lips with the tip of her tongue.

"Oh, my," she said, not with alarm, but with intrigue. "No wonder that disgusting keg of a man is running around the island as if he had even a scintilla of power here."

Birch moistened the tip of her index finger and began circling the crystal rim of her now empty wine glass. The crystal began to vibrate and the glass began to sing at a high, clear pitch. Marjory had seen Birch pull her parlor trick before, but this time it seemed a rote performance.

"Any speculation on who this dead man is?" she finally said, looking directly into Marjory's eyes. "Local? Or one of us?"

"Oh, no. Not a guest, I wouldn't dare think," Marjory said, pressing her fingers to her heart as though the possibility would be devastating. "Certainly someone would have come forward by now, don't you think?"

"I wouldn't know what to think at this point, dear," Birch said, but that look in her eye meant she soon would know as much as it was humanly possible to find out.

With her line of inquiry now set into the most extensive system of gossip and rumor on the island, Marjory moved on to equally important pursuits.

"On the subject of dinner guests," Marjory now said, as though the chit chat of a dead man and a snooping sheriff were simple diversions from the important parts of life at the Poinciana. It was her turn to give the matron a coy look. "Could you invite Mr. Foster from the steamship family to join us?"

Graham Foster was a young man in his early twenties who fit most perfectly into the Royal Poinciana's growing clientele of moneyed society. He was the son of a steamship magnate who had become fast friends with Flaglers. The railroad baron had been a prime customer of the elder Foster for the delivery of his building supplies and the transportation for his advance work crews. For the far-seeing Flagler, it was an investment in a future that he himself would control. Once his rail lines were laid, Flagler would be the main transportation for all things moving up and down the Florida east coast instead of the steam shippers. If Foster couldn't see he was cutting his own throat, let the instant gratification of money now be his bandage.

As for the son, Graham, he was also more interested in spending his father's wealth than looking ahead at a dying company that he would inherit. In many ways he was quite dense. Marjory McAdams liked that in a man.

Her request that Graham Foster join them for dinner may have caught Mrs. Birch off guard, but she was the kind of woman who could see her own traits when they showed up in other women.

"Why Marjory, you loathe that young man. What could you possibly want to use him for?"

McAdams professed to pout. "I think loathe is a bit too strong," she said. "He is a bit of a showboat, but he is also only a handful of years older than I am and unless you can find me a dinner companion less than three decades my elder, I will simply have to make due."

Birch watched her young charge's eyes, sure there was something mischievous behind them.

"Very well then. I shall invite young Mr. Foster and then deny all culpability if I am asked," Birch brushed Marjory away with a flutter of her fingertips. "Run along, dear. And do ask Abby to come pour me another of this delicious French nectar."

She had planned it all on the run, and she was amazed that so far it had gone swimmingly.

Mrs. Birch had held up her end of the bargain. When Marjory arrived for dinner that evening, the Birch's table was occupied by her husband and Marian and Robert Rothschild, he of the Manhattan real estate Rothschilds. Marjory nodded to Mrs. Rothschild as the men rose to greet her.

"You are stunning, my dear," Robert Rothschild said, and meant it.

"Why thank you, sir," she said with a light curtsy.

Marjory was dressed in a pale blue dress that was long and slim at the waistline and included the newly popular "leg-o-mutton" sleeves that billowed out and accentuated the thinness of her youthful figure. She was naturally a slip of a girl, but tonight she had gone to the trouble of lacing up her corset a few extra notches which, in addition to accenting her waspish waistline, also added a bit more umph to her breasts. Though most of the older women, including Mrs. Birch, wore a high-necked style, it was not inappropriate as evening wear to include a low-cut bodice.

"I would concur," said Mr. Birch, who, despite his reputation as a careful and circumspect banker, was a jovial man in social company and was known by most as having an appreciative but careful eye for the younger ladies, careful indeed considering his wife's strength and demeanor.

Marjory then turned to the still standing Graham Foster. He took her fingers in his and raised them to his lips but did not touch. At least he had been taught some manners in his upbringing.

"What a pleasant surprise, Graham," she said with enthusiasm. "I wasn't aware that you'd returned to the island. How wonderful to see you."

"It is an absolute pleasure, Marjory. And you do look incredibly fashionable."

As they all sat, Marjory could feel Foster's glance of appreciation into her cleavage. He was dressed in a dark waistcoat and trousers made of a carefully striped fabric. The dress was formal, as was expected for dinner at the Poinciana, but Marjory figured she knew him well enough that his concern for this clothing wouldn't cause him to hesitate when the time came.

He was a thin and angular man, sharp at the knees, elbows, shoulders and nose. He was clean-shaven but wore the standard moustache that had become popular as of late, and it partially covered his unnaturally pink, thin and almost girlish lips. His eyes were a puppyish brown, at least when she was in his company, and there never seemed to be anything behind them other than an obsequiousness to please her. She smiled at him and felt a slight trickle of shame.

The dinner was of typical fare for the Royal Poinciana, exquisite in every respect. The table linen was impeccably white at the hands of the laundresses

Marjory had visited that very afternoon. The silver and crystal were of the finest European style.

The six diners went luxuriously through four courses: green turtle soup, heart of palm salads, oven-baked salmon, a potpourri of shrimp and scallops and clams casino from the Bahamian islands, a sampling of cheeses and apple wedges and—for all at the table—a serving of a strange and succulent fruit called kiwi. Mrs. Birch continued a steady diet of red wines, and the rest also imbibed on a variety from the Poinciana's well-stocked collection.

The conversation ran from a discussion of summer plays they had all missed in the city, a room by room recitation tour by Mrs. Rothschild of her sister's opulent home in Hyde Park, a highly political debate by the two elder men over the Spanish American conflict and its effect on the U.S. economy, which was put to an end by a then-braying Mrs. Birch that "no country that produces such lousy wine is worth conquering" and finally an agreeable assessment of this year's hotel baseball team and a promise by all to attend this Friday's game against the visiting team from Ashville, North Carolina.

Throughout the evening, Marjory listened with forced intent to Graham Foster's descriptions of his family's plan to offer steamship service to Cuba from the terminus of Flagler's train in Miami, his braggadocio over a new type of steam engine he himself was building for use on a single-passenger personal vehicle, and his plan to break a land speed record in such a contraption.

All the while she smiled coyly, feigned great concern for his safety, looked adoringly into his too close-set eyes and ate a half dozen oysters with such slow, deliberate and sensuous care that even Mrs. Birch (who'd been watching the couple closely) was forced to clear her throat with either admonition or glee.

It had taken only one after-dinner dance to the hotel orchestra's rendition of "And the Band Played On" for Marjory to convince Foster to walk with her in the gardens. With her fingers laid on his forearm and the smell of night-blooming jasmine in the air, it was hardly fair how easily it was for her to talk Foster into taking her on a ride on the lake in his company's row boat.

"It is such a beautiful evening and you do know how I love to float, Graham."

The young man was bewildered.

"I thought you hated the last time we went out in that tiny boat," he said. "In fact if I recall, Marjory, you said you'd rather be swimming."

"Yes, well, I do enjoy the swimming. But then I would have to remove this lovely dress," she said, again employing the coy smile and using her off hand to gesture down along her delicate waist and long skirts. He went silent. Perhaps he was envisioning it.

"I believe the boat is up on the ramp at the company dockage," he said. "It may indeed be under guard by the watchman, but it shouldn't take any time at all to fetch it."

So now they were out on the water, the oar locks creaking gently as Foster rowed without haste onto Lake Worth. Marjory had situated herself in the bow at a half turn, looking out at the lights of the Poinciana, keeping track of their progress north so she would know when to guide her "beau" to shore and a rendezvous near the old dredge wharf by nine o'clock.

"The stars are so beautiful tonight," she said. "Perhaps if we get farther north out of the glare of the hotel they will be even brighter."

Foster quickened his pace.

"They are beautiful but much colder than the sparkle in your eyes, Marjory."

Demurely, she turned her cheek away with a smile. Where did he come up with these lines? Was there a cheap magazine like the Farmer's Almanac of trite phrases men studied to woo the women they hoped to impress?

Foster waited a few beats, letting the work of his silver tongue do its duty. Surely she was enjoying his company. Hadn't she touched his arm just so? Hadn't she had a grand time dancing in his grasp? Her suggestion of the boat ride was certainly proof that her feelings had changed toward him.

"Frankly, Marjory, if I may, I wasn't sure that after our last meeting I would have the pleasure of seeing you again."

"I do apologize if you took my attitude in the wrong way," she said, recalling that the last time they'd been tossed together by a lady friend of her father's it had been a disaster. She had taken umbrage at Foster's braggadocio of why men were superior to women in any field of outdoor pursuits such as game hunting or fishing. Her father did not have the time to deflect young Foster's perilous line before Marjory had challenged him to a fishing contest aboard Captain Connelly's deep sea yacht. The next day, Marjory pulled in the largest swordfish of the outing, and then she added insult to injury on the return by announcing at about the one mile marker from Palm Beach Island that she was overheated and was going to swim the rest of the way to the beach. Infuriated by Foster's smiling dismissal, she stared him directly in the eye and then stunned three of the four men aboard by removing one layer of her overclothing, mounting the rail and then diving like a true professional into the aqua water. It took several minutes for her father to convince the captain that Marjory was an excellent swimmer and would probably be back in their hotel suite long before they made dockage.

She had not seen Graham Foster since. But she knew he had access to a rowboat.

As they moved easily to the north, Marjory now listened with half an ear to her companion's monologue about the subject he was most familiar with—himself—and the other half on the night sounds along the lakefront. An owl called its kaweek, kaweek from a hunting perch somewhere in the water oaks on the island shore. A splash off to the west, but not more than thirty yards away, gave truth to the fishermen's tales that large tarpon did indeed feed in the nighttime waters of the lake. Marjory turned away from Foster to check on their progress to the dredge dock, and as they drew near turned on her charm once more.

"Might we just drift a bit, Graham? I so love the quiet here and the stars truly are a wonder."

Foster stopped rowing and talking. He had been facing back toward the receding lights of the Poinciana, turned and saw her view of the blackness to the north and was, at least for a moment, transfixed by the sight of the constellation Virgo hanging low in the sky and the star field around it dipping down to the horizon.

"You do have the constant touch of the dramatic that follows you," he said. It was perhaps the first statement of truth she'd heard from him, and she felt a twinge of regret at what she was about to do. But the feeling did not stop her. She slid forward to the edge of her seat, moving closer to him. He reacted as she knew he would to the subtle invitation, shipped his oars and matched her movement until their lips met.

When he pressed, she retreated.

"Oh, my, Graham," she said, feigning breathlessness. She reached out to clutch both sides of the boat as if to steady herself. "I, I...oh, my."

Now her right hand went to her throat, though she knew in the darkness he would not see the lack of any sort of blush to her skin.

"I do believe I'm becoming quite dizzy. You have taken me by surprise." She looked at him with that learned woman's technique of peering up with the eyes while keeping her chin low. Foster did not move; he was still leaning forward, frozen in an awkward pose.

"Not unpleasantly," Marjory added. She then looked about, as if unfamiliar with where exactly they were. "Could we possibly go ashore here? The lack of solid ground beneath my feet is quite, umm, unsettling."

Foster settled back in his seat as if commanded and reached for the oars.

"Absolutely," he said, scanning the shore line and picking up the obvious dark outline of the dredge dock. "I apologize, my dear. My intentions were honorable and I did not mean to cause you to swoon."

The slightest touch of bravado was in his voice. A man taking responsibility for his manliness, thought Marjory. Ha! All her previous inklings of guilt disappeared.

"Just there." She pointed to the dock. "Could we go ashore there?"

Foster pulled the last few strokes and beached the bow onto the rim of wet mash that served as the shore. Without hesitation he removed his shoes, rolled up his pants cuffs and got out to push the rowboat higher onto solid ground so Marjory could get out without soiling too much of her gown. He took her arm, and they walked up to high ground while she breathed deeply and appeared to be gathering herself.

"My," she said again, using a word she rarely uttered when she was not in the company of people she wished to socially impress or to con into thinking she was weak. "I'm not sure what came over me. But I'm certainly better now."

"Are you sure?" Foster said, looking into her eyes but again injecting that touch of overconfidence and double meaning into his voice.

McAdams noted the question was lacking in true concern and she showed her confusion with a questioning face.

"I mean are you sure that you don't know what came over you?"

Now he was smiling. Did he really think his kiss had caused her to swoon? She turned her face away, hoping it was taken as a blushing moment instead of a mild chagrin. Men, she thought, and then without looking up she took his arm and turned south toward the hotel.

"There is a path made by the workers. Can we walk together back to the hotel?"

Foster looked back once at the rowboat, and she read his hesitation.

"Surely everyone knows whose boat she is and will not dare to move it." She squeezed his arm just so. "And it was been such a wonderful night. Let's not let it end so soon."

As they walked arm-in-arm through the brush along the lakeshore, McAdams knew that she would not see the baseball player and the young woman even if they were close by. But she did hear the unfamiliar trill of a bird she knew was not native to the island, the whistle low and sounding too much like a pigeon from Brooklyn to be real. Foster made no reaction to the sound; he was again listening to himself. As McAdams moved more quickly down the path and away from the dredge dock, he was again expounding.

"Mr. Flagler has certainly done a marvelous job with the hotel and the beginnings of the town on shore. Business has doubled since his arrival, and that means at the very least a doubling of my own trade."

McAdams was perplexed at where he was going with such conversation and afraid she was losing his focus. He was looking out on the lights of the Poinciana and the approaching paths of the manicured lawns and golf course. He stopped and turned to her.

"I will be a rich man," he said, the statement full of what was not being said. He grasped her other arm and pulled her closer.

Damn, she thought. I've gone too far. He's actually going to propose to me.

"I will inherit my father's steamship business and be set for life. The more people who hear about the beauty and climate of this place, the more we'll ferry them and their necessities for building and living here. There are plans to widen and deepen an intracoastal waterway that for the next one hundred years will be the major transportation line to the very tip of Florida. People will forever flock to our boats."

Foster turned his head just so, waiting for her to raise her face to his. "You can be part of all that, Marjory."

"Why, Graham Foster," she said, much louder than his romantic whisper. She freed her arms, planted all ten fingertips into Foster's chest and pressed him back. "Aren't you just the forward thinking one? And a bit too forward in other ways I might add."

She stepped back, turned toward the hotel and began to walk.

"By the way, if you intend to inherit Florida's transportation world with your steamships, you should have a conversation with my father when he arrives on the island tomorrow. I do recall on his last trip he talked of some fellow named Ransom Olds who was interested in coming to Daytona Beach, where he said people were sure to go absolutely ga-ga over his new invention called the motor car."

CHAPTER TEN

Look at yourself, lad!"

Harris had come forward to the train engine landing, where Byrne had stationed himself ever since the dynamite fiasco some three hours before. Byrne followed the order, looked down at himself and noted that he was indeed covered with soot and coal oils, even though he thought he'd positioned himself out of the stream of smoke and ash.

"We'll be pullin' into West Palm soon enough, and before we cross over to the island you'd best be lookin' smart, son.

"Go on back and change into something clean, if you've got any. Mr. Flagler is entering his domain and I promise you you're going to be damned embarrassed to be in the company of such opulence lookin' like a coal peddler."

Byrne headed for the caboose. Harris cut his eyes at the engineer and fireman who were equally soiled and gave them a shrug. "No offense, men."

Within the hour Byrne was stationed at his place on the rear platform. He'd brushed his coat, inspected his shirts and picked the one with the least dirt around the collar and polished his brogans with Harris' boot black. By now he was used to the movement of the train and could feel it slowing as they eased into the populated area of West Palm Beach, if you wanted to call it populated. Byrne had poked his head around the corner to look forward several times, thinking that at some point he'd be able to see a skyline of the city but was disappointed each time by the continued flatness of brush and scrub pine and the seemingly endless tangle of green. Soon, off to the east he picked up the reflection of water, a lake that Harris would later call Lake Worth. To the west they passed several acres of cleared land and rows of crops that his mentor would tell him were pineapple plants. Byrne had seen the fruit once in New York when a street merchant had somehow gotten a load of the oblong, prickly looking orbs and made a show of whacking at the individual husks with a machete while guaranteeing "such sweetness and juicy flavor like you've never imagined in your lives." Byrne noted there was a crude sort of sprinkler system spewing water over the crops, which led him to believe there would be plumbing in the city. He would be proved wrong.

A dirt road began to parallel the tracks, starting as little more than a two-rut wagon trail and then turning into a hard, flat roadbed and then improving, if you could say that, into a surface tamped down with a strange, shell-like crust. As they entered the town proper, a few two-and three-story wooden buildings sprouted on the side streets with signs like O.W. Weybrecht, The Pioneer Hardware Store and E.H. Dimmick, Druggist. But many of the businesses were in tents or carts not unlike old Mrs. McReady's outside his New York tenement.

The train slowed and with the familiar hiss of the steam brakes came to a full stop. Byrne was about to hop down to take position on the ground outside Flagler's car when Harris appeared at the door.

"Not yet, lad. They're switchin us onto the island spur. Just the hotel guests in the last two cars, the parlor car and Mr. Flagler's number 90. The rest of the lot'll stop at the station in town and then be headin' south to Miami.

"We'll take you down that route in the future, Mr. Byrne. For now the boss needs us here," Harris aimed his exaggerated nod off to the east. When he disappeared inside Byrne stepped over to the other side of the platform and looked toward the lake. In the hard sun he could see an enormous gleaming white structure rising up alone on the opposite shore. He determined she was at least seven stories, with huge mansard roofs at either end and a broad cupola at the middle. It was no doubt the Royal Poinciana, but it looked out of place along the flat horizon of blue lake water and low green shrub. Byrne hadn't seen anything since Washington, D.C. to compare, and as he looked down the side of the train cars, he spotted several of the upscale passengers leaning out of their windows and pointing. They were apparently joining in his simple astonishment. The train began to move again, this time curving along a spur and then up onto a bridge that was taking them across the lake, the grand hotel growing larger and more impressive with each turn of the wheels.

Even from the slight elevation of ten feet over sea level, the greenness of the place washed over Byrne. The coastal shrubs, the hotel's manicured lawns in the distance, all ringed by aqua-colored water that itself seemed to take on a tinge of green. He could smell the salt again, the air filling by the minute with that tang, the bite that was no longer the fish monger's scent, but one all its own, simmering in the heat and carried by fresh wind.

Byrne watched what from a distance had looked like rag-topped stakes become sentries with plumed hats and then morph into impossibly straight-trunked and smooth-skinned royal palm trees with filigreed blades sprouting like fans at their heads. As the train eased off the bridge at the island end and slowed next to the hotel's southern entryway, Byrne picked up the strains of music. It was a joyful, welcoming tune he could not name, but it had the same effect of making him grin and did the same to those people gathering to greet the new arrivals. When the cars came to a hissing stop, he could see an eight-piece band tucked under a garden trellis. He jumped down off the iron stairs and smartly gained position at the door to Flagler's car as instructed.

There were some thirty people in the crowd. Byrne swept his eyes and assessed them: moneyed was the first impression, men in clean summer suits, most of light colored shades, all wearing banded boaters or white fedoras. The women were to a one draped in long dresses of white that were near blinding in the bright sun and they too were in hats of wide brim and varying shapes. Byrne's second impression was that despite seeking this extraordinary Florida sun, they had all gauzed their skin from its touch: the hats, the long sleeves, the veils.

He saw no darkness, no slouch or averted look, no movement at the edges of the group that smelled of predation. Despite the hats, the men were all openly showing their faces, smiles and grins abounded. The music stopped, spontaneous clapping began, and Byrne turned to see Harris at the foot of the steps to number 90 and Mrs. Flagler standing for a second of adoration at the top. She was dressed in the same manner as the women awaiting her, and Harris offered his meaty hand as balance as she stepped into the graces and greetings of her own endearing flock. The respectful ovation continued as Flagler appeared, he too in a straw boater, but now in an impeccable light woolen suit that seemed far too business-like for the occasion. He had already donned the darkened eyeglasses that shielded his eyes from the bright light, and stepped down unaided after graciously tipping his hat to the gathering.

Byrne followed as unobtrusively as possible to the inner circle. Harris had done the same. And so too had Mr. McAdams, Flagler's second-in-command. He took up a position immediately to Flagler's left—either bathing in his boss's greetings and adoration, or protecting him? Byrne watched the hands of those who reached out to shake hands with the patrician, tracked anyone whose fingers might go to the inside of a jacket as they approached, anyone whose eyes were down first and rose only at the last minute. The music started again as the group moved toward the hotel, the entourage stopping only long enough for a kiss to Mrs. Flagler's cheek by another white-draped woman or a pleasant bow by an apparent friend or business acquaintance of her husband. Harris was just giving Byrne an eye-rolling high sign when both of them snapped their heads forward at a completely unexpected yelping of a dog. The shoulders ahead seemed to turn at odd angles and hat brims tipped downward, Byrne pick up the movement at ground level of a white object that was moving quickly through the forest of legs in a more or less direct line to the man he was supposed to protect. His wand was already out in his hand and he flicked it out to its length and in his peripheral vision he sensed Flagler begin to bend at the waist as if doubling over. Byrne began to step into the void that seemed to be naturally forming in front of the old man before he got his first full view of the white dog and heard Flagler say in the loudest and most emotional statement since he'd met the man: "Delos!" The white dog leapt into his master's waiting arms, licked the old man's chin and engendered the only smile that Byrne would ever see on Flagler's face. Byrne retracted the baton and tried to slip it back into his coat unnoticed.

The procession continued up the steps and into the south portico of the hotel, Harris stopped at some unseen boundary and turned to his proégé, giving him the sign again that their responsibility was finished. Byrne nearly banged shoulders with Mr. McAdams.

"Interesting walking stick," McAdams said, looking into Byrne's eyes with a mixture of interest and mirth and then down to the coat pocket where the baton was now secreted. "But I assure you, young Pinkerton that if you had broken the neck of Mr. Flagler's favorite living thing, it would have been the last act of protection you would have performed on this island."

Byrne looked unblinking into McAdams' face. The man was twenty years his elder, nearly his height, had flecks of gray in his hair and the scent of eau de toilet rose from his collar in the heat. But there were also sharp creases at the corners of his eyes. The lines made him look distinguished, or perhaps deeply tired. His words had not come off as an attempt to put Byrne in his place. That would have been a tone with which Byrne had long ago become familiar when in the company of the higher class. He considered a rejoinder, perhaps a comment that if his reflexes were so poor that he couldn't check his first reaction, he truly wouldn't deserve the position of protection. But he simply said, "Yes sir."

He took a step backward then two more when a flurry of soft white fabric and a high-pitched song of "Father! Father!" seemed to push him out of the way.

Later, Byrne's sense of it would be as a cloud of bright chiffon and a waft of gardenia, a glance of tumbling auburn and a glimpse of china skin. The enveloping hug between McAdams and this sudden woman was equal parts strong, athletic, loving and dear.

"Oh, father. I did miss you so."

Byrne saw the thin waist, outlined by the pull of her dress under her father's arms. He saw the hard knot of muscled calf as she stood on tiptoe. He saw the kiss she blessed to her father's cheek and he saw the eye, green as an emerald, which caught and seemed to both notice and acknowledge him over her father's shoulder.

"Eyes right, boy!"

Harris was at Byrne's sleeve, pulling him back toward the train.

"Out of your league, lad. Out of your class. And out of your head if you think for a second more of the daughter of Mr. McAdams."

Byrne blinked and turned his attention to the hands before him as Harris was flipping through a roll of money, counting out twenty dollars and then placing it in Byrne's palm.

"That's a week's pay, Mr. Byrne, for services rendered and more to be expected," Harris said. "Get your things out of the train car. It'll cost you a nickel to walk the bridge back to the other side. Over in town I would recommend the Seminole Hotel, corner of Banyan and Narcissus. Can't miss it. It's the biggest damn building on the mainland. I'll come and get you there when you're needed.

"And I'd warn you of spendin' time on saloon alley if it would make any difference. They're a tough bunch of rail workers out there on a weekend night. But I'll figure you know how to comport yourself in such an environment."

Within minutes Byrne had his duffel containing everything he owned in hand and was walking back along the rails toward the bridge to the mainland— walking, not exactly with purpose. For some reason he kept looking back at the grand hotel, over his shoulder at first, then in an almost sidestepping crab-walk, unable to stop staring at the glow of the place, the unusual set and rustle of the long-bodied palm trees. Was he looking for another glimpse of the girl in the brilliant white dress? Or trying to set this new fairyland in the proper context of his new life? It had always been his way to assess a place — a neighborhood, a row of residences, a beer hall, a tenement alleyway. Who belonged there and who didn't. Where was the danger mostly likely to lie? Where were the escape routes? There was something here that made him wary other than its setting and smell and air of opulence. He'd known the feeling from being in the moneyed center of New York City, the feeling of not belonging and always watching it as an outsider. But this was different, and his sense was that he was both fascinated by the island and too suspicious to turn his back on it. The other thought was that this was the kind of place his brother Danny would see as an opportunity, a target and a mark.

"Pardon, sir! Pardon!"

Byrne spun at the call and was met by the sight of a contraption that was half bicycle and half wickered lounge chair rolling toward him. A black man was up on the seat, calling out for his attention, while an elderly white couple was in the settee looking out in blissful comfort. The gentleman tipped his hat to Byrne, and he returned the greeting. The driver's face was as unreadable as a pewter plate. Byrne stepped aside to let them pass and then watched the back of the skinny black man's shoulders and the sway of his hips as he peddled the carriage away toward the hotel at a pace and rhythm he might be able to keep up for the rest of his life.

At the lake a swing gate on the bridge was mounted by a boy not more than ten years of age who was collecting five cents to use the pedestrian walkway to the mainland. Byrne flipped the boy a nickel and started the six-hundred-foot trek across water. Again the opaque quality of the water captured him, but he also found himself using the handrail more often than his natural athleticism would usually need. He was an urban lad, not used to being on or above water, a new experience was throwing him off his game. He would need to master it, he thought, especially if he was going to spend time in this place where water was such a dominant feature.Nearing the end of the bridge he slowed his pace. A knot of people was stopped, perhaps a dozen men, women and a couple of children, waiting on the walkway while some form of inspection went on. He noted they were all Negros, dressed cleanly, in the way of domestic workers, and carrying a variety of satchels and bags and duffels not unlike his own. The impression was that they were a group traveling or moving, but from where? The island? He stopped and took a place next to the last man, who nodded quickly up the line as if indicating Byrne should pass them by. Byrne stayed where he was. He watched the process and noted that some official was taking little time in dismissing the men and children but more thoroughly questioning the women. The man was tall and lanky and scarecrow looking, with bony shoulders and a gaunt face. At one point he reached out a long finger and lifted the chin of a woman who had seemed not to want to look into his eyes.

"Your name, woman?" Byrne heard the official say.

"Lila Jane Struthers," the woman replied in a voice not defiant, but proud of the words spoken.

"Mizz Struthers. Do you know the woman called Shantice Carver? And don't lie to me now cause I been lied to too many times today."

"I know her sir, yes sir," the woman said. "But she work the maids' side sir an I work the laundry."

"Have you seen this Shantice today?"

"No, sir. Lots of days go by I don't see her."

"When was the last time you did see her?"

"I believe I seen her over here sir on the night of the carnival," the woman said, and this time Byrne did pick up the taste of defiance in her voice.

"I guess ya'll following the party line today, eh Mizz Struthers? What? You all got together and decided what to tell the sheriff's office before you even got asked?"

"I don't know nothin' about no party, sir," the woman said. "An this the only line I been in today."

The inspector made a dismissive sound in the back of his throat and moved his attention to an elderly man. Byrne took a new assessment of the scarecrow, concentrated on the man's eyes, the line of his nose, the set of his feet for balance and another, longer look at the man's hands to determine their strength. Was his thin build deceiving? How quick would he be to deliver a blow, or avoid one? Did all the sheriff's men wear such black coats? And what exactly did the insignia on his lapel badge say? The official dismissed the old man and moved down to Byrne, took in the length of him from eyes to feet.

"No reason for you to wait, sir. Move on."

Byrne didn't move. From this close distance he could read the letters stamped into the man's badge: "Deputy Sheriff."

"Do I gather that there is some kind of search being performed?" Byrne said, turning his language level up a notch for the fellow. "A woman, I presume?"

The deputy's assessment of Byrne stopped for an additional second at his feet.

"Not to be concerned, sir. Strictly a local matter."

"Would that be local as on the island, deputy?" Byrne said. "And would the matter have anything to do with the train?"

The deputy stepped in close to Byrne, turning his head away from the workers.

"It's a matter of a Negro prostitute shankin' some poor bastard over in the island backwoods, sir," the deputy said. "Not something that the Pinkertons need be bothered with."

Byrne stepped back thinking: I've got to do something about these shoes. It's like wearing a bloody sign across my forehead.

The first stop he made was at the telegraph office located in the town's new railroad depot. The office consisted of a single planked window where the dispatcher, ticket seller, weigh master, and telegraph operator where all embodied in the same man, a large and surprisingly friendly man with eyes as bright as blue marbles anxious to help anyone in line, which, when Byrne arrived, numbered zero.

"Uh, yes sir, Mr. Byrne. I can check on that right away sir. Only take a second, sir, if you don't mind, sir," the clerk said after collecting the worn telegram Byrne had offered him in the way of introduction. The man spun to collect a shoebox from the wooden table behind him. Byrne could see the wired teletype machine sitting lonely and motionless.

"Any correspondence to this office is kept here and in confidence, sir, as required by the government and reiterated in the training of each and every operator within the system, sir, which in this case would only be me of course," the clerk said breathlessly, with a smile on his face that had not a hint of cynicism. His fat fingers were flipping through the box in search of a message that Byrne's telegram had been retrieved, but when the man finally pulled out a sheet and handed it to him, it was only the copy of the message he had originally sent.

coming to meet you in three days...ma is dead...

"No, sir," the clerk answered to Byrne's question. "No one has came to collect it sir, and it was received as you can see right there on the date, sir, on the very same day, or close to it anyways, that it was sent from New York City."

Byrne pinched the paper between his fingers. "Would you know this man, Daniel Byrne, the one to whom the telegram was sent?"

The clerk looked down at the paper as if there might be a photograph there. "Uh, no sir. I don't believe so. Though they is a lot of folks who come through here, sir," the clerk said while letting his gaze focus behind Byrne. The juxtaposition of his statement and the empty room seemed to have no ironic effect on the man. "But then I am not required by regulations, nor am I trained, sir, to know on sight each and every person who sends or receives messages, sir."

Byrne pointed again at his brother's worn telegram.

"The man I'm speaking of sent that message from your office four weeks ago according to the date."

The clerk again studied the paper.

"Yes, sir. That would be from here, sir, according to the identifying numbers, sir."

"But you don't recall the man who sent it?"

The clerk shook his head.

"Very well, then," Byrne said, refolding the telegram.

"Was it your daddy?" the clerk said as Byrne turned to leave.

"Excuse me?"

The clerk pointed his finger at the pocket where Byrne had tucked the telegram.

"Ya'll got the same name."

"No, it's my brother," Byrne answered. He walked away. In strict confidence my ass, he was thinking as he made his way back out onto the street.

Harris of course had been right about the Seminole Hotel, named, Byrne soon found out, after the Indian tribe that now occupied southern areas of the Florida peninsula. It was a four-story structure that towered above the rest of the wooden shops and tents and pole barns that created a wobbly-legged colt of a downtown. Byrne could smell the fresh sawn lumber, hear the hammering of nails nearby and practically taste the sun-heated flavor of newness. It was the frontier town he'd read about and heard stories of in those Wild West reenactments along Tin Pan Alley in New York. But this was not the West. This place was called Florida.

"Yes, that's right, Michael Byrne, with a Y after the B and an E at the end," he said to the hotel clerk at the check-in desk at the Seminole. "No. No specific length of stay. Might be a day. Might be a week. I'm with Mr. Flagler's security team. A Pinkerton."

What the hell, he thought. Since everyone could guess his occupation by looking at his shoes, he may as well use the status and that threat of authority that he and his boys exuded to gain advantage on the streets of New York City.

"Certainly, Mr. Byrne. We do have a fine room available fronting the lake on the fourth floor with a wondrous view of your employer's island," the clerk said with a new smile.

"Something on the second floor, if you will," Byrne said, his tenement background speaking without consideration of his new surroundings.

"Yes, sir. Of course, sir."

The room was spare. The furniture was fine and sturdy and quite possibly newly hewn in hardwood. The floor was of a dark, close-grained pine he didn't recognize. There was a throw rug in the middle that was brand new. The single bed had a chenille coverlet, and he tossed his duffel onto it and went to the window. Even from the second floor, the Royal Poinciana stood monolithic across the lake. He raised the double-hung casement window, felt the breeze blow in off the water and again took a deep breath of the wondrously new scent of sun-warmed salt air.

He stripped off his coat and shirt and filled the dresser-top wash basin. The china bowl was polished and had a gold leaf band around the rim. It was free of any chips or scratches. He cupped the water in his hands and splashed it up into his eyes and rubbed his face, repeating the gesture three times before picking up a hand towel and wiping himself dry. While dabbing his neck and shoulders he looked up into a face that had a slight stubble of beard and a new sheen of red sunburn on its nose and cheekbones, and in his father's Irish tone the face whispered: "Jaysus. What the hell are ye doin' here, Mikey?"

When he returned to the front desk he again used his already established authority to ask a question: "I'm looking for a man who left word he was awaiting me in town. His name is Daniel Byrne. Has he ever registered here?"

The clerk looked up into Byrne's face.

"A relative?"

"Yes."

"With the same spelling then?"

"Obviously."

"I believe I would have recognized it then, sir. I don't recall anyone using that particular name before. But I've only been employed here for the past few months."

Byrne asked for the names of other hotels in the city; the clerk gave him a list of three.

"Unless of course your relative is on the island, sir."

"That I can check myself, thank you," Byrne said. From what he had seen so far of the island, Danny would have indeed had to strike it rich to be ensconced across the lake. Inquiring for dinner he was told that the Midway Plaisance saloon and restaurant on Banyan Street had just received a new brew that had become quite the rage and that they could serve up a fine fresh catch of the day that would provide a taste Mr. Byrne had mostly likely never encountered in his previous life. He'd tipped his cap to the clerk, thanked him, and covered a brief smile. They might have a sun and smell and heat that could not be encountered in New York, he thought, but certainly nothing that couldn't be presented on a table. The restaurants of the city were unmatched in any corner of the world if, of course, you had the money. He would see about this catch of the day and this supposed new brew.

Byrne rolled up the sleeves of his white shirt two turns to the middle of his forearms and stepped down from the hotel porch to the street. His telescoping wand was in the deep pocket of his trousers, and now he had a mighty ache for a beer. The walk to the saloon took him less than ten minutes during which he was offered: the finest hot bath and shave, the foremost in leather boots, the most affordable and profitable piece of real estate left in the Palm Beach area, and a "trip upstairs mister that will be your slice of heaven on earth." The blatant bray of merchants and hookers brought on the first fit of nostalgia for his native city he'd felt since arriving. His reaction was the same as if he were home. He ignored the hype and kept his wallet in his front pocket with a light chain attaching it to one of his belt loops. He also registered every face he saw. Danny could not have changed too much in three years time. He would know him from a hundred paces. But he had seen enough to surprise him in the last few days that he was taking no chances.

It was past four in the afternoon when he stepped into the wooden saloon of the Midway. It being the dinner hour the place was near full of men in both work clothes and respectable suits. The smell of fried fish was in the air and that unmistakable scent of fresh hops and barley and yeast that conjured a liquid that would cut the dust from your throat and take the pout off your face.

Byrne shouldered his way to the bar and bought a pint of Anheiser beer that he would later find out was part of the first load of keg beer delivered to the town of West Palm Beach. He took a deep draught, closed his eyes in appreciation, and then worked his way out to the canvas-covered porch area of outside tables. He scanned the gathering, memorizing faces and modes of dress as well as anything sinister attached to belts or stuck down into boots and listened intently to the sound of voices and accents. He heard a familiar tone from one corner and moved to a huge wooden cable spool that was making due for a table top. His three binder boy acquaintances from the train were sitting at the nine, twelve and three o'clock positions of the round top. Byrne picked up one of many wooden crates being used as chairs and took the six o'clock spot.

"Top o' the day to you, Pinkerton," the man from the Tenderloin said. He waited until Byrne was settled in his seat. "Please, join us."

The cynicism was cast as a joke, made even more so by the creamy foam he left dripping from his mustache.

"What brings you slumming here on the west side, Pinkerton?" said the Italian. "Figured you to be settling in the island castle near the boss man."

"No, I'm just a junior lifeguard, Pauley," Byrne said, watching the street boys' eyes for a reaction to the fact that Byrne had gone out of his way to check the train's passenger manifest and had figured who was who among the small group. Gerald Haney had used the same name on the manifest. The German was Henry, a common Americanization for the name Hienrick. The Italian from Cherry Hill was probably Paulo originally. His face went blank, trying not to react to Byrne's correct guess, which was a reaction in itself.

"Besides, I don't think they serve good beer to the champagne crowd over there." Byrne raised his glass to the group and took another long swallow, gaining his own foam line above his lip.

The group joined him in the toast, and that common thread of young men and drink gained him another tenuous link.

"So, I thought you boy'os were on your way to Miami," Byrne said. "It must be something more than the arrival of keg beer to keep you from your date with fortune."

Gerald Haney smiled to his mates and they grinned in return. It seemed a learned response to deflect questions of their questionable business.

"Aye, Pinkerton. Fortune is where you find it," he said. "And when you hear tell of it on the street, only a fool ignores the call."

"And the call is?"

Haney drained his glass before answering.

"No more free courses in real estate business, Irish. You'll have to be buying."

Byrne acceded to that logic and bought the next two rounds while Haney, with an occasional word from Paul and Henry, told him the word on the street was that Flagler had been buying up even more property on the west side than he already owned. They'd heard that the entire hotel working class was transferring to the West side of the lake.

"They all got up in mass and moved?" Byrne said, thinking of the stoic face of the black man driving the bicycle carriage. "Sounds like a bit of a phenomenon."

"Word is that they were burned out," Paul said. "Accordin' to those that know, their little village over there called the Styx was set fire in the night and the entire place gutted." Paul's chin came out with the statement, proud that he had gleaned information off the street so soon after his arrival. For his trouble he got an immediate glare from Haney.

"The real word is that prices on the island are going to skyrocket," Haney said quickly. "But the hard part is getting hold of the sellers. They're already being wined and dined by the gentry. To get ahold of any of those land titles the speculators are going to have to be connected and sharp," Haney said. "Might be worth stickin' round for a bit, though. Never know when the trickle down might start. Some guy tradin' up wants to dump what he already has on the mainland so he can qualify for something on the island."

He leaned in conspiratorially to Byrne.

"Knowledge is money, boy'o, and since your ear is closer to the rich than ours, keep us in mind should ya hear somethin' juicy, eh?"

Byrne did not dismiss the possibility. Being noncommittal, he'd learned, kept doors open. Haney was right about one thing, information is what the world ran on, be it business or law enforcement. It was a lesson he'd learned firsthand from Danny. He'd have to build a network if he was going to find his brother and survive in this land of sun and heat and haves and have nots. Eventually the binder boys all rose and bid him farewell. A waiter arrived and asked if he was going to use the table for more than drinking and Byrne asked for a lunch recommendation. In minutes was served the finest tasting fish—called yellowtail snapper—that he'd ever put to fork. He stayed for another forty-five minutes, eating and drinking and recording the faces around him. If he was a smoking man, he'd of lit a cigar. Fine fish and fine beer. What more could a man want while sitting in the sun with money in his pocket? The answer surprised him when it came sidelong out of his head. It was the memory of bright chiffon and a waft of gardenia, a glance of tumbling auburn, a glimpse of china skin and the shine of an emerald eye.

CHAPTER ELEVEN

ALL RIGHT MARJORY. I'M LISTENING. TELL me what you know." The McAdams had retired to their quarters in the Poinciana, a suite of rooms that were not the equal of the Birch's, but the tiffany, Ming, fine leather and dark mahogany were still extraordinary for an employee. Mr. McAdams had loosened his collar, kicked off his shoes and made himself a heavy glass of scotch. He was exhausted from the New York trip but took his favorite place in a high-backed wing chair with a view of the golf course and asked again.

"Tell me what this urgent matter is all about."

Mr. McAdams was always accommodating to his daughter. Since his wife's death he had been more lenient than perhaps he should have been. He recognized that he had somehow transferred from his wife to his daughter the need to listen and to some degree share his confidences. He saw it as a way of gaining insight into himself, having the feedback from those who loved and knew him best. They wouldn't bullshit him. They wouldn't be sycophantic, sucking up to gain favor or advantage. And he knew they wouldn't use what they learned to knife him in the back. The conversations were frank—Marjory had inherited that characteristic from her mother. But in certain cases, like this one, he would withhold some truths, just as he had with his wife. Truths that might hurt her. Truths that might hurt his standing in her eyes. But it didn't stop him from being blunt.

"What is it with this fire that has so intrigued you? What do you know of this dead man found in the ashes?"

Marjory had to calm herself. Her telegraphs to her father had been vague by necessity. And she knew how he reacted to hyperbole and emotion in these retellings of her experiences and concerns. She adopted the style of her mother, serious and businesslike, when she could.

"On Monday, Papa, the servant's village, the Styx, was burned to the ground. I was out on the porch at the Breakers that night with a friend. A female friend," she added. This was, after all, her father.

"We smelled the smoke and then saw the glow of flames in the trees and went to investigate."

"Yes." McAdams had already been advised of these facts. He already knew who the friend was, the senior housekeeper who his daughter had often been seen in company with. He had decided not to fight that battle, his daughter's penchant for fraternizing with the staff. He had never wanted to stifle her inquisitiveness or shield her from knowing the ways of people, especially those outside of her class. Such associations had served him well as Flagler's front man, his forward scout so to speak. "You learn the truth by listening" had been his own private motto, and he would not hamstring his own daughter by denying her that knowledge. In this situation, though, he was concerned his broadmindedness would come back to haunt him.

"Go on, dear."

"So I went out to the fire site," she said. "To help if I could."

McAdams raised one questioning eyebrow. The look was not unfamiliar to Marjory. It was disapproval of her actions, of her logic, but her father would never say a word, just give the eyebrow, point made.

"We watched the fire, while it ate everything up. It was hor..."

Marjory stopped herself short of stepping across the emotional line she knew her father disliked.

"It destroyed nearly everything. The homes and that wooden dance hall and most of their belongings. They were left with nothing."

"I know you're concerned. And Mr. Flagler has already taken steps to build accommodations for his workers across the lake. I do believe they will in fact be an improvement in the housing those people had thrown together in the Styx," McAdams said.

Marjory now abandoned the rule against displaying emotion. "Yes, I know. But it will be no benefit to the poor woman who that abominable blob of a sheriff has accused of killing that man."

McAdams held up his hand, lowered his head, showing her his acquiescence to the fierceness his daughter owned.

"I know about the body. But please tell me that you did not also witness this."

"I'm sorry, but yes, a few of us did see the body. It was not so bad as when Mama and I saw that dead little boy in the Bowery that day."

The memory tightened the skin around Mr. McAdams's eyes. It was one of the few times in their marriage that he had admonished his wife. Her penchant for social work in the city had led her numerous times into undesirable neighborhoods in the lower bowels of Manhattan, but she had always reassured him with explanations that these were group trips with other like-minded women and they never traveled without escort, often off-duty police officers handpicked by trusted commanders close to prominent members of their society.

But the idea that his wife would take ten-year-old Marjory along with her crossed all bounds of acceptance. While the entire group was walking near Chatham Square, ostensibly scouting out a location for some cockamamie poor house for unwed mothers, a child half Marjory's age fell, or was pushed, or simply thrown from the window of a six-story building they were passing. In relating the story his wife had been unable to determine whether she'd heard the gasps before the thud of the body or the other way round. She said she'd tried to shield Marjory's eyes from the crumpled body that lay before them. But Marjory later had dreams of birds losing flight in midair and reacted with a twitching shock whenever she heard a thump from some innocent occurrence out of sight. She had actually taken one of her dolls and positioned its arms and legs in a horrific tableau that his wife said was a remarkable reconstruction of the dead child's position on the sidewalk. In time Marjory seemed to have forgotten the incident, but obviously not altogether.

Mr. McAdams, in his dry manner, stated only the facts as he knew them.

"And I understand, Marjory, that the sheriff—and I do wish you would be more circumspect in your descriptions of the man—has conducted an investigation."

"Which is the entire problem. This so-called investigation has led to a ludicrous assumption that a poor Negro housemaid put a knife into the man and then tried to burn his body to cover the crime and led to the destruction of her own home and entire village."

Mr. McAdams put his chin in the crux between the forefinger and thumb of his right hand and tilted his head just so. It was a sign Marjory recognized as the point in which the conversation had turned from an exercise in listening to one bordering on argument.

"And this accused woman, did you know her, dear?"

"No."

"Had not Mizz Fluery introduced you to her?"

"No, Papa." She hated lying to her father.

"So you did not know that she was a known, shall we say, escort of sorts with a rather tawdry reputation?"

"I did not know she was a prostitute, no," Marjory said, rising to the debate that was now growing into the kind of lecture from her father she always railed against.

Mr. McAdams closed his eyes at the sound of the word prostitute, as if it were a glob of spittle that sullied both her upbringing and her beauty.

Marjory recognized her limits, and knew from her father's look that she may have stepped over them. Logic had always been his game. She retreated to it quickly.

"There were several people at the fair on the mainland that saw the woman there. She wasn't even on the island at the time of the fire." This of course was speculation and was in fact Marjory's entire motivation. Had Shantice Carver actually seen something she was never intended to see or not?

McAdams took a sip from his glass and remained stoically silent, but listening.

"And it is quite possible that Mr. Pearson himself recognized the dead man," Marjory added, letting her ace come out of her hand in an effort to gain favor. "You can ask his opinion. I know he'll speak to you with candor."

Mr. McAdams remained quiet in the face of his daughter's salvo. It was not the effect she was looking for. He finished his scotch with a slight flourish, a signal that the conversation was over.

"I shall speak with Mr. Pearson. And I will also attempt a meeting with the sheriff. Those things I can do under my limited authority," he said. McAdams lowered his chin, dipping his forehead just so, and looked up at his daughter with his eyebrows raised. It was his conciliatory look, the one that asked for her patience, her discretion and her obedience.

"But please, my dear. Go no further with this until we talk again. I promise I'll share with you what I can. But please, Marjory, leave this alone for now."

The look and the slightly pleading tone always cut to her heart, made her feel guilty for adding burden to her father's life.

"I will," she said, standing and stepping to his chair. He would get to the truth, to what was known by whom. And then he would share that knowledge with her. That she was sure of. She bent to kiss his cheek. "It is wonderful to have you here."

CHAPTER TWELVE

WHEN BYRNE EMERGED FROM THE SEMINOLE Hotel the next morning he made sure not to step directly into the light. He'd learned that the sunrise in Florida was not the same event as in New York. Unfiltered by smoke and ash and undiffused by a hundred tall buildings and their cast of shadows, the sun here had the power to create temporary blindness to a Yankee whose immediate response was to squint and shade his eyes with a raised hand.

Today the lesson paid off. Byrne stayed back under the shadow of an awning. He spotted Mr. Faustus, leaning against a hitching post in front of shop baring the sign "L.A. Willson, Fine Boot and Shoemaker. Perfect Fits and Most Approved Styles Assured. No Cheap Work."

Faustus was dressed in dark trousers and a white long-sleeved shirt buttoned tight to the neck and at the wrists. He had apparently left his tailed coat and his vest at home but still wore his high hat. Despite the early hour, he had a lit cigar in his mouth, the scent of which Byrne caught in the mild breeze. Since Faustus' boots were shined, perfectly sound and in no need of repair, Byrne assumed he was waiting for him.

"Good morning, young Mr. Byrne," Faustus said, coming off one haunch.

Byrne, his eyes adjusted, stepped down off the porch and joined the man.

"Good day to you, sir."

"A fine day in paradise, Mr. Byrne," Faustus said with a flourish of the cigar. "With this mild wind blowing in from the north, the ocean will assuredly be as a child's soft blanket and it is a perfect morning for fishing."

"Fishing, sir?"

"Why yes, young Pinkerton. Have you never been fishing on the deep blue sea?"

What Byrne knew of fish was the odor of the docks on Canal Street in the Lower forties, the mongers wheeling their carts up Broadway, the chopped-away heads washing in the slush of the gutters. But his memory of last night's dinner, combined with Faustus' use of the description of this fabulous water, caused a spark of interest to flash in his mind. He looked into Faustus' eyes where there was a certain liveliness that he'd not seen before: no business, no cunning, no historical lesson, just an inkling of adventure.

"Fishing?" he repeated. Faustus raised his immense eyebrows in invitation. Byrne thought of the bait-and-switch of the Bowery, but knew he was too smart if that was the man's ploy. Besides, Faustus was turning into someone who seemed quite connected in this new town. Perhaps connected enough to know where to find someone named Danny Byrne even if his brother had changed his name. Byrne felt as if Faustus was investigating him as much as he was Faustus. As a result, the man intrigued him. Why not come right out and ask if he knew of Danny and get it over with? Surely he'd been blunt with everyone else. But bluntness did not seem to be Faustus' style, a trait that Byrne recognized as his own in the past. Could he be an ally, or nemesis? And if he was being subtly recruited, to what end?

Within an hour they were aboard a twenty-six-foot sailing launch, pushing off onto the lake from the docks of A.T. Rose, Boat Builder, on the southern boundary of the city.

When Byrne had agreed to Faustus' excursion he'd first asked if he would require anything special: clothing, equipment, food.

"Not a thing, young Pinkerton. Just your curiosity," Faustus had said and winked.

Within short walking distance of the hotel they passed through a boatyard of sorts with hulls in partial repair or stages of construction. The smell of fresh cut wood mixed with that of thick lacquer and paint. Faustus tipped his hat to a craftsman who was at the task of shaving what looked like a pole of fine ash wood into what Byrne assumed would eventually be a mast. Other workers were scraping the dried scales and what appeared to be barnacles from the bottom of a launch that had been pulled from the water with ropes and pulleys up onto a cradle of sorts. The equipment and docks and the wood itself looked new and fresh and hardened in the sun instead of the dank and rotted pilings and the stench of fish and oils and filth Byrne had experienced on the wharfs of New York.

On a dock jutting out into the lake was a waiting vessel. Faustus called to the man coiling lines on the bow and introduced him to Byrne as Captain Abbott.

"All loaded with rigging and lunch for two as requested, Mr. Faustus," the captain said, taking the older man's elbow and guiding him onto the deck. Byrne waved off the offer of help and stepped down onto the gunwale and then to the deck boards while trying to lock his eyes onto Faustus's. The fact that the old Mason had anticipated that Byrne would automatically agree to the fishing offer bothered him. But his irritation at being manipulated was soon overwhelmed by his fascination with this new enterprise.

After pushing off from the dock, Captain Abbott yanked on a line that unfurled a fabric sail. "Watch your head, boy!"

A heavy wooden beam swung by just as Byrne ducked and the sail filled with a woof. The forward movement underfoot almost felled him, but Byrne caught his balance and stood with his feet apart as the captain cleated the line and then skittered past him to gain control of the tiller handle. Byrne's head and eyes swung in three directions trying to keep up with the mariner's actions, the swing of the boat, and the relation with the land.

"Ha!" yelped Mr. Faustus. "That beam that nearly took your head off is called a boom, young Pinkerton. That's the one to watch when Captain Abbott starts yelling 'Coming about!' or it will certainly boom you up side the noggin'."

"I see," Byrne said, trying to be cynical but unable to keep a smile from starting at the corners of his mouth.

When Abbott yanked on yet another line and the boom pulled in, the boat heeled a bit to one side, Byrne moved to the other and sat on the raised gunwale, now looking ahead to see where they might be going and feeling the pleasant rush of wind in his ears. The only times he'd been on the water in New York was in a stolen rowboat on the East River with Danny or on the ferry to New Jersey. The wobbling rowboat and the crowded ferry were nothing like this. As the canvas stretched and the lines tightened he could feel the craft's speed increase and took the chance of leaning out to watch the pointed bow slice through the lake, sending out the V-shaped lines of disturbed water. The lack of motor noise and the pure physical pull of the sail were intoxicating. It was almost what he imagined flying to be like.

Off to the northeast he could see the diminishing view of the upper floors of the Poinciana. For the next half hour Byrne remained quiet, studying the movements of the captain and inspecting the craft: the sturdy brass of the cleats and fittings, the polish of the teak decking and the weaving in the rope lines. He finally relaxed after deeming the whole operation seaworthy despite his lack of experience to tell him any different. While the captain continued to make small adjustments to the sail and tension of the lines, Mr. Faustus was now pulling out what Byrne assumed to be the fishing poles and equipment and what must be the bait they were to use in catching fish.

"Step on down here, Mr. Byrne, and let me show you what we've got," Faustus said.

What he had were four long rods from six to eight feet in length. Faustus explained that they were made from split Tonkin bamboo and Calcutta reed. He picked one up at the base and wiggled it, causing the pliable fiber to bend and whip at the end.

"A little more give in the shaft than you're used to," Faustus said, without looking up. "But it gives you much more control of the fish once he's got the hook in his mouth."

Byrne said nothing. He knew Faustus had seen him use his telescoping rod to manage the crowd of farmers during the train ride. Even now the weapon was in the deep pocket of his pants.

"I'm sure you'll get the feel of it," Faustus said, handing one of the poles to Byrne.

It was light in his fingers. The base appeared to be made of maple and there were simple wire loops attached at equa-distant points along its length. He took his own turn flexing the pole, snapping its end and creating a whipping noise not unlike that which his own metal rod made when he was using it with a fury. Next Faustus brought out a box and removed two large brass reels about the size of a child's head. Byrne could tell they were heavy by the strain that showed in the old man's forearms and tendons when he lifted them and set them on the deck. He showed Byrne the iron gears and brass casings and the cork handle that spun the device. On an interior spool was wound some sort of linen line. Faustus pinched a loose end and pulled off a length of the line.

"Twenty-four threads spun together," he said. "Maximum strength when it's dry is about sixty-six pounds. But that won't matter out here. We won't be picking them up out the sea like some hangman. The idea is to hook them and then outguess them. Let them pull the line through the water until they wear out their hearts, but keep them from breaking free just the same.

"Oh, you'll see, my friend. It's a glorious thing."

The captain sniggered behind them, not in derision of the words but in a shared recognition of another man's addiction. Byrne himself was surprised by the old Mason's excitement and by the fact that every minute closer to the fishing grounds seemed to peel another year off his aged face.

Captain Abbott yanked in a length of what Byrne had now learned was the mainsail sheet line and hollered out a word of advice: "Hold onto somethin' fellas, the inlet's a bit choppy today."

Byrne saw a rise and fall of ocean swells he'd never witnessed before. Ditches and troughs, was his instant thought. Mounds and hollows to split any axle. He held fast to the edge of the gunwale and felt the bow rise on the first wave and then braced himself as it plunged down into the following trough. He expected impact. But the boat's bow knifed through the water and the landing was not nearly what he'd expected. The next forward plunge sent a spray of sea out either side of the bow like sheets of snow from a plow blade. By the fourth such rise and fall Byrne was studying the angles the captain was taking, admiring his expertise at controlling the boat's pitch and roll with the tiller. By the sixth swell, he was humbled.

Within minutes they were through the inlet and onto the smoother, rolling ocean. Captain Abbott let out the boom and took a more southerly course. Faustus stepped up onto the gunwale with a hand-hold on one of the mast stays and stared out onto open water. Byrne followed suit on his side of the cockpit, worried now that he would miss another new experience. The sky was cloudless and blue, and the sea borrowed its color and then bent it into greens and turquoise depending on the depths.

"Your employer loves these waters and this coastline as much as anyone with an appreciation of such beauty," Faustus said without turning. The statement took Byrne by surprise, but since there didn't seem to be a question invoked, he let it stand without comment. Captain Abbott, on the other hand, responded with a derisive snort.

"Did you know that Mr. Flagler's first forays into this part of Florida were by sailboat? No one who rides this sea could not miss its Edenic pull."

Byrne let the old man's words stand alone. There will be a point in them, he thought. Faustus, he'd already determined, was not a man without a point.

"But I fear Flagler's island is not just a single jewel to delight his friends and rejuvenate their spirits for the business of business in the north," Faustus continued, finally turning to look Byrne in the eye. "There will be trouble in that paradise, young Pinkerton. And in your position, it will be trouble you won't be able to avoid."

"I appreciate your concern, sir," Byrne said, deciding whether he should rise to what he was already perceiving to be bait. "And from what I've heard on the street, trouble is already there."

Faustus stepped back down onto the cockpit deck.

"I'm glad I did not underestimate your abilities at intelligence gathering. Would you be speaking of the death of a white man in the Negro quarters on the island?"

"There was talk of it on the street," Byrne said.

"And did the speakers have any idea who the unfortunate fellow was or what his business might have been there?" Faustus said, carefully watching for reaction.

"I don't recall any talk of business, no. Did you understand him to be a businessman?" Byrne asked, playing the game, giving what he could to get what he might.

Faustus moved on, but Byrne had seen a twinge of pain in the old man's eyes.

"At this point in this virgin land everyone is in business. There are people buying, people selling. Be it the labor of their hands, the guile of their intellect, the dreams they lust after or the lust itself."

"And your business, Mr. Faustus? What exactly is it that you do?" Byrne kept his tone as innocent as possible although he perceived he'd made a fine move in their little chess game.

Faustus sat on the starboard gunwale and began the process of attaching the reel to the heavy end of one of the poles.

"I've been involved in a wide variety of enterprise in life, my friend. I've used my hands as a shipwright in Biloxi, my intellect as a student of medicine in New Orleans, my tongue as a merchant of everything from ladies' plumed hats in Savanah to gunpowder in Charleston.

"I served as a field surgeon in the Civil War and afterward worked as a surveyor of the broken land of the South."

Faustus turned his face up to the sun with a look that showed neither pride nor regret.

"I have been blessed and cursed in the activities of commerce and men for many years, my young fisherman," he said, handing Byrne the completed pole. "And either way, it can be a befuddling thing to see.

"Presently, I admit I'm in search of good men. Men with honesty and moral fiber in their souls. Men who believe in the goodness of others and are adept at bringing that quality out. Men who, instead of taking advantage for their own gain, recognize that gain can and should be shared."

Ah, the pitch, Byrne thought.

"And have you met such men, Mr. Faustus?" he said.

"Oh, yes," Faustus said. "But I have also been fooled by those with the look and intelligence and talent for such things, only to be disappointed."

The old Mason was now looking into Byrne's face as if it was familiar to him, as if he were speaking to Byrne himself in this obviously heartfelt sense of disappointment. Such accusation had no basis as far as Byrne's actions were concerned, still he had a nagging sense of responsibility. It was Faustus who broke the spell.

"For now, young Pinkerton, let us lure the beasts from the deep and see what challenge they may afford us."

Byrne shook off his apprehension and watched while the man opened the hatch of a wooden barrel lashed into one corner of the cockpit and came out with a small silver-sided fish, which he proceeded to carefully skewer with the finger-sized hook he'd tied to the linen line.

"First we'll do a little trolling on our way to the stream, eh Captain Abbott?" Faustus said.

Abbott was a man whose eyes seemed nearly colorless and thus able to reflect the intense shimmering light off the water rather than absorb it. His skin was dark and seamed. His lips formed a taut line and were the color and consistency of red onion skin. Perhaps they would split and bleed if he used them to excess, Byrne thought. Maybe that's why he so rarely spoke.

"As you will, sir," he said, and although Byrne saw the man's Adam's apple move, his lips did not. Byrne thought instantly of a ventriloquist he'd seen in the Bowery.

Faustus baited his own hook and showed Byrne how simple it was to cast the fish into the bubbling wake behind them and let the line spin off his reel. He'd put a canvas glove on one hand and used his thumb to occasionally slow down the rate of the linen leaving. In less than five minutes the old man suddenly jerked the tip of the rod up, like Byrne might have done with his own baton, and then began to turn the handle of the spinning reel. Without hesitation, Capt. Abbott turned the boat into the wind to slow it. The boom swung to the middle of the cockpit and almost smashed into Byrne's head. He was captivated by the sudden tightening of Faustus' line and the deft way the old man reeled and then stopped, apparently feeling the direction of the pull on the other end and then reeling again. There was a small sweat and an obvious joy on Faustus' face.

"It appears we've got ourselves a nice dolphin," Faustus yelled over the popping of canvas as the sail went loose in the wind. "Grab that gaff over there so you can hook him when I bring him along the starboard side!"

Byrne searched in the direction Faustus had indicated but had no inkling what a "gaff" might be. Without taking his pale eyes off the battle, Captain Abbott reached out a leg, put his foot on a cork handled hook like Byrne had seen ice delivery men use to handle their blocks, and kicked it over to him. Byrne picked it up and thus armed stared back at the sea, following Faustus' line into blue water. Minutes passed as Faustus coaxed and maneuvered, reeled and stopped. The flexible tip of the rod bent and swung like a willow in the wind. Finally Byrne saw a flash of silver light below, then the body of the fish, slowing in its struggle and soon he could see the dark circle of its eye.

"Alongside, son," Faustus said, now pulling the defeated catch to starboard. "Hook her in the gills if you would."

Byrne bent and reached overboard. He was talented with a piece of metal in his hand and gaffed the fish and pulled it up out of the water, surprised by its heft, forty pounds at least. He flopped it down into the foot of the cockpit and withdrew the gaff while Faustus pressed his polished shoe across its broad side.

"Comin' about!" Capt. Abbott called out, and this time Byrne reacted to the words and ducked. He felt the jolt as wind filled the sail and the boat was again underway. Faustus bent to remove his hook from the fish's mouth. "She'll make a fine meal, this one," he said.

Byrne continued watching the fish, its tail still waving as if it could propel itself to escape in the air as it had always done in water. But it was a different world up here and old defenses didn't work. Finally Faustus grasped the dolphin and slid it into a shuttered bin filled with chopped ice.

"All right, Mr. Byrne. Time for your own lesson on the finest fishing grounds in the world."

Faustus baited the hook on Byrne's rod and tossed his line overboard. During the next hour the men pulled in a dozen fish: several pompano, two more dolphin of equal size to the first, three of what Faustus called redfish, and a four-foot-long shark the face of which Byrne openly compared to that of a Tamany police sergeant.

Byrne snapped only one line when a dolphin dove unexpectedly and he yanked back to stop it instead of letting it run. His observations of Faustus' moves and technique were so thorough that several times Byrne would make the correction just before the words were out of the old man's mouth.

"You're a quick study," Faustus said while removing the hook from yet another fish's mouth. "As I knew you would be.

"But we've a much bigger challenge ahead and it's in water you still have never imagined in your deepest dreams."

The look in the old man's eyes was disconcerting in its almost religious anticipation. Byrne found his skin tingling with the excitement to come after already being flabbergasted by the experience of fighting the running, instinctual muscle of big fish with a simple bending length of wood and a spool of linen thread. What could the old Mason now have up his sleeve?

"Into the stream, sir!" Capt. Abbott called out, and when Byrne followed Faustus' gaze he had an answer.

"Jesus, Mary and Joseph," he whispered, looking out and then down into an opaque blue water that was like no color he'd ever witnessed nor thought possible.

Byrne felt the shift of current below them, the boat being pushed against its will to the north. He looked first to Faustus, but the man's face had taken on a look of one witnessing a deity. Even the craggy Abbott appeared to have a glint of smile on his slash of a mouth.

"It's the Gulf Stream, son," Faustus said. "She's nothing less than a magical river that circles the Gulf of Mexico and then comes surging round the tip of Florida off Key West and runs like a fire hose northbound to New York and on to Nova Scotia.

"Ships have been using her muscle to take a free ride north for centuries. If you just sat on her in a rowboat you'd float your way to shores of Europe herself without taking a single stroke. There's a whole troupe of Norwegians who pluck tiny sea hearts off their beaches that were once washed off the shores of the Caribbean and simply got lost in the stream and took the ride for thousands of miles."

Byrne had no doubt of Faustus' geography lesson, but it was the color of the water that hypnotized him. He laid his chest across the starboard gunwale and reached down to actually touch the water, convinced that if he scooped up a handful he would have a puddle of blue in his palm.

"This is where the finest of the breed work their own fishing grounds, Mr. Byrne. Where they can run as fast as lightening and strike at will then flash away into their own deep universe."

Faustus was working again at the rigging. Byrne looked over and saw that he was attaching an odd-looking piece of metal to the end of his line. Oblong in shape, like a teardrop, the thin leaf of shiny tin had a hook protruding from the fat end, and unlike Faustus' other lures, there was a strange barb at the very tip akin to whaling harpoons Byrne had seen at the city docks. It was obvious by its design that such a hook was not going to slip easily out once it speared through the mouth flesh of a fish.

"I had this spoon custom-made by a friend in Philadelphia name of Samuel H. Jones," Faustus said, tying the pointed end of the teardrop to his line and clamping a series of split lead weights the size of peas to the line to pull it deep. "Sam claims he caught the most beautiful fish he'd ever seen in Florida on a spoon like this up on the Indian River inlet. A tarpon, he called it, as big as a man."

The old man dropped the lure into the blue and Byrne watched it glitter in the deep light as it sunk deeper and deeper, maybe thirty yards, maybe forty before he could no longer track it. He looked up into Faustus' eyes and saw a mixture of anticipation, lust and competition that unsettled him at first and then stirred a tingle in his own hands that he recognized as the energy that came only when he had his metal baton in his palm and the threat of violence in his veins.

"Let's drag her south a bit, captain," Faustus called out, and Abbott swung the boat about and set a wide sail. Since nothing was said about casting Byrne's line, he settled a haunch on the gunwale and was content to stare into the water, the depths somehow haunting, as if calling him to fall in and glide down into its warmth. The sun was high now, the reflection causing Byrne to shade his eyes whenever he looked out to follow Faustus' line into the sea. Despite the breeze he could feel a light sweat under his shirt and also the sting of sunburn on the back of his neck.

"She'll take it if she wants to," Faustus said once, though the statement seemed to be directed at no one in the boat. "That's the power she holds, to do what she wants in a sea of possibilities."

The words caused Byrne to conjure a glimpse of the white of fabric and green eyes of McAdams' daughter, a recollection that despite his surroundings and the thrill of the day had not left him.

"Ever had a woman like that, young Pinkerton?" Faustus said, and Byrne looked up to see the old man looking at him instead of the water. "One with the power to snatch and hold you?"

If the old man was performing some Masonic magic trick, reading his mind, Byrne would not have been more taken aback.

"No, sir. Never."

Faustus chuckled.

"Well if you do young man, hold on just as tight as she does and enjoy the hell out of the adventure."

The pole in the old man's hand yanked forward and the linen line started spinning off the reel like a strike of heat lightening. He instinctively pulled back on the rod. It bent in a U-shape, and Byrne was sure the laminate would splinter in Faustus' hands. He could have sworn he heard the sound of cracking wood but it may have been line zinging off the sides of the cast metal.

"My god!" Faustus pointed the tip of the rod toward the water and let the line and the fish run. When he felt the beast turn, Faustus raised the rod, took in a few turns of the reel, and felt just a bit of the weight of muscle that was at its end. Now the surprise had left his face and been replaced by a startled joy.

"Oh, my, lad, what have we got?"

Byrne was staring after the line, watching it rip through the water like a sharp knife through satin and creating a similar sound. Then before his eyes, it went slack.

Snapped, he thought. But Faustus didn't move.

"Wait, wait, just you wait now," he said.

The moment Faustus had hooked the fish, Capt. Abbott had again swung into the wind and even he could not keep his eyes from the sea where the linen line now lay like a string of spittle.

"Wait, wait." The captain repeated Faustus' words and Byrne felt the hairs on the back of his neck tingle.

The explosion erupted less than thirty yards off the starboard stern. Byrne swore he saw it coming, a sun glint in the depths, a flurry of silver bubbles rising. It then let loose like a fire hose just below the surface, a burst of water sprayed into the air, a fountain that contained in its middle the body of a silver fish like some scaled angel.

Byrne could not have been more stunned if he'd witnessed a rogue firework explode from a Lower East Side manhole cover.

In midair the beast bent its back to match the arc of Faustus' fishing rod and then twisted its body in a violent shake and plunged back into the sea.

"Christ on a cross!" said Capt. Abbott, the first non-nautical utterance that had come out of the old sea dog during the entire trip. The boat had come to a standstill, rocking in the long waves. Byrne looked at Faustus for a clue. Both old men watched the water and the tip of the rod. Again like a rip of lightning through a cloud the fish burst the surface, flying higher still while shaking its huge body like a dog trying to dry itself with a shiver and twist.

"She's a hundert an twenty if she's a pound, sir," Abbott said, still in reverence.

"And bound to run, captain."

"Yes, sir. Coming about, sir."

Abbott swung the boat by pumping the tiller until the sail could catch wind. Faustus made his way forward in the cockpit, keeping the fish on the port side. Again the line went taut as a guitar string and Faustus let it spool out.

"The line will put a drag on her," he said. "She'll have to swim against it. All we can do is follow and hope she's not strong enough to break it." For the next hour the men worked the line and the boat, Faustus trying to anticipate the moves of the fish, Abbott following his called out direction.

Byrne could already tell from the beads of sweat rolling off the old man's face and the bend in his back and bow of his shoulders that he was tiring. The joy had diminished from his face, along with a certain degree of grit.

"Damn, she's strong," he said in admiration. He took his eyes off the ocean for a second to look at Byrne, who could do nothing but wipe the old man's face with a cloth dipped in fresh water. "She'll run for awhile, but at some point she's going to buck again, son. And truth be known, I don't think I'm strong enough anymore to match her."

Byrne turned to look at the captain.

"No. You son," Faustus said. "First, get my holster out of the bin there."

Byrne was used to taking orders, and conceded that Faustus was the one in charge. He went directly to the bin and realized what the man had asked for. Holster? He glanced back at the old man, who was back to the business of horsing the fish.

Byrne began pawing through the bin, searching for and finally finding a dark leather holster wrapped tightly and pressed into one corner. He pulled it out and stood with a .36 caliber Griswold revolver in his hands. What the hell was he planning to do, shoot the damn fish?

"Strap it on, lad," said Abbott without looking. "Loose like."

Byrne uncoiled the belt, buckled it around his waist and notched it so the old leather settled on his hips, the gun handle at his right side, all the while wondering what the hell.

"OK," he said.

Faustus grinned at the gunslinger pose.

"Get rid of the gun, young Pinkerton, though I do not doubt your proficiency with such a mechanism.

"And slide the holster round to the front. Next time she gives us a lull, we're going to stick the butt of the pole right into that pocket. That way you'll be able to use that back of yours, son."

Byrne got the picture, pulled the gun and held it for a second in his hand, the familiar weight of it and the warm metal against his palm. He laid it in the bin and then twisted the holster so it was positioned between his legs and moved to Faustus' side. On the old man's command he grabbed the pole with both hands and they jammed the butt down into the holster. For the first time Byrne felt the power of the fish below.

"Jaysus."

"You got that right, Irish," he heard the captain say behind him.

"Now, son. Visualize the line below. It's working in a long curve. The beast pulling it this way and then changing course and pulling it the other," Faustus waved his hand in a wide motion to describe the movement. "When you feel the pressure ease, you know she's changed course and you've got to move the tip to make sure the line doesn't snap when it catches up to the turn."

For the next hour Byrne felt and listened, watched the line, leaned back with the holster digging into his crotch but glad for the leverage it afforded him. His own young muscles began to ache and each long minute he gained respect for Faustus and the fish. While he worked, Faustus talked, giving him what knowledge he had. The old man also fed him fresh water so he wouldn't have to take his hands off the pole. At one point Abbott removed his own captain's hat, doused it in the drinking water and then without a word unceremoniously flopped it on top of Byrne's head and left it there, the shaded coolness running down his face and neck.

All three men could feel the fish slowly turning its easterly course more and more to the north to follow the current of the Gulf Stream.

"Path of least resistance," Faustus said. "Just like all living things when we tire.

"But beware of the heart in this one, she'll give it one last try to escape."

The Florida sun was now in the western sky. Byrne could feel the tightness on the skin of his neck like it had shrunk as it sizzled under the direct heat. They were into the third hour, but he had refused to ask how long this could go on. His back felt like one giant muscle, bunched and aching. At Faustus' instructions he'd let his arms extend, giving up on flexing them except to reel a small amount of line when he felt the need. The wind continued to blow but mercifully did not increase. Their ride on the swells had become so rhythmic there was almost a music to it.

Byrne was about to turn the rod again when the line went slack.

"No pressure," he said, alarm in his voice. He let the tip go down toward the water and looked at Faustus. "Did it break? Has she broken it?"

"No!" Faustus reached out to push the rod back in high position. "She's turning on us. Reel the line, son. Reel the line."

Byrne spun the handle. Abbott stalled the boat into the wind. All three stared out to the northwest, waiting.

Sun glanced off the wave fronts and tossed deep blue shadows on the backsides. Each glimmer on the sea's surface caught the men's attention. Byrne's knuckles were white on the sweat-stained wood of the rod, his fingers nearly numb as they worked the reel.

The captain saw it first, his sea-trained eyes, despite their age, picked up the silver below the surface.

"There!"

A finger jutted out due north.

Again came the rise of silver and the rip of water. The fish was closer this time, like she needed to see who had beaten her. The long body cleared the ocean but not nearly as high as the first times. The twist was not as violent. The buck was almost listless. But the shine of scaled flesh was even more spectacular in the glancing sun.

After the splash no one said a word. Byrne felt the tension return to the line but it was decidedly feeble.

"Keep reeling," Faustus said.

In another thirty minutes they pulled the fish up from the blue and alongside. Faustus leaned over and grabbed the line, twisting it once around his palm and drew the tarpon near. But when Byrne went to fetch the gaff the old man said, "No. Just hand me those pliers, son."

Abbott had left the tiller. "I was wrong, sir," he said, looking over the gunwale. "It's a hundert and fifty easy."

The mouth of the fish was huge and gasping, its boney structures stretching the tough skin.

"Reach down and grab a gill," he said to Byrne while he probed the inside of the fish's mouth with the pliers to find the hook. In a second he twisted his wrist and Byrne heard the pop of gristle being torn. The hook was removed. When Byrne started to lift, Faustus again said no, traded handholds and grasped the gill himself and lowered the fish's mouth back into the blueness. Then he let go and they watched six feet of silver float down behind them and with a mere twitch of the tail, turn and disappear.

Faustus stood for a long minute, watching. His starched white shirt was soaked with sea water and sweat. A streak of fish blood tracked across the front. His polished shoes squished in the puddle of scum, guts, water and fish oil on the cockpit floor. His look was at once both humble and majestic.

"Time to go home, captain," Faustus said. Abbott pulled in a sheet line, called "Comin' about" and the sail popped in the wind, heading southwest.

Byrne said nothing, partly stunned, partly exhausted, partly understanding. He unlatched the holster and gave it to Faustus. He handed Abbott's hat back to the captain, who shook it once and then pulled it tight over his grey head.

"Might have been a record, sir," Abbott said, yanking down the brim to shield whatever look there might have been in his eyes.

"Aye," said Faustus, who reached into the bin and took out the handgun, replaced it in the holster and rewound the belt. He looked up with that grin of his on a now tired face.

"But would that have made it any more glorious?"

Even Abbott smiled. No need to answer.

"As for you, young Pinkerton, it was a job well done. A lesser man would have given in. And an even lesser man would have screamed bloody murder at the thought of letting that one go."

Byrne remained quiet.

"I do not think that I misjudged you, despite my inclinations from influences past," Faustus said and now their eyes were locked.

"Did you think that I was like my brother?" Byrne said, guessing what he now felt in his bones.

"The family resemblance is unequivocal," Faustus said.

"Do you know where he is?"

"Yes," Faustus said. "I believe I do."

CHAPTER THIRTEEN

HE DID NOT WANT TO MOVE from his bed the next morning, but the pounding on the door demanded it. Faustus had refused to elaborate on his comment that he might know where Danny was and would only say that he would make his inquiries and update him when he could. But Faustus was not the kind of man who came bashing at your door.

Byrne rolled to one shoulder, first feeling the sting of crisp skin on his neck fairly scrapping across the pillowcase and second the ache of muscle in his back. He made it up onto one haunch, his ass the only place he didn't feel pain.

The fist on the door continued.

"Rise and shine, lad. I know yer in there," Harris's voice boomed from the hallway. "Shake the hangover out of yer head, you've work to do."

Byrne got to his feet. The heat in the room went straight to his face. He ran his tongue over his lips and discovered the cracked layer of blister that had formed there.

"Coming," he said with a rasp, and even the inside of his throat felt sunburned. He crossed the room with his cotton boxers on and opened the door. Harris was at first taken aback at the sight and then let an infrequent smile show up on his big pie-shaped face.

"Well, well, Michael. It wasn't the devil of drink at all that struck you, lad. 'Twas your introduction to the great Florida sun, eh?"

"I went fishing," Byrne said, moving back to let Harris enter.

"Indeed you did, lad. And caught more than you bargained for, eh?"

Byrne thought of the tarpon in flight, the twisting, beautiful look of the thing.

"Yes," he said. "Much more."

"Well, you're not the first nor the last white-skinned New Yorker turned crispy red and you won't be the last. But that won't excuse you from your duties.

"Here's another dole of spending money." Harris peeled off bills from a wad that had materialized in his big fist. "You'll have to go over to Buholtz's on Banyan and buy yourself a proper suit. We've been asked to be present at Mrs. Flagler's society ball this evening and we'll both have to be in costume, like nobody's going to recognize a couple of Irish mugs like us bumpin' round in a mix of them.

"Still, we'll make an attempt to watch over the old man. Be at the grand ball room at six. I'll be honest with you, it's a first for me. We've never gone off and away from the train before so I'm not sure what they might be expecting. But someone's nervous these days."

Byrne thought of the rumors that someone had been killed on the island during a fire in the servant's quarters. Should he share this intelligence with Harris? He wasn't sure he should but couldn't say why. Did he not trust his own sergeant? That wouldn't be a first considering the lessons learned doing his corruption work as a New York police officer. He'd be surprised of course if Harris wasn't already aware of the rumor, but since he'd not mentioned it, Byrne decided to hold his own cards for now.

Harris had tightened his Irish mug during his giving of orders, but couldn't hold it when once again he looked at Byrne's ruby red nose and cheeks.

"Ask the desk clerk where you can find some aloe, lad," he said with a look of empathy on his face. "It's a plant they use here to give you some relief. You cut the leaf and squeeze out the gel inside and rub it on that sunburn. You'll survive."

Byrne went to the mirror after Harris left. His eyes were swollen. His nose looked like one of the old regulars at McSorely's, red and wrinkled, his cheekbones like they'd been rouged in one of the Tin Pan Alley follies. He'd of laughed if not for the pain. Harris was right, he'd live. But he sure as hell wasn't going to shave until he had to.

Byrne pulled a shirt over his burned shoulders and neck and gathered his dirty clothes in one of the hotel pillow cases. At the front desk he asked the clerk for both a laundry and where he might obtain some of Harris's mysterious aloe plant. The answer to both queries was the same. On Banyan to the north was Joe Cheong's laundry in the back of the Jones' cigar factory.

Byrne was able to locate Cheong's, which was little more than a wooden lean-to with tubs of fresh water and an old steam press. Under the awning was a covey of small, bird-like women fluttering about. He was reminded of similar businesses in corners of the Lower East Side. The needs of men—and the commerce that went with it—had quickly been transplanted from the established streets of New York to the new Florida. After negotiating a price for the laundry, Byrne spent several moments of awkward pantomime and pidgin English asking for the aloe. The head woman, a diminutive Chinese with gray hair and an abrupt air, simply stared at his odd gestures and finally took up a sharp bladed knife from under the counter and signaled for him to follow her. She led him to a small private garden of sorts. Several plants he did not recognize had been hand-planted and carefully tended. The woman went directly to a dark green, crown-shaped bush that Byrne took for a cactus of some kind. The woman hacked off three of the stiff leaves with her knife and held them out to him. When he hesitated to take them, she singled one out, scored it across its three-inch width, snapped it in half and then with her fingers kneaded the middle of the leaf, milking out a yellowish gel. Without touching his face, she showed how Byrne should dab the gel onto the tips of his fingers and then smear it on his own skin.

He followed her instructions and immediately felt relief. The woman accepted a dollar as payment. When she returned to the laundry, Byrne took off his shirt and applied the gel to his neck and shoulders, ears, and forehead. Whether the juice from the plant truly had any medicinal value was of no consequence to him. It diminished the pain of his sunburn and was thus well worth the money.

With his spirits buoyed, Byrne made his way through the streets. The walking loosened the muscles in his back and legs. Near Narcissus he began to walk past the shop of Hawthorn & Dorsey, which had a small, almost toy-like red and white barber pole out front. He remembered the crowd he'd seen in front of the Royal Poinciana, their clothes and their fine ways, and he hesitated. He thought of the young Miss McAdams and did a U-turn, put his hands in his pockets and walked into the shop. It was impossible to be unobtrusive. One man, be it Hawthorn or Dorsey, was sitting in a high wooden chair reading a copy of *The Gazetter*. There was a single chest of drawers against the wall, scissors and razors, brushes and wash bowls on its top. A mirror was mounted behind.

"Good morning, young sir," the man said, hopping to his feet and folding the newspaper. "Shave and a haircut?"

Byrne had never had anyone but his mother cut his hair and had never had a calm man come close to his throat with a razor.

"The cost?" Byrne said.

"Twenty cents," the barber answered and added: "Each."

"Very well," Byrne said, giving the barber a look that was meant to say "I know the bait and switch trick but will give you the business regardless."

The man smiled and reached out a hand: "D. H. Hawthorn. A pleasure to serve you, sir."

The barber helped Byrne remove his coat and set him on the stool. He snapped open a folded sheet with a flourish and wrapped it round Byrne's neck.

"New to these parts, sir?"

"Yes," Byrne said. "Just in."

"Nasty business the sun down here. I shall be extra careful of the sunburn."

"Thank you."

"Care for the newspaper while we work, sir? I'll do the haircut first."

"Fine," Byrne said, and Mr. Hawthorn not only unfolded the small paper and lay it across Byrne's lap, but then proceeded to tell him everything that the journal had printed that day and then some. By the time the haircut was done Byrne knew all about the feud between the liberal newspaper editor and the sheriff, which had come to the point of the editor being arrested, that J. T. Berry and J. B. Thomas had killed a bear on the west side of Cedar Lake Tuesday morning, that a lighthouse at the preposterous cost of $90,000 had been recommended for the mouth of the Hillsboro River well south of the city, and that a young man such as himself would do well—if he had a mind and the means—to attend a land auction along the East Coast Railway tracks just up the line next week "which very few folks know about and could result in a fine and profitable acquisition if you get my meaning, sir."

When asked what kind of business he was in, Byrne answered only that he was in "security" and then tapped the heels of his brogans. From that point on the barber was quiet and seemed particularly careful with the razor when it came time for Byrne's shave. Pleased with the clean look he saw in the mirror, Byrne tipped Mr. Hawthorn a dime and proceeded down the street to Buholtz's.

While the New York shopping districts, even along Bowery, had increasingly featured specialty shops with specific goods for specific needs, Buholtz's was a general merchandise store that despite its small size overwhelmed with its variety of dry goods stacked and hung and pigeonholed into every conceivable place: hats and caps, boots and shoes, bolts of multicolored and multitextured cloth, racks of dishes and cutlery, cooking utensils and pots, stacks of baskets, blankets and ladies' bloomers.

Byrne stood, feeling as out of place as a young man could, until a salesman came up and asked if he could help. Byrne chose to state his predicament rather than try to hide his social ignorance.

"I need a proper suit for one of Mrs. Flagler's formal dinners at the Poinciana tonight," he said.

The salesman began to look him over, no doubt for size. But Byrne took it as an assessment.

"As a guest," he added.

"Certainly, sir. My name is Bob Campbell and I will be pleased to assist. This way please."

He was led to a deep corner of the store, behind piles of boxes and crates that created a semiprivate area with several jackets and trousers and vests hung against a wall and a full-length mirror on one wall.

"My, you are certainly tall and broad shouldered," the salesman said. "And it is very short notice. But our specialty, Mr. uh?"

"Byrne."

"Our specialty, Mr. Byrne, is our line of ready-made clothing," Campbell said, again taking a step back and eyeing him. Byrne thought of the time Harvey Cannon measured him up at the Rockaway Pub before asking him outside for a fight. He'd whipped Harvey's ass without once taking out his baton.

"I'd say a thirty-eight long might do," Campbell said and began going through the racks.

In less than forty minutes Byrne had been outfitted with a dark suit of tails with a finely brocaded vest and a monumentally stiff white shirt that made him wince when buttoned against his sunburn. Though Bob Campbell pushed, Byrne declined new shoes, much to Campbell's chagrin. When the total bill came to forty-two dollars and change, he swallowed hard, decided against the hat that was suggested, and paid. Alterations to take in the waist of the pants and to accommodate Byrne's unusual request to lengthen the right hand pocket and add a leather sheath to its interior would be completed in an hour. With the remains of Harris' fifty dollars, he went down to the corner of Banyan and Olive and had two beers and a fillet of yellow tail at J.C. Lauther's Saloon and Restaurant.

After lunch Byrne picked up his packages and returned to his hotel room. He stripped to his underwear, split open the aloe leaves as the Chinese woman had shown him and used the rest of the balm to again cover his face and neck. Then he raised his window, let the ocean breeze flow in and lay down. Within minutes his dreams came with jumping fish and gang members swinging heavy clubs, of the clean smell of salt air and the stench of running sewage, of the feel of squinting into bright sunlight and doing the same in an effort to see down dark alleys, of the vision of a young prostitute outside of Harry Hill's concert saloon in the Bowery and that of woman in dazzling white chiffon and bright green eyes who seemed to be watching him through it all. He awoke with a start, positive that he'd overslept. But when he checked his watch it read four fifteen. He laid for a few minutes more, staring at the ceiling, recounting his half dream visits and jumbled recollections. For years his mother had a strange addiction to the palmists and so-called seers who haunted the neighborhoods of the poor in New York. His father called them shysters and purveyors of a fool's hope and forbade her from spending money on them. She did anyway. She once told Michael that dreams were the windows to the future and that she took her dreams to the seers for interpretation. She saw great things for both him and Danny.

"It's a world here of democracy, boys," she would tell them. "No grand marquees or lords keepin' ya down. Your work and your brains is what you need, and you both have plenty of that."

At the time Danny was all bravado and spunk, yelping about becoming the "king of the Bowery." All Byrne could do was answer "Yes, mama." He thought of her now and his own disparate dreams and what they might mean. Where the hell was Danny? And did Faustus really know the answer to that question?

In twenty minutes he was washed and dressed and polished. The man he saw in the mirror was a version that should have made him uncomfortable but instead let him straighten his shoulders and give himself an uncharacteristic wink. When he passed the clerk downstairs he saw the man's face brighten, though when he recognized Byrne the look turned sober. As Byrne approached the bridge to the island he actually looked forward to greeting the deputy who'd been scrutinizing the pedestrians the two days previous. But he noted that although the boy collecting a nickel for passing was in place, the lawman was absent.

"What, no one here to go through everyone's pockets today?" he said to the boy.

"They all went south on a fugitive hunt, sir."

"A fugitive hunt?" Byrne recalled Harris's anxiety over unknown threats to Flagler on this night. "What kind of fugitive?"

The boy gave him a look that insinuated there was no way he was giving up valuable information without remuneration. Byrne dug into his pocket for change, dropped the nickel fare in the boy's hand but pinched a half-dollar piece between his fingers and let it speak for itself.

"That one they been lookin' for. The niggra lady. The one that killed the man on the island. They done found her in Key West," the boy said, whispering conspiratorially and holding out his palm. "They say she was dressed in men's clothes and tried to get aboard a northbound ship."

"They plan to bring her back here?"

"Damn straight. An if they ever find out who that dead man is, they just might be a lynchin'."

The boy's demeanor and language reminded Byrne of young Screechy back in Tompkins Square. He dropped the half dollar in his palm. When it comes to the young and wise, the streets are the streets.

A lynching, Byrne thought, moving on across the bridge. His newfound friends, the binder boys, had spoken of one only days before, and he had no reason to doubt the veracity of their story. How did a place with the architectural splendor and rich sophistication that he was walking to put up with something as crude as a lynching? He'd heard the stories told by the old ones from Dublin of the beheadings and such by the English, but Jaysus, that was ancient times. Public hangings! Across the lake from Mr. Flagler's golf course!

Halfway across the bridge he gave up the ruminations and took off his new coat and unbuttoned his collar. It may have been early evening but there was still a heat in the air and he was sweating. He would readjust his wardrobe once he got to the other side. Once more he took in the view of the Palm Beach Island, measuring her, memorizing her coastline and the movement of the water beneath him. His attention fell on a dockside gathering of boats and people. A half-dozen men were moving about a centerpiece that he still could not make out. Something large was being raised on some form of block and tackle. The huge object spun and caught the low sun. Thirty steps closer and Byrne recognized the thing as a fish! It was roped at its scythe-like tail and was being raised to hang upside down. The thing was at least ten feet long, a fantastic-looking beast with a long pointed bill that seemed impossibly fragile, as at one point in the hoisting the entire body, at least four hundred pounds, appeared to balance on that sword-like tip. Men gathered as a gang around the suspended fish and it became obvious that a photographer had set up his tripod and was capturing the moment. Closer still, Byrne could see that the men, with the exception of the bandy-legged one dressed in light-colored dungarees and a black-brimmed captain's hat, were no doubt guests of the hotel with their florid faces and estimable paunches. After the flash of the photography powder, they all shook hands and moved up from the dock, back-slapping and nodding in their accomplishment. The captain and what was later identified to Byrne as a blue marlin were left behind, the fish slowly spinning in the breeze, its color draining in the failing light. Byrne thought of the tarpon, silvered and flashing as Faustus had removed his hook and let it go and the old man's words: "But would that have made it anymore glorious?"

As he approached the Poinciana's grand ballroom Byrne was already convinced that he was a poseur and was equally sure that he didn't give a shit. He knew the minute he walked up the steps to the hotel entrance and caught the same changing smile from the tuxedoed greeter that he got from the clerk at the Seminole. You might pass at a distance, but never up close. The greeter stepped forward. Upon inspection, the employee's suit was at least two cuts above the forty-dollar variety Byrne felt so proud in: the fabric finer, the lapels silk, the tailoring perfect. But even the high polish he'd given his brogans did not cover their street look. Still, he held a higher power and used it.

"Michael Byrne," he answered to the greeter's request for an invitation. "Mr. Flagler's Pinkerton." The man made a sour face, but passed him through. Security breach, Byrne thought. Anyone could say they were Pinkerton and the boy at the door would wave them in.

He passed through the lobby, purposely not looking up at the grand ceiling like some tourist and then scanned the crowd to find Harris standing near the doors to the ballroom. When Byrne joined him, Harris' mouth held that grin at the corner of his mouth. He'd read Byrne's expression.

"I tol ya to lose the shoes, lad. Didn't I?"

"I'm not one of them and don't want to be," Byrne said through his teeth. "Fuck 'em."

"Aye, now that's the spirit," Harris said. "And it's also the idea of havin' us here. Nobody who might want to start trouble is going to mistake us for busboys either. And that might be enough deterrent on its own.

"You just use that photographic memory of yours. Mr. Flagler's true friends and relatives will be near him at the front of the ballroom. I've confidence you'll have them down pat early enough. After that you can spot any strangers."

"What kind of threat are we talking about, sergeant?" Byrne asked, puzzled. "A bloody assassination?"

Harris chuckled deep in his throat, the sound of an echo in a big wooden barrel.

"No, lad. It's the pissed off ones we're watching tonight. Mr. Flagler's land acquisitions can make him enemies, even those of the higher society and not just those hick farmers at the train sidings.

"In this rarified air, boy, the more money you have, the less you like to lose it."

Christ, the rich, Byrne sneered.

"Stay on the edges, lad. Use the walls and keep your eyes open. Don't get caught up in the finery, if you know what I mean." A trio of middle-aged women floated by in gowns that were low-cut and dragging trains behind.

"Watch for the angry faces. We'll be fine."

Harris led the way into the grand ballroom, and once again Byrne had to consciously remember to keep his mouth from gaping open.

The hall was some two hundred feet in length with a soaring ceiling lined around its edges with electric bulbs that highlighted the frescoed painting that adorned it. Romanesque white columns lined the walls for the first fifteen feet up and then large scalloped arches framed a dozen high windows.

The dance floor was a polished parquet wood of the kind Byrne had never seen even though he'd witnessed the ballroom at the Astoria Hotel from the kitchen doors. A cop friend of his had smuggled him into the newly built hotel on Thirty-fourth and Fifth Avenue to meet a girl selling perfume at a boutique inside and they couldn't help but poke around. But New York's finest had nothing on this place. The orchestra was at the far end of the hall playing something classic and staid, and though most in attendance were sitting in the straight-backed chairs that lined the dance floor, a few couples were out moving with grace. Byrne could hear the swooshing of the fine dress fabric brushing the elegant wood. He and Harris split up and Byrne moved behind the arched columns to "work the walls." He was watching the men, most of whom were dressed in black tailcoats with vests made of white pique. Byrne did not have to be reminded that he had been talked into spending extra on the dark brocaded vest he wore and did not look down.

As he moved closer to the front he could see a subtle change in both the finery and the distinct smell of money. The chains on pocket watches became more delicate, the gold metal taking on a shine of higher carat. Stick pins appeared in ascots and four-in-hand ties. An elderly man whom Byrne had scene dancing with aplomb was now carrying a walking stick with an ostentatious silver lion's head. Finally, at a table nearest the orchestra he spotted Flagler's shock of white hair. The railway baron was standing in a circle of men who were listening closely to his every utterance. Byrne focused on their faces. Not an angry look in the crowd, although he quickly determined that all of them would be acquiescent to the man's words even if he were mumbling horse shit. Byrne widened his circle about Flagler, eyeing the corners and the space behind the columns that he himself was using for cover.

His gaze landed on Mr. McAdams, who was also entertaining a gathering of men of means who had found a quieter place far to the left of the orchestra. McAdams was, as seemed to be his practice, leaning into the man beside him, talking directly into the listener's ear as if the words were only for him. Byrne watched long enough to memorize the listener's face and then went directly to the nearby seats. If the father was here, where was the daughter?

He scanned the crowd, first the women sitting nearby. Their hands, many in gloves matching their gowns, were in their laps or holding small beaded purses. Most of them were wearing hats ornamented with feathers and ribbon that partially obscured their faces. Byrne was convinced that Miss McAdams would not be wearing a hat. He concentrated next on the dance floor, which was now filling up with couples, the more graceful turning figures and stylish poses to the waltz music, but even the less adventurous moved in soft, reaching, confident steps. He checked the younger women, those with waspish waists and athletic movements, but did not see her. For nearly an hour he moved among the crowd, nodding at those who nodded at him.

He was watching a demonstrative gent with a bulbous nose and a voice like shoveled gravel rattling on about some soldier unit he'd seen in Tampa across the state called "Roosevelt's Rough Riders" on their way to Cuba. As if on cue the orchestra struck up a quick tempo to drown the man out, and the careful dancers began to leave the floor. With a clearer view across the room Byrne caught sight off a flash of white fabric and a glimpse of red curl and shifted from behind a pillar to see Miss McAdams in the arms of a tall man, both moving fluidly to the new beat. The gent was in a tuxedo that stood out from the rest, with a sharp center crease in the pants and cuffs dusting the tops of a pair of patent leather shoes covered with cream-colored spats. The tune carried the same one, two, three count of the previous waltzes, but at a pace that seemed to energize Miss McAdams while keeping her partner on his toes. Hers was a driving, aggressive and reaching step that seemed utterly confident, while the man worked at keeping up. Others on the dance floor moved from the middle and let the couple take over, and Byrne began to lose out to an obstructed view. Still he watched, catching a blur and a smile, mostly the man's due to his height or his showmanship, until the final strains when McAdams struck an ending pose that was pure sculpture. It was the first time in Byrne's life that he wished his feet had rhythm.

Before the next song began the couple exited the floor, several men complimenting McAdams. Her partner trailed behind her and shook every hand offered. They seemed to be coming directly at Byrne, who decided to simply stand his ground. From several feet away he couldn't tell if McAdams' cheeks were colored from cosmetics, the blush of unsolicited compliments, or the exertion. Just before she reached him she spun on the heel of one slipper, the train of her dress swishing up onto his own brogans. "Graham," she said. "Could you fetch me something to drink, you dear. I am absolutely parched."

"Delighted, Marjory," the one called Graham said and moved away.

Without hesitation McAdams continued a full rotation and looked directly into Byrne's eyes.

"And delighted to meet you, sir," she said, offering her hand. "I am Marjory McAdams."

Byrne took her fingers and bowed but wouldn't pretend to kiss them. He'd seen a hundred such scenes during special event details and thought it prissy at best.

"Of that I am fully aware, Miss McAdams," he said and then added, "Nice dancing."

She tilted her head, just so, and hesitated. The silence made him uncomfortable. There was a heat coming off her, and she smelled of newly planted oleander, sweet flowers and musk. Up close, her complexion was unblemished. Byrne was fighting a losing battle to keep his eyes off from hers.

"So, do I call you Mr. Pinkerton, sir, as my father does?"

"I would hope not," he said and then realized he still had not dropped her fingers. She slipped the rest of her hand into his without looking down and shook it slightly before letting go.

"Michael Byrne," he said.

"A pleasure, Mr. Byrne. And do you like the waltz?"

"Very much."

"And do you dance?"

"No."

A pout formed on her lips, and even though it was an obvious tease, Byrne couldn't keep the look from tripping his heart.

"I am simply an observer," he said, trying to recover.

She smiled. "I'm told that Pinkertons do quite a bit more than observe."

"I've heard that too, Miss McAdams," he said, enjoying the sparring if it could hold her before him for even a minute more.

"And from the look of your sunburn, your observations have mostly been from outside, Mr. Byrne."

His hand started to go to his face but he stopped it.

"Boating," he said, "on the sea."

He picked up on the instant brightening of her eyes, the green almost magically taking on a bit of blue at the edges of the iris, as if his own recollection of the Gulf Stream color was reflecting there.

"The ocean is one of my favorite things about being here," she said. "Obviously you are wasting no time enjoying the uniqueness of Florida."

"Like I said, I'm an observer."

Now she smiled without teasing, a natural smile, one that he had brought out.

"So you are a boatman. Are you a swimmer as well? An ocean swimmer?"

He thought of the blue again, how he had wanted to simply fall in and let it take him, but he also thought of the taste of the salt when he had seen the ocean for the first time, what, two days ago, three?

"I have managed the East River," he said, without elaborating that on that single occasion he had fallen in while trying to steal an armload of oysters and was pulled back spitting and gasping by the hand of his brother.

McAdams raised an eyebrow, whether surprised by his audacity to swim in that putrid river or his stupidity in doing so, he could not tell.

"Well, perhaps you may join me for a more pleasant bathing hour in the ocean some time, Mr. Byrne. The beach off the Breakers is quite lovely this time of year, and the water temperature should be much more to your liking than the rivers around Manhattan."

Byrne was trying to find another word of wit to make the conversation last when the dandy she'd called Graham returned, holding a crystal goblet of clear liquid.

"Water, Marjory," he said, though his eyes were on Byrne rather than McAdams.

"Good evening, sir. I don't believe we've met," the man said, offering his hand to Byrne.

"Oh, do forgive me. Mr. Michael Byrne, this is Mr. Graham Foster," McAdams said.

Byrne did not like Foster's shoes. He did not like the crease in Foster's pants or the silk brocade of his vest. He did not like the smart handshake he gave or the glisten of some kind of pomade in his hair. And over the man's shoulder, Byrne did not like the look of a hurried and sober conversation between a messenger boy and an older gentleman whom he'd spotted earlier and took for a hotelman, noting that although he greeted the guests and seemed to be well known, he did not participate in the guests' conversations and was not necessarily anxious to have Flagler's ear like the others.

"Since you are both boatmen," McAdams was saying, without a hint of fun or sarcasm, "you may have tales to share."

Byrne may have let an unconscious grin twitch at the corner of his mouth, but he was no longer paying attention. He watched as the hotelman moved unhurried, but with a purpose, to the other side of the room and pulled Mr. McAdams aside, turning him away from his group and whispering something into his ear. The stoic expression on the men's faces was what alerted Byrne. They did not crinkle their eyes in even customary pleasure. They did not tighten their jaws in consternation or masked alarm. Their faces simply went blank, passive, and reflexively, internal. Something was up.

He shifted his eyes back to Foster and Marjory McAdams.

"A pleasure to meet you sir," he said, with a slight bow but no handshake.

"Miss McAdams." He took her fingers, looked at the lines of question form at her brow. "As you know too well, I'm working. Excuse me," he said and moved away without another word.

Byrne moved to the nearest wall and watched Mr. McAdams across the room. The man was extremely cool, carefully holding his new knowledge, working it in his head, looking around as if unhurried and unbothered. He shook a guest's hand, touched an elderly woman's forearm just so. And then he moved ever so gentlemanly toward Flagler's table. Byrne slid to the other side of the column and followed with his eyes. McAdams approached Flagler, but moved behind the white and regal head, and then slipped past. He continued down the line, beyond the seated Cornelius Vanderbilt and his wife and then to a man whom Byrne almost immediately recognized from

New York. A businessman, Byrne thought, and then began his own internal way of finding the face inside his mental collection. Uptown? No. During some special occasion when Byrne was a guard? No. It was during a police action, he was sure. The businessman rose, excused himself, and moved off with McAdams to a corner, where they were joined by the hotelman. The way the businessman dipped his head in acquiescence was the tip-off. Such a man of power was not used to subservience and thus when he showed it to McAdams, the moment glared. Byrne was now sure that he had seen him before. It was at a prostitution bust at the Haymarket Dance Hall on Sixth Avenue just south of Thirtieth Street. Byrne had been a simple cop at the time, called in to provide manpower and muscle for the raids that were done for show when the press shook up city hall and the pols needed to look like they were doing something to control the sex trade in the city. The businessman was one of the society types that got caught up in the dragnet one night. Byrne had seen the man take the commanding lieutenant aside and peel off a number of bills into his palm, enabling him to simply walk out onto the street. Since the man was never booked, Byrne did not know his name, but he also never forgot a face.

Harris was still on the other side of the dance floor.

"There's news running round the room," Byrne said quietly when he got to his sergeant's side.

"Indeed," Harris said, without alarm or question. "It's not a matter of concern to us, lad."

"Care to fill me in? It seems to be of interest to a few in power, including the man sitting next to Mr. Vanderbilt," Byrne said, nodding toward the Flagler table, where the businessman was now retaking his seat.

"That's Birch, a Manhattan real estate man and a banker friend of the lot of them," Harris said.

"And the one in the tailless coat on his way out of the room," Byrne asked, directing Harris' attention to the hotelman who had first sought out McAdams.

"That's Pearson. He's the hotel manager. Deals with every crisis, big or small."

"OK, what's the crisis?"

"Not our concern, Mr. Byrne. We are here solely to protect Mr. Flagler."

Byrne coughed into his hand and then looked into Harris' face with a grin meant to match the old Irishman's now famous tic.

"And since when did good intelligence and an ear to rumor not serve that cause, Mr. Harris?" Byrne said.

The sergeant looked pointedly into Byrne's face, any sign of playfulness on his own completely gone.

"Go back to work," he said and then walked away.

CHAPTER FOURTEEN

Byrne watched Harris disappear into the crowd before he looped around a column and made for the exit. Go back to work indeed, he thought. He'd heard the expression too many times as a cop when he'd noticed the graft of the captains, the politicians on Bowery and the shake-downs by the Tammany crowd. He had no taste for turning his back.

He went through the lobby and out onto the wide porch entrance, walking at a slow pace, acting unhurried, like a guest seeking a bit of fresh air. If he smoked, he would have taken one out and lit it. Rather he put his hands in his trouser pockets, one touching the baton, the other pinching his fold of money, and made his way down the steps to the driveway apron. When the livery boy looked up, Byrne engaged him.

"Stunning evening," he said. The boy was dark-eyed and impossibly skinny. He cut his eyes left and right, making sure the man in the evening clothes was talking to him.

"Yes, sir," the boy said, keeping his face forward.

"Hard to believe anything could ruin the peacefulness of such a night." Byrne shifted his own gaze toward the boy, making sure he knew to whom the conversation was being directed.

"Yes, sir," was again the answer.

Byrne took his left hand out of his pocket, the fold of bills held loosely within sight.

"If there were something happening, something unusual being talked about on such a night as this, how much would you think that information might be worth?" he said.

Now the boy shifted his own gaze, first to the money, then up, furtively, to Byrne's face.

"Might be somethin' like two dollars," he said, starting at a bit of a higher figure than he might realistically make, leaving room for negotiation, just like any street-smart kid in New York.

Byrne didn't have time for negotiation. He peeled off two dollars and put the rest back in his pocket.

"Word is they bringin' that whore back to town," the boy said, looking at the money. "The housewoman that kilt that white man in the Styx. Sheriff Cox done caught her runnin' and is draggin' her back to jail."

Byrne let the idea settle on him and then handed the boy his money.

"Tonight?" he said.

"Boy comin' in from West Palm says right about now."

Byrne looked out on the dark water and could make out a few lights from his own hotel and a few sprinkled north in the city. He thought about the lynching he'd read about in the Jacksonville newspaper and the hanging of the accused killer of the tax assessor. Harris was probably right. The information was the kind of gossip that would spread fast, even to the group of men inside. Byrne decided he would tuck the knowledge away. It had no relevance to his work. He went back up the stairs and was moving toward the entrance when he saw Marjory McAdams hurrying across the lobby toward him. He fixed his face, trying to look more charming than he was, trying to find something sophisticated to say. She blew past him without recognition. He couldn't gauge whether the look on her face was a hard anxiety or angry fire, but he watched her pass through the doors and then followed. She skipped down the steps with her dress trailing. There was one of those odd bicycle contraptions waiting. A large black man, athletic and handsome, helped her into the carriage and then moved like silk up onto the seat, stepped on the pedals and started to roll. He looked up once as Byrne hurried down the steps and caught his eyes, held them for an instant with a look that said "Don't even try to stop her" and then sped off toward the ferry dock.

Byrne stood frozen for a minute, heard the engine of the ferry grind and pop in the distance, and marched inside to find Harris. His sergeant was now near the front of the room, behind the orchestra, watching Flagler's table. Byrne went to his side, took his elbow and whispered into his ear.

"I have to leave."

Harris turned only his head, looked into his charg's eyes and said: "Give me a reason."

"Intelligence gathering and a bit of protection."

"Protection for who?"

"The daughter of Mr. Flagler's acquisitions engineer, his right-hand man, McAdams. I believe she's gone to the mainland to get involved in a prisoner being brought to the jail, a hotel worker, a Flagler employee if you will."

"It's a rumor," Harris said. "I've already told you isn't our business."

"It's a rumor flying all over, including to the management of our boss's hotel," Byrne said.

Harris turned away, perhaps assessing all he knew about Byrne, his abilities, his talents and his seriousness.

"Make sure she's safe, but bloody damn stay out of the rest of it," Harris said. "The sheriff is a shite, but we don't need to antagonize the bastard." Harris might have only perceived the nod of agreement because when he turned, there was nothing but air behind him.

Byrne went down the front stairs in two gliding jumps. He had the coat off and the top button of his shirt loosed before he reached the pedestrian bridge. He scanned the lake on the south side for a glimpse of the ferry and saw the lamp it carried far ahead, swinging already into the docks on the other side. His brogans had long been broken in for running the city streets and he lengthened his stride. The moon was still down, the sky above black velvet and sprinkled with stars that afforded little light. Still he ran with a purpose, remembering the feel of the bridge from his walks, aware of keeping his step high to avoid tripping on a raised wooden slat. He focused on a light at the end of the walkway where the boy should still be standing and made his path straight and unwavering.

He was breathing hard when he got to where the bridge tender was standing. The boy looked him up and down, the sweat-soaked evening shirt, the face red and chest heaving.

"Someone chase you out, then, sir?"

Byrne was looking south at the ferry dock. The boat was empty. The passengers, McAdams and the big Negro, were nowhere in sight. He reached into his pocket and brought out a dollar.

"Take me to the jail," he said, thrusting the money at the boy.

The kid looked at the money

"You're kidding," he said, his tone skeptical to an offer to get paid to go where he'd wanted to be all night. Byrne brought out another two dollars and pushed all of it into the boy's hand.

"Right. This way," the kid said, grabbing the cash and leaving his post behind.

They went west on Clematis, crossed Narcissus where the shops and restaurants were darkened and the street nearly empty. But Byrne could hear music and laughter coming from a block north on Banyan where most of the saloons would still be open and evening drinkers would do what they ultimately did late into the night. The boy seemed more anxious than he was and skipped a few steps ahead. They crossed Olive Street and before they were halfway up the block Byrne could see the flickering glow of torches being held high at the next corner. Closer still he counted nearly a dozen people gathered in the street, keeping their distance from an enclosed, box-like wagon with barred windows high on the sides and a small square in the door to the back.

"It's the prison wagon," the boy said over his shoulder. "They ain't took her out yet."

The jailhouse was a two-story wood framed structure with four small windows set high on the first floor and flanking a slated door. There were three standard windows on the second floor, their panes flickering with reflected firelight. An outside staircase led up along one side. Byrne scanned the crowd. The first person demanding attention was a black-suited man the size of a finely fatted heifer who was planted near the jailhouse door. His hat was clamped on his head like the cover on a teapot. Byrne could not see his eyes, but the man was digging between his thin lips with a toothpick like there was something worthwhile in there. There was an aura about him, perhaps it was the distance that everyone else kept from him or the nonchalance he showed at what was clearly a tense event. Byrne pegged him as the sheriff. At the other side of the door stood the skinny armed deputy who had questioned Byrne at the bridge two days ago. His eyes were down and he was in low conversation with the bulging man. The shadows were such that Byrne could not see his bobbing Adam's apple. Another man dressed in the same dark utilitarian suit as the others appeared at the top of the staircase. He hurried down, his heels banging on the steps, the sound of gangling keys in his hands. At the plank door he twisted a key in the lock and pushed it open, the entrance now like a black maw in the firelight. Though the wagon could have been stopped just outside the jail door so that the prisoner would endure barely seconds of exposure to the gathering crowd, the sheriff had obviously set the stage for a bit of drama. He got more than he bargained for.

The key man crossed to the wagon, stepped up to the rear door and unlocked it. When he swung open the hinges and climbed inside, people turned and whispered to one another. An obvious drunk from Banyan Street openly blurted: "They ought to hang the nigger bitch right now." There was a short silence and then Byrne heard an almost imperceptible thud, something hard against something soft, but when he turned he could see nothing in the shadows. The low sound of violence escaped everyone else's attention except for the fat sheriff, who cocked his head and also looked briefly out into the darkness but then seemed to disregard it.

After a few moments the key man backed out of the wagon. At the end of his extended arm came the shackled thin wrists of a smallish Negro woman. Byrne could see that in addition to the handcuffs she was also wearing leg irons. There was a white kerchief tying up her hair and she was wearing a man's shirt and the same style of pants with the single stripe on the leg that Byrne had seen on the prison work crew at Jacksonville Beach. The key man yanked her toward the jail and she stumbled and went down. The cry that escaped her was small and bird-like and made up of both pain and fear. The key man did not turn his head but continued to drag her across the hard pack.

"Dear God in heaven," came an exclamation of anger from the crowd, and for the first time Byrne caught sight of Marjory McAdams marching in from the shadows, her Negro companion rubbing his knuckles and trailing behind her.

"Must you treat this woman like some kind of animal?" Marjory shouted.

The key man stopped in his tracks at the sound of an authoritative female voice. Marjory stomped directly to the jailer's side, gave him a frozen stare and then bent to the woman, touching her hands and then her face and mewing consolations that Byrne could not hear. No one moved at first. The sight of a young woman dressed in high fashion, her flowing ball gown dragging in the dirt, coming to the aid of a Negro working girl being hauled into the calaboose on a murder charge stunned them. The heavy man at the jail door seemed the only one not affected. He tipped his hat up as if to better absorb the scene and then motioned to the deputy to intervene, saying something that Byrne could only hear as a low rumble.

The deputy crossed the distance in three elongated steps and said: "Ma'am, ya'll gonna have to step back now. This is a official transfer of a prisoner and they ain't no time for your whinnin'."

When the deputy grabbed McAdams' shoulder Byrne wasn't sure whether it was his touch or his statement that lit her fuse, but Marjory came bolt upright, the crown of her head barely missing the deputy's chin and then stared into his face.

"If you touch me again, sir, I will abandon my duty as a civilized woman and scratch your eyes out."

The deputy tucked his chin and pulled back as if he'd been slapped. The entire gathering went quiet for a full beat and then someone at the edge of the darkness guffawed.

"Ha!"

The deputy blinked, gathered himself, and raised his free hand over his shoulder while uttering: "Why you prissy, high-fallutin' bitch I'll..."

Three men moved—Byrne and the Negro chauffer with incredibly similar speed and fluidity, and the sheriff with a single step and the forming of the word "STOP!" at the edges of his mouth. Everyone else sucked in their breath.

The deputy's face was no more than a foot from Marjory's and his hand had not yet begun its forward motion when the whooshing sound of a steel whip split the space between their noses. Both sets of eyes went large with the feeling of cut air. The baton instantly retraced its path between them but this time stopped like an immovable girder across the deputy's raised wrist. His hand would be going no farther.

The deputy first looked to the Negro, guessing wrongly that he must be responsible. But the chauffeur was staring at Byrne, not believing someone could have been so fast and accurate. Marjory's eyes followed the gleaming steel shaft from the deputy's hand to Byrne's fist and then to his face.

"STOP RIGHT THERE!" The sheriff's voice finally escaped his mouth, and the resonance was nearly as arresting as Byrne's baton had been.

"Morgan, back off!" he said to the deputy and strode across the street, bringing more than just his girth to bear on the scene. It was as if his huge presence itself forced the deputy and the Negro and Marjory to move simultaneously apart. Only Byrne seemed unaffected. He'd been in the company of large powerful men before. Still, he was so focused that his baton was still raised to the level of the deputy's hand, which the lawman had taken with him.

The sheriff waded in.

"Miss McAdams, I believe," he said, his lowered voice now dripping with courtesy. "Surely this is no place for a lady like yourself. Such an unseemly event."

Marjory squared her shoulders. "Unseemly, indeed, Mr. Cox," she said. "The idea that you would be dragging this poor woman through the streets like some animal carcass from a hunting party of yours certainly qualifies for the term."

Sheriff Cox did not avert his eyes. "This negress is a killer, Miss McAdams. I believe that disqualifies her from your description, ma'am."

"As I expected Sheriff, you have a failed understanding of the law of civilized countries, including this one, that anyone accused of a crime is presumed to be innocent until they are declared guilty by a court," McAdams said. "She is not a killer until a judge and jury says she is."

The fat man's eyes narrowed and his thin lips went tight.

"In fact, Sheriff, I doubt that you even have a sworn warrant for this woman's arrest," McAdams said. The sheriff stayed silent, searching, it appeared, for some kind of rejoinder. But the deputy called Morgan couldn't stand it.

"Now just a goddamn minute, you little smart ass. This nigger bitch don't have no rights and she done shanked a white man in the belly an' that's enough law for us." He pointed a long finger at Marjory and then took a step toward Shantice, who still lay curled on the ground. Byrne saw or felt a dark shadow move beside him. The big Negro had appeared like a wall between the deputy and the tiny woman. The deputy came up short, astounded either by the man's fluid speed or his audacity.

"Why you..." His face was flushing while he reached into his coat. A long-barreled revolver came out with his hand. The flash of Byrne's baton swept the air and snapped the deputy's wrist like a limb cracking in the wind. The man yelped and the gun fell to the ground.

Now it was the sheriff whose movements were quick and sudden. He stepped forward and with an amazing strength grabbed a handful of his own deputy's jacket and pulled him back as if he were weightless.

"Now just hold on, by God," he boomed, his voice reverberating off the storefronts of Clematis Street. He put his palm up to Byrne as if it were the hand of the deity he'd just claimed. "Ya'll just calm down, boys."

The Negro chauffeur seemed to shrink in the face of an authority he knew almost by instinct to obey. Byrne lowered his baton to his side.

"Pinkerton, this ain't none of your affair," Sheriff Cox said. "I'm the law here, even if Miss McAdams believes she's the lawyer. And I am lawfully taking this prisoner into custody."

Byrne was only slightly surprised that the sheriff would know of him and his Pinkerton affiliation. He stepped back.

The sheriff motioned for his key man to help Shantice Carver to her feet.

"If you wish to attend the woman's arraignment by the judge on Friday afternoon, Miss McAdams," he said, matching her diction and turning to face her. "Then you are, as a citizen of these United States, fully within your right. The charge will be murder.

"Now folks, clear the damn streets," he commanded, and all involved began to move in opposite directions.

Byrne looked over his shoulder once to see the deputy scuttle back across the yard, holding his wrist to his belly.

The trio of Byrne, Marjory and her chauffeur moved up the street to where the bicycle carriage was parked. Marjory was still flushed with anger. The two men were uncomfortable and independently decided to let her cool.

Byrne held his hand out first.

"Michael Byrne," he said.

"My name is Santos," the man said, shaking Byrne's hand. "Carlos Santos."

Santos' big hands and strength reminded Byrne of his friend, Jack. His voice and look reminded him of west side neighborhood called Little Africa in Greenwich Village where the Italians and blacks had been razor fighting for years. Byrne couldn't see a lick of Spanish in the man, but his protection of Marjory McAdams stood him well as far as he cared. The handshake was a bond.

"My apologies, gentlemen, for not introducing you," McAdams finally said, her fists still clenched in knots. "But that fat bastard, pardonnez-moi."

"Pardon which, your French, Miss McAdams, or your manners?" Byrne said. Santos looked at him and started to smile. Marjory lost an edge off her anger.

"That man is infuriating and dangerous," she said, civilizing her tone.

"He's a lawman with power," Byrne said. "They get that way."

Now Marjory was concentrating on his face.

"And why is it, Mr. Byrne, that you are here in the first place. This, as the sheriff said, is not your concern. Your only duty would be the protection of Mr. Flagler and his trains if I recall correctly."

"Yes, well, protection can take many forms," Byrne said, trying out the explanation he'd have to give Sergeant Harris. "The fact that a wanted killer was being returned to the jail was too close to ignore."

"I see. And your reason for stepping in with that, that, metal whippet of yours?"

Byrne could see no better answer than the truth.

"It seemed like the right thing to do."

Marjory continued to assess him. "Very well then, Mr. Byrne. If you are of a mind to do the right thing, come with us." She turned to Santos. "We need to visit those who had taken responsibility for Miss Carver's safety and find out what happened."

The big man held out his hands in a questioning gesture.

"But ma'am, that's a three mile journey north and this carriage isn't going to make it past the city streets." He was looking to Byrne for help, but none was forthcoming.

"Then we will walk the final two miles," Marjory said and swung herself up into the seat. "Mr. Byrne tells me he is a fine swimmer and boatman so I'm sure he has the physical abilities to stride alongside."

Byrne shrugged at the challenge. Santos looked between the two of them, climbed aboard the bicycle seat and turned up the kerosene lantern that hung on his handlebars. He swung the rig north and quietly said, "More like two and a half final miles," under his breath.

While Santos peddled, Byrne kept even alongside by half jogging as Marjory exercised only her vocal cords while she filled Byrne in on her version of events. She told him about the island's workers all being asked to celebrate on the West Palm Beach side of the lake, enticed by free food and carnival rides and music. She described the late night fire in their compound, how only she and Miss Fluery had responded and how the dry wood had simply flashed into flames and destroyed nearly everything.

She told him of the aftermath, the rummaging through the ashes in the morning light and the shocking discovery by Miss Carver of the body of a white man in a lean-to behind her burned-out home. At that point she looked carefully at Byrne, searching for reaction to that piece of news.

"And no one recognized this man, this white man who you say was dressed in fine clothing?" Byrne said, thinking only marginally of his own new clothes and the way they had made him feel as if he were in costume, pretending to be something he was not. "Are you sure that he wasn't a customer of Mizz Carver? I mean, you did say she was a lady of the evening."

In the lamplight he could see Marjory's eyes. It was the same look he got from Faustus, the assessing one, the unsure one, almost as if they were trying to catch him in a lie. But she relaxed.

"Yes, Mr. Byrne, she may be a prostitute. But if you had been there to hear the poor woman's anguish you would know she was truly shocked."

"Yes, sir," piped in Santos, who was taking it all in from his seat above. "Mizz Shantice was damned scared. Too scared to be makin' it up, sir."

"And she described the dead man as having a roll of money stuffed into his mouth," Marjory said. "And surely everyone who looked could see it plain and simple when we got to the place where his body lay burned."

They were near the edge of town now and the darkness was so complete Byrne could only see parts of Marjory's face in the flicker of the lamp.

"Now, in your experience, Mr. Byrne," she said, "could you imagine a prostitute who would kill a customer, leave a substantial amount of money in his mouth and then proceed to scream his location to all within earshot?"

Byrne spoke in the direction of her voice. "No, Miss McAdams. In my experience, no."

A second later the wheels hit a series of ruts that nearly tossed her from her seat.

"Walkin' time," Santos said, unable to peddle hard enough to get the contraption going again. "But ma'am, it's still a couple of miles and I don't know how you going to manage in that dress."

He and Byrne heard the extended sound of fabric ripping. Then came the distinct whoosh and fop of a large bundle of cloth being tossed out behind the carriage and landing in the two-track rut of a roadway. There was enough light for them to see Marjory's white figure jump out of the whicker seat and land lightly on her feet in the dirt. The train to her dress had been removed and her petticoat was hanging just above her dancing slippers.

"Let us walk gentlemen," she said as if she'd simply disposed of a hat. "You may lead, Mr. Santos."

Santos carried the lantern, but it was of little use out here, the circle of light it tossed was like a bubble in the deep black. Byrne had long since sweated through his shirt, and he could swear that the combination of perspiration and Santo's light was drawing the clouds of mosquitoes that feasted on them. On occasion they would hear the call of owls hunting in the night or the rustle of brush that could have been any wild animal from opossum to fox to the well regarded panthers that roamed the area. Byrne had already heard tales of hunting from men at the restaurant bar and wished he'd picked up the deputy's damn pistol when he'd had the chance.

Marjory kept pace and continued to talk, maybe covering for her nerves at being in such a dark and insect-infested place. She told Byrne about the efforts of the hotel staff to secret Miss Carver off the island once they'd heard that the sheriff was accusing her of stabbing the dead man. She told him of the way Santos had taken Carver across the lake at night, though did not go into detail as to how a rowboat had come available.

"And Mr. Santos assured me that he had found people up the way who could keep her safe," she said, with an edge of accusation in her voice.

"I swear they are good people, Miss McAdams," Santos said, not afraid to defend himself. "They were with the underground railroad up in North Carolina. They got people from Georgia all the ways to New York, ma'am."

Marjory went silent for several moments.

"We'll just have to see what happened, Carlos. I apologize for judging you or them."

They continued on for more than an hour, the lamplight thrown out ahead of them. The palmetto and scrub pines thickened on either side, as did the insect cloud. More than once Byrne had to use the back of his hand to wipe mosquitoes from his lips, and he heard Marjory cough sharply at one point and then spit with disgust. But she never stopped and never complained. He was impressed by the pace she kept and wondered at her motivation. She was a rich young woman with a fancy ballroom and a feast fit for royalty awaiting her back at the Poinciana. Was this naïve sense of justice for a Negro chambermaid really strong enough on its own to drag her out into the steaming wilderness? He'd spent most of his life studying people and anticipating their moves based on hunger, lust or greed. None of those were driving her. The most devout who prayed aloud for compassion had their priorities, even if it was to smooth their way to heaven. But McAdams didn't appear to be one for religion. So what the hell was driving her?

You're a cynical bastard, Michael, he said to himself. Marjory kept up until the trail ran into a clearing that opened out in front of them.

"Windella Plantation's pineapple fields," Santos said. "The Wilson's place is just the other side."

Coming out of the bush, the trio was met by a freshening breeze off the lake, and with the horizon now in sight Byrne could see the glow of the Poinciana far in the distance like a lighthouse beacon on the sea. A memory of waltz music played in his head and the smell of women's perfume and clink of fine crystal.

"What was the name of that tune you danced to tonight?" he said to Marjory, whose face was lit only on one side by the lantern. She turned and looked at him as if he'd spoken in tongues.

"The 'Voice of the Waves,'" she said. "A John Hill Hewitt song, but why in God's name would you bring up such a question, Mr. Byrne? We are as far from that silly moment as we are from the moon."

"That's what I was thinking," Byrne said and moved on.

Crossing several acres of pineapple plants, as yet in the shape of small cabbage heads, Santos led them into the trees. In a few minutes all three could detect the low yellow glow of a light. Closer yet they could make out a squared window in a small clapboard house. When they were within calling range, Santos cupped his hand and yelled: "Mr. Claude! Mr. Claude Augusta Wilson! It's me, Mr. Claude, third-base Santos. We comin' in, sir!"

Before their circle of light could hit the front steps a thin black man with wide shoulders, dressed only in a pair of bib overalls, stepped out of the door. His head was peppered in tufts of white hair, which also sprouted from his chest. In one hand he raised a lantern of his own and in the other hung a shotgun the length of his own leg. He returned the call.

"Third Base? That really you, son? God in heaven, boy. What are you doin' visitin' in the middle of the night?"

The man called Mr. Claude never raised the gun barrel, even when it became obvious that Santos was not alone. But he stood his ground as strangers—a white woman in a torn-away ball gown and a white man in a sweat-soaked tuxedo—stepped onto his raised porch. Santos began explaining and Mr. Claude listened, all the time casting his eyes at Marjory, surveying the damp and drooping hairstyle, the expensive necklace, the dirt-spackled dancing slippers. He also checked Byrne, the formal getup, the straight and athletic posture, and the fact that the white man kept his right hand in his deep trouser pocket despite the sweat and heat.

"And now the sheriff done brought Mizz Shantice back to the jailhouse and says she's gone to be charged a killer," Santos said, finishing up.

The statement snapped the man's head around. "I'm truly sorry to hear that, son. Really I am. We been workin' sunup to sundown here what with the dry weather an all tryin' to keep them apples watered an alive an' we didn't hear nothin' 'bout it," Mr. Claude said.

Marjory stepped forward, brushing back a strand of hair from her face and smoothing what was left of her skirts in an attempt to be presentable.

"Sir, can you tell us what happened? It was our understanding that Mizz Carver would be safe here out of the hands of the sheriff, who is simply looking to blame and punish her for a killing she obviously had nothing to do with."

He looked up with his eyes only. "You Miss McAdams? The one Third Base here tol' us about?"

"Yes. Forgive me," she said, adjusting her voice. "Yes, I am Marjory McAdams and this is an, an associate of ours who has offered to help, Mr. Michael Byrne."

The man reached out to take Marjory's offered fingers and when Byrne leaned in, Mr. Claude met him halfway, watching to see what the stranger might draw from his pocket. When Byrne offered only an empty hand, Mr. Claude made note of the fact that the pocket did not pull heavy as it would have if a handgun had been left there.

"Claude Augusta Wilson," he said as introduction. "Please, ya'll come inside before the insects done carry us all away."

Inside was a single room divided by a curtain that hung at an angle from the middle of one wall to the middle of the wall adjacent, ostensibly creating privacy to one triangular corner of the square. The room was smoky from a dark smudge pot that sputtered in one corner and kept the mosquitoes at bay. Mr. Claude set his lantern on the middle of a long wooden table, pulled out a chair and motioned the others to sit. In the glow Byrne could see a rough cabinet of dishes against one wall, a shelf loaded down with books along another. A spinning wheel and what appeared to be a loom dominated one corner and was surrounded by wicker baskets of cloth. Another door, he figured, must lead to a kitchen of sorts, and when he looked up he realized that the ceiling was open to the high palmetto fronds that thatched the roof. Byrne was used to the meager furnishings of his own Lower East Side dwellings and did not judge. But he noted that a carefully made area rug covering one part of the wood slat floor came alive with color when the light spilled onto it. Thus the loom made sense. He recalled his own mother's piece work.

"Tina," Mr. Claude called out toward the curtain. "It's OK, Tina. It's Third Base and some of his friends come lookin' for Mizz Shantice. I'll come out and make some coffee now. An the rest of ya'll stay in bed, hear?"

A tiny black woman emerged from behind the curtain in a simple housedress that she smoothed with her hands just as McAdams had done before on the porch. Mr. Claude introduced her as his wife and she curtsied, said "Evenin'" and went through the side door. No noise came from behind the curtain, leaving Byrne to only guess how many children there might have been behind it having been told to stay in bed.

Mr. Claude sat at the head of the table and took a deep breath as though clearing his mind.

"That was one scared woman you brought us, Third Base," he said. "An' I swear she done curled up on one of the chillin's beds and was up to nightmares that wouldn't let her close her eyes."

"Tina and I thought we could get the word out to folks up the line in Titusville an' then to Georgia and get her movin' in a few days but then Thomas and the boys heard the sheriff an' his deputies were slap askin' every Negro in town if they seen her."

"An' I ain't tell 'em nothin' daddy!" came a shout in a child's voice from behind the curtain. "If they smack me all day I ain't tell 'em nothin'."

"Ya'll hush up, Thomas, an' go to sleep," Mr. Claude said, raising his voice though his anger was only half there.

"Now you know we ain't scared off by such," he continued. "We been through it before. When a brother of mine come by and offered to get Mizz Shantice down to Miami on the train and then on a boat to New York City, I was certain he had the connections to get it done.

"We dressed her up in men's clothing for some disguise. The brother give her a wad a' money an' off she went. First I heard of her being caught was you just now tellin' me."

Mr. Claude had been succinct in his explanation, leaving few questions to be asked. The table went quiet. His wife came into the room with a coffee pot and four cups and poured. Byrne sat back in his chair and sipped the coffee but was alarmed by the taste and had to control his face not to show displeasure. But Mr. Claude noticed.

"I apologize we don't have no real coffee. That's just made up of parched corn, sir. But you can add you some sugar and it's all right."

His wife set a small china bowl of sugar in the middle of the table and Byrne allowed himself a pinch. As they all drank he was again drawn by the colors of the rug and then spotted an insect the size of a man's finger that he'd already been told was called a Palmetto bug. The thing sneaked in from some dark corner, perhaps drawn by the smell of sugar in the air. Byrne watched it scuttle across the floor toward the table. And he noticed for the first time that all four table legs were set down into open tin cans. The bug climbed up the side of the can and then down inside. Byrne waited for it to emerge on the wooden leg and continue its way up but the thing never came out.

"It's the kerosene, sir," Tina Wilson said. She too had been watching the bug and the strange white man in her home at the same time. "The cans are half-filled with kerosene and it kills 'em dead 'fo they can get up to the table. Onliest way to stop the insects in Florida they eat you out of house and home."

Marjory gathered her skirts around her. All the rest in the room returned to the discussion.

"Did Mizz Carver describe for you what occurred on the night of the fire?" Marjory said, keeping her voice neutral. "That is, who she saw, if anyone at all?"

"Like I said, she was awful scared," Mr. Claude reiterated. "Said only that she found a dead white man and just repeatin' it made her even more scared."

"You say you know this brother and trusted him," Santos said. "Do I know him?"

"I don't suppose you do, Third Base," Mr. Claude said. "He's a white man, a Mason like me." Claude raised his left hand to show the Masonic ring on his finger, the emblem was too small for Byrne to see but he knew what it looked like.

"You know this brother's name?" Santos said.

Mr. Claude hesitated and looked at his wife.

Byrne cut in: "Is he an older man, white hair and goatee, tends toward frock coats and polished boots and a show-off hat?"

"You know him," Mr. Claude said, a statement, not a question.

"Yes. Amadeus Faustus. I was fishing with him yesterday."

"Yeah, he do like goin' out on the sea an catchin' them big fish," Mr. Claude said. "But he don't never bring none back to eat. I never did understand it."

Byrne turned to the others.

"I can talk with Faustus. I'm due to meet with him tomorrow."

They all got up to leave. Marjory had left her coffee barely touched. Mr. Claude was in despair as he stood on his porch. In his experience, little good could come of the situation, unless someone intervened, and that meant someone of standing and wealth and very white skin.

"Will you be able to help her, Miss McAdams?" he said, the tone almost pleading, which was something that did not come easy to the man's voice.

"We will try," McAdams said. She stepped closer and touched her cheek to the old black man's. "Thank you," she whispered.

The three of them walked again in the glow of the lantern. They crossed the field, each keeping their own counsel.

Byrne finally broke the silence.

"Interesting fellow," he said to no one in particular but then to Santos: "What was that Third Base all about?"

"Baseball," Santos said.

"Ah." Byrne was familiar with the game. He'd heard stories of the New York Giants, but had only seen the Italians play near Old St. Patrick's Cathedral near Mott and Prince Streets. He'd never seen a Negro man play.

"Mr. Santos is the best player on the hotel's seasonal baseball team and is most likely the finest third baseman in the world," Marjory said, an actual touch of pride in her voice.

"Some of the fans like Mr. Claude just call me Third Base," Santos said. "They know we have to use Cuban names to play on the team an' it's like slave names to them. They know it ain't real so they give us a nickname."

Where each of their thoughts went from there was a secret. No one spoke until they reached the carriage. McAdams climbed up into the seat. "I'm not sure we accomplished a damned thing."

"Did you expect to? Other than relieving your anger?" Byrne answered and was immediately sorry he'd spoken his mind.

Marjory held her tongue for long moment. "No, I suppose not," she finally said. "Though it's never a bad tactic to do some intelligence gathering."

Touché," Byrne said, thinking of his conversation with Sergeant Harris.

"Ah, French, Mr. Byrne?" McAdams said. "Shall we now pardon you?"

"Hell no," he said, his smile matching hers in the flicker of flame.

CHAPTER FIFTEEN

THE IMAGE FLOATED UP IN HIS dreams all night: Marjory, her white dress dusted with dirt and torn to the calf but still swirling in the ocean breeze as she stood outside the Poinciana. Her hair was damp from sweat, tendrils pasted against her neck. Her eyes, the greenness now visible in the light of the hotel, tired from the journey, but still holding a glow that told you her passion was part of her, awaiting a challenge.

She had sent Santos away after they arrived back at the ball, which had long since wound down. They were at the south entrance and stood away from the porches, she being wary of being seen in such disarray. Byrne offered to walk her to the Breakers, but she declined with that hint of stubbornness in her voice that kept him from insisting. He repeated that he would find Faustus in the morning, but first had to explain himself to his Pinkerton sergeant.

"You made a selfless sacrifice tonight, Michael Byrne," she'd said. "Interesting."

She'd stepped forward and put her cheek next to his just as she had done with Mr. Claude, but Byrne could not imagine the old man having the same reaction as his. Despite the evening's trials he could smell the lavender, warm lavender, rising up from her skin and her cheek felt as smooth as a whisper.

"Thank you, sir." She turned and walked east toward the ocean. Maybe he'd closed his eyes at that instant, but the same image had come to him every time he woke during the night and was with him now.

He rose from his bed in the Seminole Hotel and washed in the basin. He'd hung his new clothes from last night on the closet door, dirt halfway up the legs of the trousers, which were also peppered with tiny brambles that were spiked and painful to pick away. The shirt was no longer white, though he hadn't lost a button during the entire adventure. His coat, which he'd draped across his arm or tossed in the carriage, was the only part of his forty-dollar purchase that had somewhat survived. After being chewed out by Harris last night for leaving his post and chasing "your bloody intelligence" he wished he'd kept the money he'd spent as he might need it when he became unemployed. Harris had only calmed a bit when Byrne described how he'd escorted Mr. McAdams' daughter and had indeed been forced to step in and prevent a physical altercation between her and the sheriff.

"With your magic wand?" Harris said, that twitch of a grin at the corner of his mouth.

"Aye."

"Oh, what I'd of paid to see that fat bastard's eyes when that came out."

Byrne was gruffly dismissed and warned to be available in the morning.

The recollection now caused him to dress quickly and head downstairs to breakfast. Having tasted, with admiration and appetite, scrambled turtle eggs and ham with cornbread, Byrne headed out on to the street in search of Faustus. The old man had nearly promised to find Danny, hadn't he? Last night's shenanigans aside, it was time to find his brother.

The air was dead still outside, not a breeze from the ocean. Byrne started for the docks first, walking south along the lakefront; the water was silent, stretching out like a hot pane of glass. In the distance he could see a sharpie, its sails hanging limp and useless, the boat seemingly stuck in the calm a hundred feet from shore like a tired wagon with its wheels plunged solid into mud.

When he got to the docks he spotted Captain Abbott sitting on a crate mending a net.

"Ain't seen 'im," was his answer. "It's no day for fishin' less you want to shore cast and hell, it ain't worth it anymore. Hell, the fishin' here has all but dried up what with all these tourists. We'll be lucky to have a fish in Florida in another ten years."

Grumpy old man, Byrne thought.

"Where might I find Mr. Faustus on a day such as this, then?"

"Two places." Captain Abbott did not look up. "Watchin' 'em dig holes on that plot of land of his on Clematis, or drinkin' beer at the tavern cross the street. Course why a man would drink that swill instead of God's own elixir of rum from the islands is beyond me."

Byrne left Abbott to his grumbling. The captain was correct on where best to find Faustus. As Byrne approached Olive Street along Clematis, he spotted the man standing in front of a cleared piece of land watching brick masons working a line of about fifty feet. Survey string mapped out the rest of the foundation that ran some sixty feet deep into the plot. Faustus was leaning on his cane and dressed as if he'd attended his own shabby ball the night before: his top hat was tipped to shade his eyes and his tailed jacket and trousers were again of a fine but faded cloth.

"Mr. Faustus, good morning, sir," Byrne said.

"Ahh, Mr. Byrne. I trust a fine evening was had by all at the Flagler's welcome home ball in the palace?"

Byrne let the greeting sit, considered his tactics then decided to hell with being polite or patient.

"Have you obtained the whereabouts of my brother, Mr. Faustus? I am anxious to find him."

Faustus stared ahead at the work before him. The fact that the old man would not meet his eyes sent a shiver of dread through Byrne. It was well-known body language on the street—a man who will not look you in the eye is either hiding bad news or lying to you.

"In due time, young man. In due time," Faustus finally said. "First tell me of your exploits of last night. Rumor is abounding."

Byrne fought back an anger that was rising in him. Was Faustus playing him for some reason? Maybe he had no information about Danny. Maybe he was just keeping Byrne on the hook like one of his fish, enjoying some game.

Well, if he wanted games: "All had a good night I'm sure with the exception of Shantice Carver and of course Mr. Claude Augustus Wilson, who probably did not enjoy being awakened in the middle of the night."

Byrne watched the names register on Faustus' profile. The old man seemed to work the angles in his own head.

"Yes, well. We did try with Mizz Carver. Unfortunately, despite our efforts to sneak her aboard a ship going north, she was obviously apprehended.

"But also obvious is your knowledge of the occurrence," he added, "which does surprise me. I've not yet heard from my dear friend Mr. Claude, but you have done some diligence. Congratulations."

It was now Byrne who watched the brick-layers, slapping and tapping the stones into place in front of them.

"Masons building a Masonic Temple?" Byrne said, and this time the statement turned Faustus' head around.

"You are indeed an extraordinarily informed and perceptive young man, Mr. Byrne. You continue to impress. Yes, this will be the location of the first temple to be built in this region of Florida. And we will need men of strong moral fiber and dignity to fill her, sir.

"They will be men who voluntarily ask to join and they will be accepted because they were good men who believe in God and hold high ethical and moral ideals. It will be a place to learn and to teach what friendship, morality, and truth really involve, and to practice on a small scale the reality of brotherhood."

If it was an invitation to join Faustus' group, Byrne ignored it. He knew nothing of the organization and had more pressing concerns.

"Do you know where my brother is or do you not?"

Faustus seemed *to* think about the question for a moment.

"Floridians do not stand out in the sun for nothing, Mr. Byrne. May I buy you a chilled beer?"

It was nine o'clock when they walked into the Midway Plaisance, and before Faustus made the distance between the door and the bar rail, a pint of beer was standing and waiting.

"Morning, Mr. Faustus," said the woman behind the bar. "Hot already, eh sir?"

"Indeed, Miss Graham. A draft for my friend here if you please." It was unusual to see a woman tending bar, but considering the hour, Byrne dismissed the propriety and motioned for a beer of his own.

Whatever the beliefs of Faustus' brotherhood of Masons, Byrne was glad they didn't include abstinence. The draft was as excellent as the first time he'd drunk it here with the binder boys. After taking a few swallows, Byrne decided that his approach with Faustus on the street had perhaps too disingenuous. He changed it.

"I'm no lawyer, sir, but it seems to me that there are some inquiries to be made about this incident of the man killed during a fire on the island. I mean, there are folks who say this Carver woman was not even there at the time of the man's death."

Faustus took a drink and made perhaps the same decision on candor as Byrne had.

"And you come across this information from which folks, Mr. Byrne? Miss McAdams from the hotel?"

Byrne gave up trying to plumb the breadth of Faustus' connections to information.

"Yes. And some of the hotel workers who are in position to know."

"And therein lies the problem, Mr. Byrne," Faustus said. "As a Northerner, you may not understand the ancient mores that still hold this land and the law that still governs it. The sheriff is not a forward thinking Southern man. If a Negro woman has been accused of killing a white man it would be a foregone conclusion that she is not only guilty, but should in all practicality be hanged for such offense."

Byrne had seen enough on the streets of New York to know that neighborhoods of Greeks, Italians, Poles and Jews operated on their own laws and precepts just like anywhere else. The "we deal with our own" attitude was one that the police had always worked both with and against to keep a lid on crime and to protect the moneyed civilians of the city. But even in a frontier like this he believed logic could still prevail.

"So let's prove she didn't do it. Certainly that doesn't get ignored in a place that's trying to become civilized."

Faustus took another silent drink. He wiped away the residual foam.

"Let us?" he said. "Did you use the contraction 'let's' as in you and I, Mr. Byrne?"

Byrne took a breath. "From my understanding, you are a lawyer, sir. And from your mouth to my ear you have admitted a medical background. And from my observation you also know most of the prominent people in this small town. So unless I'm a fool, I'd bet you know the coroner and you know how to do a basic autopsy and there is no better way to find out how a man was killed than to look for yourself."

If he'd read Faustus correctly, the old man was avoiding some knowledge of his brother. An uncomfortable knowledge. Maybe a terrible knowledge. Maybe a knowledge that now lay in the coroner's office.

Faustus absorbed the young man's challenge. "A fine presentation, Mr. Byrne," he said, draining his glass and spilling a few coins on the bar. He stood up and with cane in hand motioned to the front door. "Let us."

The undertaker's was on Clematis in a low-slung wooden building with a tin roof and double-wide doors in the front. There were sawed out places in the front wall for windows, but any view was blocked by paper hung from the inside. Wagon tracks led from the street to the back.

Faustus knocked at the door and without waiting for an answer walked in as if it were a storefront, which in effect, it was. George Maltby made his living by burying local folks, preparing the bodies of nonlocals for transportation north to their hometowns, and on occasion doing contract work for the county government, including holding the unclaimed bodies of victims of crime until given the order to move them either into the ground or to a family claimant.

When Byrne stepped into the building he noted that it was unnaturally cool. He was to learn later that the undertaker's building was directly behind the G. G. Springer's Ice Making Factory. Maltby had talked Springer into running a duct into the back of his place. The decision pleased both men as it kept down the odor of Maltby's particular business from passersby as well as from Springer's customers who came to load their own ice blocks from his factory's back door. But when he first walked in, Byrne took the chill as a sign of death and it unnerved him. The room was, like many of its day, a single square structure. But this one was halved by a plush, purple curtain like that of a Broadway stage. When Faustus called out Maltby's name, a plump and unusually jovial man swept away the corner of the curtain and stepped out like some master of ceremony for the Herald Square Theater in the Bowery.

"Well hello, hello, Mr. Faustus and friend," said Maltby, recognizing Faustus at once and making Byrne wonder how often the old man had occasion to visit the undertaker.

"To what do I owe the honor, sir? I hope most sincerely that it is not a personal matter, meaning not a personal friend who may have fallen to an early departure from this grand and glorious world."

Though the undertaker reminded Byrne of the sheriff in size and girth, his face was in direct opposition: florid and fat with pumped up cheeks that resembled a clown's, eyes that seemed perpetually large and wide open, and lips that seemed unnaturally red.

"Thank you, George, for your concern," said Faustus, tapping his cane. "But no, we've come on a bit of unofficial business and mean to inquire if you have taken possession of a body brought the other day from a fire on the island?

"My understanding is that the victim has not yet been identified, and for medical inquiry, it is my hope that I may spend a few moments in examination of the remains."

Maltby's expression fell immediately from the laughing clown to that of the down-turned smile of its forlorn opposite.

"Well, um, gosh, Mr. Faustus. You know, Doc Lansing already did that for the sheriff. I mean, he came in and took a look and said he was going to file a report with the sheriff's office on the cause of death and all."

"I was aware of that," Faustus lied, and he did it well, Byrne thought. "But my inquiry is of a different nature, George. And as I said it will take only a few minutes. I require no extensive cutting or probing or further altering of the body from what you may have already accomplished."

Maltby was still wary. He may not have been under specific instructions from the sheriff to shield the body, but it was a criminal case. And even though Faustus was a well-respected, if not always present, member of the community and a man known for his broad knowledge and a true Southerner like himself... Oh, what the hell.

"Well, I don't see any harm in that, Mr. Faustus. I mean, it is science and all, eh?" Maltby extended his hand to show the way.

Behind the heavy curtain there were three waist-high tables lined up in the middle of the space and all were occupied, and carefully shrouded, except for the middle one where Maltby had obviously been . working before he was interrupted. A table sat next to that corpse upon which rested a tray of took, a leather box of what looked like rolls of hair samples in a variety of colors, and a collection of jars and bottles of makeup, lipstick and moisturizing creams. There was also some kind of hand pump that brought to Byrne's mind a plunger the likes of which the reluctant railway bombers might have used only a few days ago. Byrne was struck by the odor of chemicals that suffused the air, not so unpleasant that he had to cover his nose but enough to warn him that worse may be yet to come.

"I was just now preparing to do a formaldehyde transfer for this poor soul," Maltby said when he noticed Byrne's gaze. "He's going home on the train to New York tomorrow and the family very much wants him to look as if he has a tan when he arrives."

Faustus paid no attention and moved directly to the far table, where a corpse was wrapped in a simple wool blanket.

"I, uh, was reluctant, sir to begin the process of embalming on this gentleman, though," Maltby said, quickening his own pace to catch up with Faustus before he began uncovering the body. "I mean, since no relative or representative has claimed the deceased..."

"Yes, why waste the expensive arsenic or formaldehyde if you're only going to dump him into a pauper's grave," Faustus said abruptly. "I understand, George."

Faustus stood at the head of the corpse and waited for Byrne to come alongside. There was a long pause, both men anticipating the possibilities which they had both been dancing around for days.

"Are you prepared for this, Mr. Byrne?" Faustus said quietly.

"Yes."

Faustus pulled back the blanket and looked down at the burned and partially decomposed face of the corpse. Despite its condition, the look of the body confirmed the rumors of not only the fire, but the identity of the dead.

Byrne's face was stoic, unwavering. His eyes went first to the head and stayed there, studying, it seemed, the contours of nose and cheekbone and then chin. His brother could lose many things in death—color and flesh and dancing eyes and muscle mass—but not that chin. It had always been out there, up and defiant when he had to be, turned just so to the right when he was pretending to ponder a trade or study a situation, tucked and careful when he was in a fight. Danny's eyes were closed, whether by death or by the coroner, and Byrne was relieved not to have to see their blueness, or the opposite, an unseeing lack of color and light.

Faustus watched as Byrne's own hand carefully reached out to place just his fingertips on the corpse's wrist. On Byrne's face, a single tear rolled down his left cheek.

After allowing the moment to pass, Faustus leaned in to the body and carefully examined it from the face down. He was careful not to touch anything, in deference to Byrne, whose reaction had confirmed what Faustus had been surmising all along. When it seemed obvious that Byrne would hold back any more show of emotion, Faustus shifted into professional mode.

"You have done some work here, George," Faustus said and Maltby stepped closer.

"No sir, not really. I did tap the internal organs to keep them from bloating, but certainly no cosmetic work and an extensive work it certainly would be if his family did indeed contact me and requested some form of restoration..."

"Ah, but George," Faustus said. "Here at the throat it appears you've done some stitching and a bit of cover with, what is that, clay?"

There was silence from the mortician. Faustus turned and picked up a steel probe from the tray behind him and then pointed at a circular area of the corpse's throat that was obviously a different color from the pale flesh. Faustus poked at the area and in so doing uncovered a series of white stitches that had been used to close a hole.

"Oh, yes. Well, it was a nasty-looking wound and seemed quite inappropriate to leave open," Maltby started, but Faustus looked up and held the undertaker's eyes. "Getting squeamish in your old age, George? I somehow find that hard to believe."

Faustus turned the body's head to the side with some difficulty against the rigor and examined the back of the neck.

"I see no one had to repair an exit wound. Does that mean, George, that you found the bullet that entered this man's throat? Lodged perhaps in the cervical vertebra of the spinal column?"

"Well, certainly not, Mr. Faustus. That would not be of my purview," said Maltby, who was now sweating despite the coolness of the room. "If such a thing was discovered it would have been by Dr. Lansing who was, as I said, contacted by the sheriff to do an autopsy of the victim."

Faustus ignored the undertaker and was examining the body's torso.

"And as for the knife wound that was originally given as cause of death," he said, now to no one in particular, "I see no indications here of such a wound nor an attempt to cover it up if there had been one. Can you help me out with that, sir?"

Maltby had obviously had enough. He stepped to the table, took hold of the blanket and pulled it up over the corpse. Despite his profession—and one would think an innate sense for such things—the undertaker had not picked up on the slight show of grief and emotion on Byrne's face.

"Mr. Faustus," he said. "I don't see how this serves a scientific purpose and really I must ask that this line of questioning be directed to the sheriff or Dr. Lansing as I do not find them appropriate here, sir, with all due respect."

The undertaker had taken a defensive stance, arms now folded over his chest and standing in front of the corpse as if now he was willing to defend it.

"That's fine, George. Really," said Faustus, gathering his cane and hat. "I certainly didn't mean to upset you, sir. We'll be on our way."

Byrne showed no unwillingness to follow, but as they were making their way through the curtain and out of the shop the undertaker shuffled behind them. "And excuse me, sir," he said to Byrne. "I didn't get your name or title, sir?"

Byrne was about to answer when Faustus cut him off.

"He didn't give it, George."

Outside, the heat and humidity wrapped about Byrne's face. He stood staring out into the brightness of the sun, wondering why he had come to this place called Florida. Why had he not just left it alone? Let his constant admonishment over the last few years stand—Danny had left and was simply never coming back. At least there would have been that tiny sliver of hope that his brother was still alive. He took a deep breath and turned to Faustus, who stood silent beside him.

"You knew it was him, my brother?"

"I could certainly see the family resemblance," Faustus said. "The locale of your own origins and the sound of your heritage were in both of your voices. I surmised it to be a distinct possibility."

"You talked to Danny?"

Faustus seemed to study the head of his cane. "I had met him, but under a different name," he said. "He had introduced himself as a Mr. Bingham. Conrad Bingham.

"This is a land where people are often reluctant to use their given names, especially the sort who are in the business that Mr. Bingham was in."

"Which was?"

"He introduced himself as a lawyer, an entrepreneur, a real estate broker and a representative of Northern interests," Faustus said, his voice flattened as not to show emotion. "He was extremely bright, like you, Mr. Byrne. He had your talent for observation and recollection. I rather liked him at first."

"And then?" Byrne said.

Faustus cleared his throat. "At our introduction he was wearing a Mason's ring. At first, I tried not to pry, but after a few days of friendly conversation I made him out to be a fraud. He was using the symbol as a way to meet those he might take advantage of."

"A big sin among the brotherhood, I suppose?"

"Yes. A big sin. No more though I suppose than a man who wears a cross of Christ around his neck while coveting his neighbor's wife."

Byrne had never been one for religion, and he'd learned in the city bars that the discussion of same was better avoided.

"Is that why you were testing me? To see if I was like my brother?" Byrne said.

"Precisely. Your attributes are admirable. And as I said, your brother shared many of them. I couldn't be sure that a sibling might have the same powers of deception as well. Trick me once, shame on you. But trick me twice, shame on me."

"So the coin, the fishing trip, even the beer this morning were all part of your litmus test?" Byrne let a slice of sarcasm slip into his voice.

"Yes. Had you bitten my coin, taken advantage of my largesse, or shot me and Captain Abbott dead on the sea and taken off with our boat, I would have judged you differently, even in the afterlife."

"But I didn't."

"No sir, you didn't. And now, with the possibility that a young woman is being railroaded into a murder charge, you have come to see if WE can find the truth of the matter."

Byrne did not have to state the obvious. His purpose may have been selfless last night. Now he had a distinct reason for finding out the truth. Now he was looking for the killer of his brother.

"So where's the bullet?" he said without hesitation. It would be the first question any good investigator would now ask, the logical question.

"I believe we will have to inquire of Dr. Lansing to answer that, my young friend."

Faustus turned on his heel and began walking back to Olive Street. Byrne had to lengthen his stride to keep up. The old man had taken on a fired energy, and this time it was neither by the lure of fighting fish or deep opaque water. Byrne could see a pursuit of something in Faustus' eyes that was being pushed by an anger that he hadn't shown before. The old Mason doesn't like being lied to, he thought.

When they got to a small storefront with a druggist's symbol and the title Dr. Lansing painted above the wooden door, Faustus turned. "I will only be a minute. Could you please wait outside, Mr. Byrne?"

Byrne started to object, but second-guessed his reaction and instead took up a place in the shade of the tin awning as a group of raggedy farm workers trudging north toward the fields. A mule-drawn wagon, loaded with green tomatoes, passed on its way to the rail station. Behind Byrne's eyes was a vision: he and Danny as boys, scouring the streets of their East Side neighborhood, watching like small animals but considering it a game, a race for some piece of food that fell from the back of a wagon. They'd skitter out into the traffic and snatch the gift from the cobblestone. Danny with that laugh of his that went gleeful at the thought of winning some prize, even if it was actually no prize at all but a morsel to add to their empty stomachs. Danny, always with that pride that he'd somehow gotten over on someone else. Danny with his dreams of finagling his way to "land and money" for a family whose members were now all dead.

Byrne's head was turned at the sound of a man's angry voice coming from inside the pharmacy, but he was unsure whose since he had never heard Faustus raise his voice except in joy of hooking a tarpon, and this was not a note of joy. He moved in front of the door and put his back to it, hearing the sharp smack of wood against wood, like the sound a cane might make when it is rapped flat and hard against a countertop. A woman in a long day dress and carrying her purse stepped toward Byrne, meaning to enter the shop. He tipped his hat: "I'm sorry, ma'am, but the doc is presently treating a difficult patient. It would be best if you came back in a few minutes." He did not move from blocking the door and she gave him her back and continued down the street. Moments later Faustus stepped out into the sunlight. He seemed unusually calm, but there was color in his cheeks that was just beginning to subside.

"A single .38-calibre round," he said. "Lodged in the vertebra as suspected. The bullet was removed and presented along with the findings of the autopsy to Sheriff Cox."

Faustus started off in the direction of the saloon. "Pity," he said, disappointment in his voice, and when Byrne, following, looked over his shoulder, there was a small, thin man in suit pants and suspenders standing in the doorway of the doctor's office looking much chagrined and defeated.

CHAPTER SIXTEEN

MARJORY McADAMS AWOKE THAT DAY WITH a determination that can only be held in its unflinching doggedness by the young. It was not unlike the ocean swimming that spurred her furiously to stroke for miles out of sight of land, or the late night trudging that she'd done last evening through the dark brambles of West Palm Beach farm lands. But today it was knowledge she was after, and her first stop would be at the knee of the "motherly" Mrs. Birch. If she then had to bring Mr. Birch into it, so be it.

"Good morning, Abby," McAdams said when she was greeted at the door of the Birch suite by the maid.

"And to you, Miss McAdams."

"Is Mrs. Birch available?" McAdams walked in and glanced about the room without the normal invitation.

"No, ma'am. She is out taking her mornin' golf. She is spose to be back for lunch though."

McAdams moved deeper into the room.

"And Mr. Birch?" she said. "Is he available?"

The maid moved around McAdams, cutting her off from looking further through the rooms but doing so in a subservient way so as not to appear authoritative or defensive.

"No, ma'am. They is playin' together this morning. Mr. Birch plays with her most all the time now."

McAdams raised her chin. "Ah. I've heard that the men on the links have brought Mrs. Birch's displays of gumption to the manager," McAdams said. "Perhaps Mr. Birch has been asked to accompany her in order to keep her on the leash."

The statement may have been too gossipy to share with a maid, but McAdams took the chance. Whether she would continue to probe would be determined by the answer. The stoic face of the maid cracked, only slightly.

"Ain't nobody put no leash on Ma'am," she said. "Not even Mister."

McAdams turned in a small circle, pretending to look at the objects of art. "You've been with them a long time, Abby, yes?"

"Only when they come to Florida, ma'am. But that's three winters now."

"And you plan to stay with them? I mean full time? I've heard that Mr. Birch may be acquiring property here on the island, which sounds like you might be needed year round."

There was worry in the negro woman's eyes. She was trying to study her own words ahead of time, before they left her mouth.

"They talk about buyin' land all the time, ma'am. Mrs. Birch, she love that real state stuff. But they ain't said nothin' to me about winter time other than about me goin' to New York City an' I ain't much for that cold weather, ma'am."

The revelation that Mrs. Birch was more of a partner and consultant with her husband in matters of real estate than she'd ever let on caused McAdams to go silent for so long the maid became nervous.

"Like I say Miss McAdams. Ma'am spose to be back for lunch."

"Oh, yes," McAdams caught herself lost in thought and now started back toward the door. "Just tell her I stopped by to talk to her about the Carver woman."

A small gasp came from Abby and snapped McAdams back to the present.

"Mizz Shantice? Is she all right, ma'am?" Abby almost begged an answer.

"Why, yes, I suppose. If you can call being in jail under the heel of the sheriff being all right," McAdams said. She looked into the now expressive face of the maid. "I didn't know that the two of you were friends."

"Yes, ma'am. Well, we knowed each other for a long time. Course we all knowin' each other here," Abby said. "Did ya'll talk with her, ma'am? I mean in private?"

"No. Not really Abby. Why? Do you think she has something to say to me in private?" McAdams, her eyes were now intent but unable to raise the maid's own eyes from going to the floor.

"Uh, no, ma'am. I'm just worried on her, that's all."

"Well, several people are trying to help her, Abby. So hope for the best and be strong, dear." The hair was up on the back of her neck, and McAdams knew from experience that the new information was pushing her even harder. She stepped out onto the hotel veranda, where only a few couples and women strolled arm in arm on their morning constitutional.

If the Birches were actively looking to buy property on the island, which she already knew from the binders she'd obtained, if "Ma'am" was truly as deep into her husband's land acquisitions as Abby seemed to indicate, that is why McAdams had seen Mrs. Birch walking, with that aggressive and manly gait of hers, from the direction of the Styx only half and hour before Ida May Fluery smelled fire in the air.

When she got back to the Breakers, the first maid she talked to knew exactly where Ida May Fluery was: "Why, it's a baseball game on today, Miss McAdams. I spect Mizz Ida down there sneakin' a look at her boy."

Whether Henry Flagler was a baseball fan or not, he knew many of his upscale New York vacationers were. The idea that they could watch a quality game in the middle of winter was a luxury he knew they would brag about to their equally upscale friends, who were still reluctant to travel south. It was little trouble for his engineers to lay out a baseball diamond on the open land within walking distance of the hotel. Grass was cheap in Palm Beach. So were players.

By the time Marjory reached the field, the stands that were erected only a few feet from the base paths were nearly full. Vacationing men were in the majority of those sitting in the sun, giving hearty ovations for each well-executed play. But several women were also in attendance, sitting with their husbands or in groups, their wide-brimmed hats or open parasols providing shade. The men were too polite to say a word, standing or stretching around any obstructed view. The women clapped softly with gloved hands when it seemed appropriate.

Marjory had been to the games before. She admired the athletic skill, the quickness and exactness of the players, the act and react of muscle memory honed by years of repetition. The fact that the athletes spent most of their days pushing carts, carrying baggage, cooking or washing, or peddling carriages only made the game more fascinating. They did this out a pure love. A game that only gained them a few extra hours off their daily work still drove them to a glorious pursuit of perfection. The field was as meticulously manicured as any of Flagler's gardens and was probably cut and trimmed and raked by the very men who played on it. In the hard sunlight the green glowed and the white chalk lines were as bright as the women's clothing.

Marjory paid scant attention to those in the stands, instead looking down the third baseline where a few black workers gathered to watch their own. She knew that if Ida May was here she would be watching Santos. She walked behind the stands, smiling and nodding to hotel patrons as she glided by. As she passed behind home plate she stopped for a moment to watch the giant black man out on the pitcher's mound. He was tall and easily over two hundred pounds. She'd seen him before, amusing the crowd with his bear-like movements and wily, smiling presence. He knew that the game was as much entertainment for the upper class as it was a competition. Yet when it was time, his arm was ferocious. At that moment he delivered a fastball. The hard slap of the leather ball in the catcher's glove was like a rifle report, and Marjory blinked hard at the sound.

"Steeeeeriiiik," called out the umpire, an equally large but soft white man who ran the games with an authority he would doubtfully own anywhere else on the island.

Marjory moved on.

At the end of the bleachers she spotted Miss Fluery in the shade of a black umbrella, accompanied by three other housemaids Marjory recognized. She tried to catch the woman's attention but in vain. Fluery's eyes were only for Santos, who was out on the field, not thirty feet away, just inside the third base line. Santos was coiled, awaiting the next pitch, his back curved like an iron awl, his hands out in front of him, the cabled muscle in his bared forearms flexing, and his eyes staring with an intensity she had not seen in the dark of last night. Marjory heard the crack of the bat, almost felt it, and hardly had time to blink when she saw Santos launch himself, glove hand stretched high into the sun where it snatched the ball out of the air, the sheer force of the drive bending his torso back. Still he landed on his toes. It was the third out, and he flipped the ball out of his glove, caught it with his bare hand and rolled it to the pitcher's mound before jogging off the field.

From the crowd behind and to her right Marjory heard a hotel guest exclaim: "Did you see that nigger jump! Wonderful!" Santos passed the bleachers and another said, "Nice job, boy," as the rest applauded.

Only then did Ida May Fluery turn and recognize Marjory standing nearby.

"May we speak, Mizz Fluery?" Marjory said, stepping forward. The other servants discretely faded away, leaving the two women, who moved together down the white foul line.

"Have you heard?" Marjory spoke first. "That Mizz Carver has been arrested and jailed?"

"Every worker on the island knew by sunup, ma'am," Fluery said, a statement, not as caustic as it could have been.

"Yes, of course," Marjory said, instantly losing her faux motive for coming to see her. "We, umm, Mr. Santos and I that is, went across to try to speak for her last evening. She did not seem to have been abused. I mean, beaten or physically punished."

"Then the Lord have mercy," the housewoman said.

"But I fear that it will be difficult to convince the sheriff or the court, if it should go so far, that Shantice is not the one who killed the man in the Styx unless we can find someone to speak out for her."

Ida May stood silent, looking out onto the greenness of the outfield, not at Marjory. She knew she was being led.

"Do you mean someone to speak for her good name, 'cause there isn't a person on this island who didn't know Shantice was a whore," Fluery said.

"No. No, I didn't mean that," Marjory said, as if that fact actually embarrassed her. "I meant that you had said there were others with Shantice when she was across the lake at the carnival. Perhaps they would be willing to say they were with her and where exactly they were when the fire began.

"Do you know who, exactly, was with her that night?"

Again Fluery hesitated. Bringing in other's names in white men's situations was never wise. Guilt by association was something to be avoided in her world. Yet she could see no hidden agenda in McAdams' question.

"I believe Abby Campbell say she was with Shantice," she finally said. "They been close awhile, though I cain't say why."

"Abby Campbell? The girl who works for Mrs. Birch?"

"That's the one."

"Do you believe her?" Marjory said, then caught herself. "I mean, is she believable, if she had to speak, say, in front of the sheriff or an attorney?"

"She be believed as much as any negro woman might be to folks like that."

One of the opposing outfielders ran out to his position. Marjory did not see him doff his hat in their direction, so did not register if it had been to her or to the head house woman. She was rerunning her previous conversation with Abby in her mind. Why didn't the girl say she was with Shantice the night of the fire? Why not offer her help once Marjory had told her that her friend was in dire need? Had they indeed been together that night? And where? And what had they witnessed? She would need to talk with Abby again, this time with a stronger sense of authority.

"I believe we'll need to employ an attorney for Mizz Carver," Marjory finally said, turning to Fluery and delivering the statement that had motivated her to come here in the first place.

"No one has money to pay no lawyer for that girl. An' it won't make no difference if they did," Fluery said with the same tone she used when McAdams first asked if she knew of Carver's arrest. She had no tolerance for white people who disavowed the obvious. The game had resumed, and Fluery began walking back toward third base, Marjory alongside.

"I shall provide the money," Marjory said, as if working it out in her own mind. She needed a way to question Shantice Carver, to find out if she had been on the island that night, to find out what she had seen. She needed to know why and where Mrs. Birch had been when she'd seen her coming out of the woods that night. Since the Carver woman was obviously reluctant to talk, as she'd been in the laundry, maybe a lawyer in pursuit of her defense could glean some answers.

As they moved closer to the stands Marjory spotted a man, wandering, looking out of place, a bit disheveled for the paying customer, so to speak.

"And I shall also provide the attorney," she said to Ida May before taking the old woman's hands and bidding her good-bye. "Don't you worry."

Byrne had come to the ball game with one intent: to find Marjory and arrange a time for her to meet with him and Faustus, to share with her the information from the morgue and the doctor's hesitant report. In return he would get back from her anything—anything—she knew about the killing and the Styx. He would be circumspect. He would not show the anger burning in his gut. He would not go off half-cocked. He would ask questions, watch reactions, intuit meaning, just like he had always done. But he would find the person who shot his brother.

"Well, Mr. Byrne. I see you actually took up my offer," Marjory's voice came from behind him, causing Byrne to spin round.

"I, uh, well, I wouldn't have missed it," he said, raising his palms to indicate the scene around him. "It's...unexpected."

"Oh, not for them." Marjory pointed relaxed fingers to the bleachers and chairs. "They have come to expect it. After all, what is summer weather without baseball, especially now in the middle of winter when they can brag about attending a game when their friends in New York are all huddled by the fireplace?"

Was that cynicism he heard in her voice, or braggadocio? Byrne was arrested by the sight of the man now coming to home plate with a bat in his hands. Santos actually looked bigger than he had in the dark, trudging with them in the fields, sitting at a small wooden table, even peddling a carriage on a raised seat. When the man reached the plate, took his wide stance and swung the bat in an exaggerated, slow motion practice swing, he looked like something carved and regal overlooking its domain.

"Your friend?" he asked. Santos was cocked and took the first pitch, a ball off the plate. The umpire bawled, "Aaaawwwwl."

"In a sense," said Marjory, who was also watching the batter. "More of an acquaintance."

The second pitch was delivered from the thin, rope-muscled negro on the mound. Again, the batter barely flinched: "Aaaawwwwl."

"A protector, then?" Byrne said.

"I, Mr. Byrne? What would possibly make you think that I would need protection?" Marjory turned to study the side of Byrne's face, wondering if by some impossible means the Pinkerton knew more than he should.

"Someone of your charm and beauty might need someone to ward off the suitors," Byrne said, only slightly embarrassed by what had come out of his mouth. He watched the next pitch come in low and hard. Santos turned on in a flashing instant. The sound of snapping oak exploded in the air and heads turned as one to watch the ball sail up, up, up and out over the tree line. Byrne, though, kept his eyes on Santos, who also, when the outcome was obvious, turned his attention to the bat as he jogged toward the first base, studying its splinters and now angled shaft and then tossing it aside. The big man jogged around the base paths to the applause of the crowd, and Byrne unconsciously reached into his pocket to feel the thin metal baton. It would stand no chance in a face off.

"If you did need that protection, he would certainly be my choice," Byrne said. Marjory had a curious look on her face, amused yet studious.

"I shall consider it, Mr. Byrne, if the need should arise," she said. "But you didn't come out here to watch baseball nor to banter."

"Not really," he said stepping back from the crowd in small, nonchalant steps so as not to draw attention. Marjory followed. When they were out of earshot, he tipped he head to her ear. "I have located Mr. Faustus. He is a Mason and a lawyer on the mainland and has made some curious findings at the undertaker's and at the doctor's where the autopsy was done."

Now it was Marjory's turn to not to flinch, the news coming in low and hard, but she held her stance.

"Really?"

"Mr. Faustus was able to exam the body himself and obtained the paperwork submitted to the sheriff," Byrne was trying to please her, uncharacteristic territory for him. "The doctor removed a bullet from Mr. Bingham's throat."

Marjory plucked a hanky from somewhere in the folds of her skirts and pretended a speck of something in her eye, a tactic to gain a second from her surprise.

"I'm sorry, did you say Bingham? Was that the poor man's name?"

"It's the name Mr. Faustus knew him by. He apparently had a reputation as a con man. Underhanded, bit of a thief," Byrne said. He had already decided to keep secret his brother's true identity—and his connection.

"Well no wonder he was a stranger to us then. I know most of the people on the island, but in the streets on the mainland, I would be quite lost—as you could tell last night, Mr. Byrne. But such news is certainly helpful to Mizz Carver, and if your Mr. Faustus is willing, I would be delighted to employ him to speak out in her defense before the judge at her hearing on Friday."

Byrne was pleased with himself, seeing her intensity, obviously energized by his news.

"Then if I may, Miss McAdams, you could have the opportunity to ask him yourself if you would accept an invitation to dinner tonight," he said. She in turn seemed to be picking out a response but quickly a smile came to her face.

"It would be a pleasure, Mr. Byrne."

CHAPTER SEVENTEEN

THE SUN WAS HOT ON HIS shoulders, sweat running down the middle of his back, and lye soap suds flowing down his arms. A long-handled scrub brush, a pail of water and an entire rail car had met Byrne when he got back to the mainland.

Harris was waiting for him on the front porch of his hotel with a cigar stuck in the side of his face and a look of worry pushing his thick eyebrows together.

"Michael, me boy. Michael, me boy," he said in a disappointed tone that reminded Byrne of his childhood years when he was about to get the strap. A vision of his father snapped on in full color inside of his head. The old man's sunken cheek bones, eyes trying to look angry but only showing how it was going to hurt him to mete out the punishment his old world upbringing demanded. Byrne would take that strap in a second to see his father's face again.

"Too much time on yer hands, eh, Michael?" Harris continued. "Didn't yer mum tell you it was the Devil's work, those idle hands, boy?"

The sergeant failed to elaborate and simply gave him his orders: "Get yer arse down to the rail station and take the soap and brush to number ninety. Mr. Flagler will be taking a trip to Miami and the car is expected to be spotless and shining like a new coin by tomorrow."

Byrne could tell by the delivery that there was no argument and that the reasons why such duty was being foisted on a security man were not going to be given. He'd had several hours on the rail side to dwell on it. After scrubbing another section of the side boards, he gathered a different pail of fresh water and tossed it up against the car, washing down the suds. He repeated the act and then went to the nearby water pump to fill the buckets again.

Had Harris finally gotten sick of his "intelligence gathering" excuse and decided to come down on him? Had he heard about the confrontation in front of the jail and been told by the sheriff to keep his new boy in check? Had he been seen in the company of Faustus, a man Harris had once warned him to stay away from, and had that information been passed along? Or was Byrne simply been caught sticking his nose into something that the powers would just as soon see left alone?

"The hell with you all," he said to himself. He'd long decided that he didn't have enough trust in Harris to tell him that the only reason he'd signed on for this job was to find his brother. He wasn't changing tactics now just to keep from washing a train car.

He picked up the brush, sloshed it in the soap bucket and returned to scrubbing the last panel of Flagler's car. Then he'd have to tackle the bright work on the steps and doorframes and then polish the brass railings and handles.

"Now there's an enterprising Pinkerton, lads," came a voice from over Byrne's shoulder. He turned to see the binder boys lined up behind him in their scruffy suits, all with shit-eating grins on their faces. Byrne turned back to the work, hiding a grin of his own.

"So the old man is headin' out again, eh?" said the voice again. Haney, the talker as usual. "Where's he goin,' Michael? Miami?"

"Can't say for sure," Byrne lied.

"Might give us a leg up, my friend. Money goes where Flagler goes, ya know. Might be some property he's been scoutin' down the tip of the peninsula. Some say the old coot's thinking about takin' the train down the islands to Key West."

The outlandish statement brought a guffaw of incredulity from Haney's mates. Byrne picked up a bucket of fresh water and splashed the side of the train.

"Isn't that a bit daft, even for Flagler?" Byrne said, picking up the second bucket. "No one takes a train across the ocean, Haney. Even him."

"Aye, the man has a vision, Pinkerton," Haney said.

"Aye, the man would have to be drunk," Byrne said.

"Excellent invitation," Haney laughed and clapped Byrne on the shoulder. "Don't mind if we do, aye boy'os. Past lunch time anyway."

While Byrne rung out his sleeves and tucked in his shirttails, the four of them walked down to J.C. Lauther's saloon.

The saloon was barely a tent with a few hand-hewn wooden tables about. But there was construction in progress on the lot and the beer was cold.

"So you're going to Miami hunting property, eh boy'os?" he said after draining half a bottle. The keg beer at the restaurant had been tastier, but Byrne wasn't going to argue.

"Word is some rich woman from Ohio name of Tuttle talked Flagler into building the train down to her place, and he's going to build another hotel," Haney said. "The Tuttle woman has the south side of the river to herself, but we all know how that works, eh boy'os?"

"Brooklyn as soon as they built the first bridge over the East River," said Paul.

"And bets are that bridge in Miami goes up in a month after Flagler gets there," Henry said.

They were all so damned sure of themselves, Byrne thought. Like they had some secret no else had. Like no one was as smart as New Yorkers when it came to finding the angle. They were just like Danny.

"Well, good luck, gents. Just don't end up like your friend Bingham," Byrne said, dropping the name his brother had adopted and waiting for the response.

There was silence at the table as the trio absorbed the statement. As usual, it was Haney who finally spoke.

"Bobby Bingham was the fellow stabbed and burned then?"

"Word is," Byrne said, using Haney's favorite attribution for information, "he was a binder boy like the rest of you. But he was working the island."

Byrne had no knowledge of Danny's intention the night he was shot, but he figured these boys, who had always been locked out of the property grab on the island, might respond if challenged.

"Fucking Bingham!" Paul said. "He wasn't a businessman. He was a shite thief and a ripper who'd do anything to steal a dollar and your good name along with it."

The boys let that one settle, no one speaking up to refute it.

"So Bobby the con man got it stuck to 'im, eh?" Haney said, watching Byrne's eyes carefully.

"Not exactly." Byrne leaned in and the boys followed suit. Nothing like a good bit of inside information to bring heads together. "Word is he wasn't stabbed at all. Shot in the throat was the reason for Mr. Bingham's passing."

"And let me guess," said Haney. "Not by the niggra they've got locked up in the jailhouse unless she was dealin' opium or another bit of nastiness that darlin' Bobby wanted and wasn't willing to pay for."

Byrne felt a twitch at the corner of his face on that one. Danny might have been many things, but he'd never dealt in the opium and morphine game.

"Well, whatever the negotiation was about was lost on the dead man's lips," Byrne said.

Again the table went quiet. Bottles were tipped. Questions were formed and unsaid. Byrne waited them out.

"Did anyone claim Mr. Bingham's body?" Haney finally asked. "Or his things?"

"Not as of yet," Byrne answered.

"Figures for that son of a whore," Paul said.

Byrne's face tightened this time. The slur was too close to his heart. He'd been able to disguise his reaction to the words against his brother, but he couldn't hold it together when someone cursed their mother. Everyone at the table could see Byrne's reaction.

"I'd of told you before, Pinkerton," Haney finally said. "But you've a family resemblance to the now departed."

Haney's mates looked at Byrne's face like a magic shroud had suddenly been lifted, their eyes widening at what their leader now knew was true.

"He was my brother," Byrne said, looking hard into the face of the one who called Danny a son of a whore.

"Jaysus. Sorry, mate," Paul said. "I wouldn't of...you know."

Byrne waved off the apology.

Again the table went quiet, a moment of silence so to speak. But no one sitting there could put off business for long.

"Did you see his things then, Mr. Byrne, if that's the real name?" Haney asked.

"It's our real name, yes," Byrne said. "And yeah, I was at the undertaker's." The curiosity hook was out and Haney was biting.

"Bingham's, uh, I mean, your brother's valise? Was it with his effects?"

"I may have seen a leather pouch, sort of like the ones you fellows have," Byrne lied. "Why? What would have been in his valise if it was found with him?"

"Ha! Everything, man. His papers, his identification, his money, promissory notes and any binders he was still holding," Haney said.

"He was loose like the rest of us. Stayed in different places, moved from hotel to shack to tent just like everyone else. You don't leave anything anywhere. You carry everything you have with you just in case you might have to leave on the double, get me?"

"Got you," Byrne said. "Perhaps I'll have to revisit the undertaker and recanvas possessions."

"Aye, you'd do better in the sheriff's office, Mr. Byrne. Just like the roll of money word says was in your poor brother's mouth. Cox has anything of value that was found over there."

Not a man at the table, including Byrne, doubted the statement. He got up, spilled some coins out on the table and prepared to leave.

"Good luck in Miami, boy'os. I've got some polishing to do."

Byrne showed up at the appointed dinner with Marjory McAdams and Faustus before the others. Faustus had instructed him to meet at the Dellmore Cottage on the island where "I will speak to Mrs. Moore, the proprietress there and have a suitable meal prepared."

There had been no time to have his fancy new suit cleaned and repaired so Byrne made do with the jacket and tried, perhaps in vain, to match it with a clean pair of trousers. He hoped the lighting would be dim.

Faustus arrived ten minutes past the hour, impeccably dressed. Byrne noticed that his garb was relatively new, versus the frayed version he seen before. His long-tailed coat with a brocaded vest was of a finer fabric and he wore shined and pointed shoes that surely could be used as weapons if aimed toward another man's lower regions. The two men met on the porch of the Dellmore with the Poinciana in full view and stood in polite silence in a cooling ocean breeze. Mrs. Moore greeted them and offered drinks, which both declined with a sense that clear-headedness might be required for the evening. After several minutes, Byrne decided to let Faustus in on his friends' concern over a possible valise that may have been in his brother's possession at the time of his killing.

"They were certainly honest with you Mr. Byrne," he said. "The binder boys are notorious for keeping their paperwork nearby. I'm afraid I was too focused on your brother's wounds and should have asked the undertaker what if any personal effects they may have collected. The fact that his clothing was nearly burned away might have led to that unfortunate dismissal on my part."

Byrne wondered if Faustus was nervous presenting himself as a lawyer to someone of Marjory's high station. That conjecture was quickly abandoned when she arrived fashionably late.

"Absolutely charmed, my dear," Faustus said, with a show of the hat and a bow. Byrne was surprised Marjory hadn't curtsied, the pleasantries were so thick.

Byrne could not find fault with Faustus' impression. Marjory had worn a dress of the lightest shade of green that had a remarkable effect with her eye color and at the same time setting off the highlights in her auburn hair. When she turned, the flow of air around her carried a whiff of flowers so delicate that Byrne thought he'd imagined it, and the fading light from the west seemed to catch in the folds of her garments and accentuate the delicacy of her figure. He, too, was charmed.

Once they were seated at a table in the small hotel's parlor, Marjory also declined an offer of wine and a consommé Printanier was served.

"I am quite impressed, Mr. Faustus," Marjory said. "I was aware of Mrs. Moore's reputation as a fine cook, but not that she entertained private parties here."

"Ah, she is an old friend, Miss McAdams, and it was quite wonderful of her to do this on such short notice. But my understanding from Mr. Byrne is that time is of the essence."

Byrne took the first spoonful of soup. Faustus was done with the pleasantries.

"I have heard bits and pieces so far, but if I am to represent this woman in a legal hearing, I really need as much information as possible," Faustus said. "So, could you to start from the beginning, Miss McAdams?"

Marjory's fingers were entwined, her wrists resting carefully on the table's edge, her eyes focused, ever so carefully, on Faustus. The old man did not flinch, nor avert his own look as polite custom might demand. Two strong personalities were assessing, were making instant determinations, and were, perhaps, making plans.

Marjory's eyes broke first. She picked up her soup spoon and delicately took three small tastes of the consommé. "Very well, sir. On Friday of last week, I was on the southern porch of the Breakers when the maid smelled fire."

They talked through the soup and through the croquettes of shrimp, Marjory recalling the trip to the Styx as it blazed, the morning when Shantice Carver came crying out of the woods after her discovery of the body, the accusation by the sheriff and Marjory's own decision to secret the woman off the island. She made no mention of seeing the banker's wife coming out of the woods before the fire. They were into the main course of broiled plover when Faustus reminded McAdams that she had committed a crime.

"Aiding and abetting a fugitive is a punishable act," he said. "Certainly you know this, and I would have to say it was either foolish or highly commendable on your part."

"I believe the girl to be innocent, Mr. Faustus. I also know the reputation of the sheriff," she said. "He is a racist and a pig."

Faustus choked only slightly on a spoon of currant jelly. He dabbed his mouth with a napkin.

"Well, that said, can you provide me with the names of those persons who will swear that Miss Carver was at the fair at the time that our Mr. Bingham was shot to death?"

Byrne snuck a look at Faustus. They had not spoken of whether to use Danny's real name or whether to reveal his sibling relationship. Faustus had made the decision alone. Byrne was not opposed.

McAdams took the opportunity to dab at the corners of her own mouth before answering.

"Yes, I believe I can," she said without immediately offering up the name of Abby.

"And these persons would have been attending the fair themselves?"

"Yes."

"And why not you, Miss McAdams?"

"Pardon me?"

"Why were you not at the fair? My understanding is that you were active in arranging the event in the first place. In fact, I've been told that you convinced your father to talk Mr. Flagler into financing the affair. I would think you'd have attended to see how well it was carried off."

Byrne, who'd been relegated to the role of observer, one he was quite adept at, listened carefully. Faustus' voice had not changed in timbre or enunciation. In another man's mouth, the question could have come off as an accusation. In his it was merely a professional inquiry.

Marjory blushed slightly. "You are correct. It was something my father and I spoke about several times, giving the workers a sort of holiday, something to lift their spirits.

"As for attending, I thought it would be an intrusion, akin to the lordly master overseeing the dance of his slaves. It was supposed to be an event for them, not for us."

"I see," Faustus said, dipping his head as if begging her pardon. But his next question had no ring of begging in it.

"And, if I may, did you know Mr. Bingham? I mean through your travels or when you may have been visiting in West Palm?"

"The name wasn't familiar. And I certainly didn't recognize the man I saw that night."

Marjory turned her head away as if the grisly sight was revisiting.

"Do forgive me, Miss," Faustus said in reaction.

Byrne found the crack in McAdams' usual hardened core curious, but said nothing. Seeing his own brother burned and dead had put a vise around his heart that nearly squeezed him to unconsciousness.

"I would like to employ your help, Mr. Faustus, as representation for Mizz Carver. I will gladly pay the going rate for a criminal attorney. I believe there is expected to be an arraignment on Friday. Would you be willing?"

Coffee had arrived, real coffee, and Faustus took a long luxurious sip before answering.

"It has been several years, but my licensing in the state of Florida is up to date and I shall be willing to aid in Miss Carver's defense. In fact, if we are allowed to present our findings to the judge on Friday, it is quite possible that the charges will be dropped altogether.

"I would, however, have to visit with the woman tomorrow, gain her approval, and hear her side of the story."

"I'll be more than pleased to introduce you," Marjory said, her instant smile lightening the heretofore dark and moody room. "I will of course ask to sit in during your discussions. I mean, I would suppose someone other than a stranger, someone with a woman's touch, might reassure Mizz Carver of our intentions."

Faustus again seemed to hold Marjory's eyes for an extra few seconds. "We'll have to see what the sheriff's policy is on that matter. It is not usual for such discussions to be witnessed by anyone other than a client and their attorney. Privilege, of course. But certainly it is a possibility."

With all manners and pleasantries to the host concluded, the dinner broke up. On the porch outside Faustus bid good evening and walked quickly into the night, headed for the bridge to West Palm Beach. Byrne lingered for an uncomfortable minute and was rewarded for his hesitation.

Marjory was staring up at the sky, her head tilted, her pinned-up hair in danger of unraveling and falling in cascades down her back.

"Oh, look at the stars, Michael. Isn't it a gorgeous night?"

The sound of his first name in her voice struck Byrne mute.

"Or do you not like the stars?" she said to his silence.

"Uh, no. I mean absolutely," he mumbled.

She took a step toward him, hooked her arm through the crook of his elbow. "Then you will walk me back to my hotel?"

He knew she was out there, deeper in the water, though her teasing and laughter had abated. Somewhere she was floating, perhaps lying on her back in the motion of the swells, tingling in the warm ocean water while she held that curious smile on her face.

She was enticing him, luring. He knew this to be true. But he also knew that his reaction to seeing her inexplicably disappear into the beachside bushes and then come running out stark naked and sprint into the ocean was going to override any question of her motives.

On the walk back from dinner she'd used his first name three times, each one sounding like a wonderful note of music. But they'd walked mostly in silence, she lightly holding his arm and he trying not to show his enthusiasm or nervousness. When they reached the turnoff to the Breakers, she'd pulled him in the opposite direction.

"It's much too lovely a night to go in," she said. "And the beach is beautiful in the moonlight."

The moonlit sand made Byrne recall Harris' tale of once mistaking it as snow. Marjory removed her shoes and they walked near the tide mark, she pointing out the sprinkling lights of phosphorescence being washed up on the shore, he being too thrilled by both the sight of the living organisms' glow and the fact that she had taken his hand in hers as they moved south.

Then she'd stopped and stared out at the ocean and the beam of moonlight that appeared as a silver arrow to the horizon. "I have to swim. It's too gorgeous not to swim," she said and made a break for the bushes. He was still puzzled by her actions when she came bolting from cover, her long legs and torso flashing white in the light and her flowing hair catching and throwing glimmers of red.

"Come on then, Byrne! Where's the Irish in you!" she called out, launching herself like a spear into the sea. He watched the hole into which she'd disappeared, no doubt his mouth agape, and then five feet farther out her head appeared and then her arms like an amphibious butterfly's wing swooped up from her sides, reformed into a point, and without losing forward motion she again speared into the water. She repeated her dolphin-like move three or four more times, growing smaller with each piece of yardage gained and then was gone into the darkness.

It took him more time than he cared to remove all of his clothes and dump them in a stack and then run in after her. He shivered only once, when the water, perhaps seventy-eight degrees but still well below body temperature, reached his groin, but he copied Marjory's motion and dove forward. He was not nearly as graceful as she, and after a couple of attempts he stopped and gained his feet on the sandy bottom. Now he knew she was out here, but where? A collection of clouds had moved in front of the moon and the path of light had diminished. He waited until the gauzy gray passed and then spotted her, breast-stroking toward him.

"My God, isn't it marvelous," she said, stopping an arm's length away. Her auburn hair was slicked back on her head, her face pale on the side where the moonlight struck it. Droplets of water clung to her eyelashes.

"Yes. I should say it is," Byrne said, amazed that his voice even worked.

She spun and jumped high into the air, her arms going up as if trying to slap the moon itself, and exposing herself to where her hips widened slightly from her tiny waist. She disappeared again when she came down and Byrne was left looking around again until she surfaced, directly in front of him, this time closer than an arm's length. He could feel the wavelets. Both of them were holding their breaths when she moved up against him and her hard nipples brushed his skin. Then her breasts flattened against him as he pulled her close and wrapped his arms around her. He moved his lips to hers, and when they touched they were cold and salty until he felt the warmth of air come from inside her mouth. He felt the tip of her tongue flirt at the seam of his own lips, but when he opened them he got a mouthful of salt water and she laughed in her throat and bent back her head to look in his eyes. He felt himself hard against her hips.

"You are absolutely unpredictable," Byrne whispered, still quite flustered.

She laughed. "You, though, are highly predictable," she said and moved again against him.

"I won't deny that."

"Ha! Not that you could." She rolled her hip against his hardness and then broke from his embrace. She floated there for a moment, her chin just in the water, her eyes dancing a bit above it.

"Are you sure you can swim? I'd hate to leave you floundering out here."

"Well, I just might need some help," Byrne said, sensing in her words that she was either going to leave or challenge him to a race and wanting neither one. "And to be completely honest, no, I can't swim."

The look on Marjory's face suddenly turned from impish to something thoughtful, like a decision was being made.

"Neither could your brother," she said, averting her eyes. "But neither could Daniel be completely honest."

At that she quickly performed another of her dolphin-like plunges and was heading out to sea, to deeper water. After a second, Byrne recovered his voice and called several times for her. But he heard her strokes diminish as they faded in the distance.

"Christ!" he said, growing instantly flaccid and colder than when he first walked into this idiot sea. Harris was right. Out of your league. Not a chance in hell for immigrants like us. He made it back to the beach, to his clothes, dressed and sat on the sand in a direct line between Marjory's footsteps and the bushes where she'd stashed her own clothes. He sat an hour, until nine o'clock, and then gave up. If she knew Danny, then she'd have recognized his body the night she saw him dead in the Styx. If she knew they were brothers, then why the ruse? Why the game? What the hell makes sense in Florida, he thought, and put on his brogans, took one last look out to sea and walked away.

CHAPTER EIGHTEEN

THE NEXT MORNING HE WAS UP, standing ready at the rail
station next to Flagler's newly washed car long before Harris made an appearance. "Morning, sir," he said when the big man approached. Harris was in his
standard working attire. But his reluctance to make eye contact alerted Byrne
that something was up.

"Mornin'."

"She's looking good, eh?" Byrne said and instantly felt like a stable boy
asking for a compliment.

"Aye, a fine job."

"Will we be hooking up here and going across the bridge to pick up
Mr. Flagler then?"

"Aye, we will. But not you, Mr. Byrne."

The use of Byrne's proper name was a step back from Harris' now familiar
"lad." Byrne said nothing and let his silence force whatever it was out of Harris'
mouth.

"I'll be accompanying Mr. Flagler to Miami. But we've another job for you,"
he said. "We need you to go with a group of gentlemen from the hotel on a bit of
an expedition this morning."

Byrne let the query in his face do the asking.

"Mr. McAdams and some regular guests are taking in a round of hunting in the Everglades and they'd like you as some kind of security I suppose. You'll be taking a rail dingy down south a ways."

"Security?"

"Yeah, security."

"For how many?"

"Three. Plus a guide."

"Hunting?"

"Yeah. Deer and wild hogs and such. Maybe even a panther, which would be a sight, eh?"

"Four armed men who need security?" Byrne said, his voice cynical.

"Look, Byrne," Harris said, finally letting the frustration and a touch of anger slip into his own voice. "This is a request by the powers that be. Mr. McAdams works directly for our boss. If he asks for one of us to go out on the road with him, we go."

"So this is a direct request from Mr. Flagler?" Byrne said. He'd played this game with the Tammany group in New York. You ask where the orders came from, ask how high up the line the responsibility lies and hope you know when to stop asking before you cross that line and become a liability.

"Mr. McAdams came to me and asked for you," Harris said, looking Byrne in the eye. "When I balked and went straight to Mr. Flagler, he didn't object. That's what I know and that's all I know. You wait here until they fetch you."

For a moment, the two men studied each other. Harris was not going to offer more, even though more was running around in his head, Byrne knew. Harris had taken on the role of the sergeants in New York, unsatisfied with their own superiors, but unwilling to challenge them. Yet the big Irishman still couldn't help himself. He stepped forward to Byrne's side and whispered conspiratorially: "There's a stink in the air, lad. The high and mighty are talking about the fire in the Styx, askin' each other who set the damn thing. Everybody knows the land value was shootin' too high on the island to have a bunch of Negro workers livin' on it. Now they're all watchin' each other to see who comes up with the title to the piece. Somebody knows somethin' and somebody's gonna get rich."

Harris backed away. "It ain't a game a tenement kid wants to get in on, lad."

Byrne climbed up onto the railroad platform, took a seat in one of the wooden straight-backed chairs and watched the rising sun. The red orb had cleared the palms and gumbo limbo trees of the island to the east, and he could feel the heat build by degrees. The pores of his skin opened and the inevitable moisture of sweat sought a cooling breeze. He thought of the chill of the ocean water last night and then the heat between Marjory McAdams' thighs and he closed his eyes and forced his head to logic.

Danny the arsonist? He thought about the possibility. Could his brother have gotten so deep with his schemes and maneuvering to be involved in burning down a community for some sort of payoff? Byrne couldn't believe it. He'd never seen his brother as someone who could maliciously hurt innocents. Yes, he'd shyster some rube on the streets, trick a man out of his pocket money, steal a piece of food from a merchant, sweet-talk someone into paying for his drinks, even run a land scam like the one the binder boys described. But deliberately burn down people's homes? Impossible. Maybe his brother was involved in the deal, maybe he blanched at someone else's plan to burn the Styx and got a bullet in the throat for his refusal.

And where did Marjory fit in all of this? She knew Danny and had kept that from him. What did she know about his killing in her own back yard? And why was she so set on defending this Negro maid?

He looked up when he heard the train whistle from the bridge from Palm Beach Island and watched its trail of smoke crawl across the stubby townscape. He did not stand when it neared but observed the manipulations to the siding as the engineer and crew latched on to Flagler's gleaming private car. Moments later he saw Flagler and his wife pass between the cars, entering their own. The old man attended to the careful steps of his wife and then looked up at the sun-touched wall of the station where Byrne sat. Their eyes met for a brief second. Byrne swore there was a momentary look of question on Flagler's face just before he stepped into his car.

With a blast of the whistle and a huff of steam, the completed linkage of train shivered and clanked and groaned into motion. Byrne could feel the foundation of the station platform vibrate as thousands of pounds of steel moved southward toward Miami. Whatever you thought about the rich old coot, you had to admit it was a hell of an accomplishment bringing such things to this sleepy seashore world. Byrne watched for the rear platform and found Harris there, staring out. He could not tell whether it was a look of sadness or warning.

CHAPTER NINETEEN

BYRNE TOOK HIS COAT OFF, PULLED the bill of his cap down to shade his eyes and rolled up his shirtsleeves. But he remained seated at the train station, as he had been instructed. He nodded at those who greeted, trying to look nonchalant while the questions of reason and motive roiled in his stomach.

Why the hell was he here? Why was Flagler dismissing him from his personal guard duty? Why would anyone request him to go out with a group of the hotel elite on a hunting excursion? Hell, he knew it wasn't his storied proficiency as a game hunter that prompted it...a tenement kid who'd rarely even seen a rifle. And Harris said there would be a guide. So what was the danger there? The party would also include Mr. McAdams, whose young daughter had just last night been swimming naked in the ocean with him and then disappeared. So what? Do they take young men who besmirch a lady's reputation out into the swamp and shoot him? Ha! You're stinking paranoid, he said to himself. Faustus was trying to get in to interview the Carver woman this day. Marjory was going to join him. Byrne would have to wait until he got back from this charade in the glades to find out what the Negro woman would tell them. There was too much happening to endure this shite. Yet, an hour after Flagler's train pulled out, he sat there watching to the north as a hand-pumped rail cart creaked toward him. It wasn't until he recognized Mr. McAdams that he stood, dumbstruck, at the site of the transportation he and the four others were obviously taking on this impromptu hunting trip.

"Hallo, Mr. Byrne!" called out Mr. McAdams as the flat-bed cart coasted to a stop. "I see our request was successfully passed on to you."

Byrne hopped down next to the track, eyeing the cart, the men, the supplies and the stacked rifle barrels arranged on the small space. When McAdams offered a hand up, Byrne took it, stepped up on the hub of one wheel and was pulled aboard. At the center of the cart deck was a two-handled, see-saw contraption which Byrne recognized as the power behind the vehicle. And just to the front of the cart was a stiff and sturdy eight-foot-tall pole with fabric wrapped around it with sail line.

"Mr. Byrne, this is Mr. Birch and Mr. Pearson from the hotel and Mr. Ashton, a magnificent guide of the Everglades region."

Byrne touched the brim of his cap in greeting and shook hands all around. Birch was the man Byrne had recognized at Flagler's table the night of the ball, the man from New York who'd paid off Byrne's commander during the prostitution raid. He shook Byrne's hand with a simple politeness, his eyes holding no recognition.

Pearson, the general manager, had been pointed out to him before by Harris. "Tight assed and shifty" was the sergeant's assessment. Byrne studied them all, as always, making note of each man's facial hair, eye color, mode of dress. If they were nervous or uneasy with his presence, none showed it. Birch and Pearson gave nothing away. Ashton was the local. His eyes were pale and reminded Byrne of Captain Abbott's in their stoic nonchalance. He had the look of a man simply performing a job.

"We're going to go south a bit, Mr. Byrne," Mr. McAdams said, looking the part of some explorer with a white bandana knotted around his neck. "Down at the Hillsboro inlet, Cypress Creek goes west into the great swamp. You will be amazed at the wild boar, the deer, wild turkey, honestly." There was a friendly enthusiasm in the man's voice, as if he were selling a new homestead to a customer. If he knew of Byrne's assignation the night before, he wasn't acting like a put-out father. Byrne relaxed, but only a bit.

"You may even get a shot at a snowy egret, Mr. Birch," he said to the banker. "The kind with the wonderful feathers your wife loves to adorn her hats with. Treat them with a bit of arsenic for preservative and she can take them back to New York to her milliner."

Birch gave McAdams a nod but did not seem to be in the mood for jovial repartee. The guide moved to the hand pump, and with elbows locked, he put all his weight on the fore handle. The cart began to crawl southward. When the handle reached its lowest level, he quickly jumped to the now raised side and did the same. The cart gained momentum. Byrne assessed the mechanics, and when he realized none of the others intended to assist the guide he took up position at one handle and copied Ashton's labors. If Byrne expected a sign of appreciation for his assistance, he would be disappointed. Ashton simply kept pushing down at his turn and stared out at the passing landscape, his eyes seemingly searching the brush and tree copse for some movement or sign. On occasion he would turn his nose up into the air. Yeah, right, like you can smell the boar or deer or whatever the hell this group is supposed to be hunting, Byrne thought. Nice touch for the city swells. But after half an hour of steady and not overly strenuous pumping, the guide's nose did indeed lead to advantage.

"Wind switch," he said, mostly to himself, and stepped away from the pump handle. The dense vegetation had cleared somewhat and Byrne too could feel the breeze catching them from behind. While the handles continued to move up and down, Byrne kept pushing his end and the cart continued to roll. Meanwhile, Ashton unfurled the cloth from the tall pole and extended what he now recognized as a boom and voila! A sail puffed out and the cart became a land boat. The pump handle in Byrne's hands started moving on its own, and he let go. The ingenuity made him smile and the feeling was infectious, for the other men, with the exception of Ashton, also began to grin.

"Hard work often inspires ingenuity, Mr. Byrne," Mr. McAdams said, noticing the smile. "Even in as rough a place as this." Since the statement was not a question, Byrne felt no obligation to respond. He instead looked out on what he now recognized as cleared land, not unlike that of the vegetable farmers farther north where he and Harris had encountered the would-be dynamiters.

"This area will someday be a massive grove of pineapples," McAdams said. "A young Japanese man with dreams of a plantation has approached Mr. Flagler. Imagine, sweet pineapples by the crate going north to Manhattan. Some men know the possibilities of land, Mr. Byrne. That it is the foundation for everything else."

Again, Byrne did not answer. If the guy was going to pontificate in vague phrases, so be it. Byrne knew a babbling man in the Bowery who stood on a wooden box and spewed verse and quotations all day for the sake of nothing more than the sound of his own voice. If Mr. McAdams thought he was imparting knowledge with his statements, it was going over Byrne's head. The others simply nodded, as if they understood. Ashton adjusted the sail, ignoring or not caring.

Past the clearing, the wild growth filled back in, and within two hours Ashton's focus shifted to the south. When he spotted some landmark he pulled in the sail and relashed it to the mast. Minutes later Byrne spotted a rail switch and a siding ahead. They rolled to a stop, and in the resulting quiet Byrne could hear the sound of moving water. Ashton jumped down, walked the rail to the switch and, after fiddling with a lock, shoved the mechanism, which swung a diverting set of rails to the siding. He motioned for Byrne to pump the cart forward, then used the switch to realign the rails. The men began to unload. Once armed and strapped with rifles and canteens and satchels of lunch, the group moved south along the rail bed that cut through a wall of pond apple trees and small cypress and then opened to the sandy shore of a narrow river.

"Mr. Ashton will lead us up the creek," McAdams said. "But keep alert, fellows. The game is numerous and, might I say, diverse."

Byrne singled out McAdams and finally asked the obvious: "If I may, Mr. McAdams. But what exactly am I supposed to do here?"

"Why, you're to watch our backs, Mr. Byrne," he replied as though the task was obvious. "You're the Pinkerton. Security, young man, security."

The creek narrowed, the palmetto thickened, and an uneven ground cover of sedge grasses, strangler fig and cypress roots caused all but Ashton to stumble and slog. Byrne found himself stepping into unexpected troughs of standing water, the thick mud at the bottom sucking at his now ruined brogans. He had to keep his eyes on the steps before him and take circuitous routes around obstacles. The air seemed to grow heavier and wetter, and he found it increasingly difficult to breath. Spanish moss hung from the trees like dark tattered rags, filtering the sun. This was the great swamp they talked about. Faustus had told him that it ran west to the horizon, a glade of enormous size, as mysterious as any deep forest. Less than an hour in, Byrne stopped to take a drink. When he looked up, there was no one in sight. The blue shirt covering Ashton's back was gone. McAdams, with the white bandana around his throat, had disappeared into the green.

"Christ!" he said, moving off in the direction he thought they'd gone. He could make his way through a maze of backstreets and alleys in the dark, but there was nothing familiar here. He would suddenly step into a hole and feel water up to his knees, the smell of it like a ripe whiff of old Mrs. McReady's vegetable cart. Each craggy cypress looked just like the one before. His landmarks were useless. He was moving around the hump of a root ball from a downed tree when he looked into a boil of grasses and swore he saw a huge log of marled wood with a row of teeth. He stopped stock still when the log's eyes came into view and stared into his own. Byrne swore he could hear the beast breathing.

They were in a stare off, an eight-foot alligator and a tenement kid from the Lower East Side. Then, as if the gator heard or somehow presaged what was to come, the reptile lunged. Its wicked movement caused Byrne to dive in the opposite direction away from the maw of teeth. A rifle's report sounded, and at the same instant, Byrne felt his left side pull at him like a whip had slapped his hip.

The sting came after he'd spilled to the ground and a burning heat followed. He watched the alligator practically crawl over him on its way to a nearby hole. Byrne saw the tail disappear, looked down for the hot spot at his side and saw a stain of blood on his shirt growing just above his hip and under his left rib. He swung his head around in the direction of the rifle shot and went decidedly quiet.

Whoever had fired did not call out. There was in fact no noise at first as he lay there. Then he heard a careful step, the snap of a twig, a slow slosh of water. If one of the hunters had taken a shot at the gator and had hit Byrne by accident, wouldn't the man shout? But if Byrne was the target, would that gunman now move in to finish the task? Byrne sat perfectly still and listened. Another slosh. The sound of fabric brushed by a tree limb. Byrne looked for cover. The hole where the alligator had taken refuge was an arm's length away. Another tick of sound, this time the light scratch of metal on wood. Byrne chose the gator over the rifle barrel and rolled quietly into the mouth of the hole. Again he listened, but the sound was muffled by the covering of muck and root and tangle of leaves. He closed his eyes and concentrated. Was that the sound of his breathing, or that of the reptile behind him? Was the animal cowering in the back of the hole, rattled by the explosion of the gun and this human chasing him into his hole?

This time, Byrne felt the footstep as much as heard it. The water and mud around him seemed to move with the nearby compression. Byrne reached into his pocket with his right hand and withdrew the baton. He found purchase against a root and dared to peek around the edge of the opening of the hole in time to see the barrel of a rifle slide into view, then a hand on the stock, then a booted foot stepping forward.

Byrne's swing was as pure and strong as an ax-man's. The baton extended with a snap from its own momentum and the hard metal struck solid on the man's kneecap, shattering bone and causing an ungodly scream. Byrne watched the man pitch forward, burying the barrel of his rifle deep into the muck in front of him. The gator behind him burrowed deeper into the hole at the sound of another species in horrific agony.

Byrne scrambled out with a fierceness that defied the bullet wound in his side and was quickly on Ashton's blue-shirted back, riding the man with a knee on his spine and slipping the baton across his throat in a choke hold. Byrne took a deep breath and blew the anger out, then shifted the baton up under Ashton's chin and pulled his face up.

"You may be the best guide they have in these parts, sir. But you aren't much of a shot," Byrne said, letting the words seep through his clenched teeth.

Ashton gurgled.

"At any rate, you aren't going to be doing much wilderness work with that split kneecap for awhile, so how about telling me who it was that hired you to kill me?"

Aston still didn't attempt an answer. Byrne moved his knee between the man's shoulder blades and forced his face down into the standing water. After a good count to twenty he let him back up for air.

"You might as well tell me, Ashton. The money won't do you any good dead. Tell me and you might crawl out of here to spend your fee on a good hickory cane."

Ashton blew out his breath, drooling water and phlegm.

"It was them," Ashton said. "McAdams and them. They wanted a huntin' accident."

"Why? What the hell threat am I to them? I'm a Pinkerton. Did they tell you I was a Pinkerton?"

"Didn't tell me shit. Just said you was gettin' too nosey."

"Nosey about what? The Negro woman?"

Ashton took another breath, wheezing through the pinched throat space Byrne was allowing him.

"Hell no. Nobody in these parts cares about some Negro. It's the real estate. That's all they ever care about is the land."

Byrne withdrew his baton and flipped the man over. He pulled the rifle out of the muck and ejected the load, then searched Ashton's belt and pockets and collected the ammunition.

"Wouldn't want you trying to shoot me in the back again," he said. He did a sweep of the jungle around him. The others might show up any minute, reacting to the single shot Ashton had taken or even the man's scream when his kneecap exploded. Or maybe they'd just hide like the gator and wait until they figured it was safe to come out. At any rate, Byrne wasn't staying around to discover if any of them had the balls to shoot him themselves. He knew there was a rock road near the coast similar to the one that he, Marjory and Santos had walked two nights previous that was used by carriages and wagons traveling between West Palm and the new town of Miami. If he could get to that road, help might run into him. While Ashton lay on his back holding his knee, Byrne examined his own wound. It was a through and through. The bullet had gone in just below his ribcage and he found the exit wound when his index finger slipped into the hole in his back. He took his shirt off, spun it into a rope and tied it around his waist, pulling the knot tight at the point of entry near his gut. He was bleeding heavily. He picked up Ashton's canteen, took a drink for good measure and began moving carefully to the east. The guide did not beg not to left alone. All he managed was to get up on one elbow, spit once in Byrne's direction and then watch the Pinkerton disappear.

CHAPTER TWENTY

AMADEUS FAUSTUS WAS NOT UNKNOWN TO the sheriff. Although the lawman was distrustful when word began to travel that there was a sharply dressed Mason in town who appeared to be of wealth and southern breeding, he simply watched Faustus carefully at first, and then dismissed him. The man did speak a high-falutin' English, which made Cox nervous. But the rich men of the island did the same, and Cox had learned to put away his initial feelings of inadequacy. Instead he dealt with them identically: he would be deferential to a point, bend to their wishes if there was something in it for him, and always be suspicious of their motivations. He knew they were all after the same thing: more. More land, more money, more champagne, more unearned respect.

His allegiance, if one could call it that, could only be to Flagler and by proxy some of his lieutenants. Flagler and his railroad were vehicles for money, and Cox did not even try to conceal that he too was lustful of large gobs of the stuff. Thus, this man Faustus got only the most basic from Cox: a building permit for his church or whatever it was to be, an occasional word of warning when the rail workers where due to invade his favorite tavern on Clematis, and a tip of the hat and a good morning greeting when they passed on the street.

So on Friday morning when Faustus showed up at the jail on Poinsettia Street announcing that he was there to represent the negra prostitute in the matter of killing the vagabond hustler, Cox was taken aback.

"Is that right, Mr. Faustus?" Cox said when the old man, in the company of that mouthy little bitch daughter of McAdams, met him in his upstairs office and asked to interview the prisoner. The bulbous sheriff took his time answering. His eyes worked deep inside his thick face, the pupils rolling across the puffed under lids like twin black marbles, first at Faustus, then over to the McAdams woman. It was, after all, the girl's father who had telegraphed him about the killing of that scumbag Bingham and had asked him to take care of it with as little impact on the island as possible. The fact that the dead man was found in the back yard of the whore made it simple. She shived him. End of story.

So why was McAdams' daughter showing up now? He'd been pondering the answer since the night she'd confronted his deputies outside the jail. Playing the soft-hearted slave lover. Did her old man know about that episode as well? There was something going on, and Cox came to the conclusion that he'd watch it play out and decide as things went along whether there was something in it for him.

"Well, Mr. Faustus, sir. If you are the negra's legal attorney, you know that you are by law afforded an opportunity to speak with your client," the sheriff said, standing up behind his desk and making a show of searching for the keys.

"I thank you, sir," Faustus said. "And I would like Miss McAdams to accompany me as she is, as one says, footing the bill."

Cox smiled his greasiest smile, the one meant to charm all the gussied up rich bitches over on the island.

"Why of course, anything to accommodate the McAdams family."

It wasn't much of a jail. When the sheriff unlocked the door and pushed it open, a dank, sour air rolled into their faces. The tiny woman was curled up against the far wall, shielding her eyes from the brightness of the sun. Faustus had seen worse prison cells in the war and even in the modern cities of Atlanta and Memphis and New York. It was actually no more than a bare wood room with four slats for windows on each side. No iron bars, no cages, no chains. There was a simple wooden chair in one corner, a stained mattress on the floor in another, a chamber pot in yet another. Marjory followed him in, hurried to the woman's side.

"Oh you poor dear thing," she said, going down on one knee and placing her palms on either side of Shantice Carver's face. The woman's eyes looked nervous and confused to Faustus, but he hesitated to put any meaning to the observation. Two well-dressed white people had just entered her jail room, and the sheriff who had arrested her closed the door behind them. If I were a young Negro housemaid with a murder charge hanging over my head, he thought, I too would be confused.

"Hello, Mizz Carver. Please don't be afraid, ma'am," Faustus said, with the kindliest voice he could muster. "My name is Amadeus Faustus. I am a lawyer and have been asked by Miss McAdams, who you know, to try and get you out of this mess."

The woman got to her feet and looked from one to the other, completely lost.

"Where's Mizz Ida?" she asked Marjory. "She got to help me, ma'am. Ya'll know she the only one can help me."

Marjory looked up at Faustus. "Miss Ida May Fluery is the head housekeeper at the Breakers where Shantice worked. She's kind of the stepmother to all the girls."

"An' where is Mizz Abby? You got to talk to Mizz Abby, ma'am. We was together when that man got hisself kilt," Shantice said, the rush of words coming at a high, desperate pitch. "We seen him down the Styx, but when we hightailed it out of there he was standin' straight up and healthy like a high-steppin' mule and wasn't no more dead than this fella here."

Faustus raised his eyebrows at the sudden flow of information.

"OK, OK, now Shantice. It's all right," Marjory said. "You know Mizz Ida and I tried our best to get you to safety? Right? You know that? So we'll do our best to help you now. OK? We are here to help you.

"Mr. Faustus here knows the law. He needs to ask you some questions so he can take care of this business with the sheriff and with the judge when he gets here. So just calm down now."

"Please, young lady," Faustus said, pulling the lone chair to her side. "Please sit down and take a few breaths."

Carver sat before Faustus as if a child before the schoolmaster.

"Miss McAdams," he said, and the authoritarian in his voice was obvious. "I will have to ask you to leave us along at this point, ma'am. It is simply against all legal convention for a second party to be witness to an attorney/client discussion. There are things this woman may say only to me as her legal representative, things that are privileged between us."

McAdams reacted as if she had been slapped. This was not the way she had intended, not the plan, not the play she needed to make. Yet here they were. Information that she desperately needed was at hand, and an outsider was telling her only he would be privy to it. She could squelch the entire situation right now, tell Faustus the deal was off. Would such an action bring her more scrutiny? Would the Carver woman tell him who and what she saw that night, even as McAdams stood outside the door? And what would Faustus do with that information if indeed this woman had seen everything? She had employed him, wouldn't he be beholden to her as well with his attorney/client argument? McAdams saw no immediate way out. She had gone too far to turn back now.

"Very well, Mr. Faustus. I leave it to your professional wisdom," she simply said and turned and slipped out the door.

The housemaid had not changed her demeanor, an underling, awaiting some form of scolding or punishment.

Faustus started in a comforting tone: "I need only for you to tell me your story, ma'am. Tell me your story, as clearly and honestly as you can. Start where you think all of this business with the dead man and the night of his undoing, the night of the carnival, began."

Carver took the few breaths as directed and balled her hands into fists in her lap as if a decision had been made. The truth was coming and damned be those whom the light would not be kind to.

"It was all Mizz Abby's idea," she began. "I ain't sayin' I didn't go along with it, but it wasn't me that come up with it."

"And who, exactly, is this Mizz Abby?" Faustus said.

"She Mizz Birch's housemaid. We been knowin' each other for a long time, since we was girls growin' up and workin' and such. She's my friend and don't pass no judgment on me because of what I do to get along."

"You mean the prostitution?"

"Tha's right," Carver said, her chin high. It was not pride, but any shame or need for justification had long been reconciled in her.

"We is friends an' we talk a lot together cause she on the inside of the hotel and I mostly worked outside, at the laundry and cleaning the kitchens and such. She mostly is with the rich folks and she knows things."

"OK," Faustus said, only needing to prime the pump at this point, keep the woman talking, the story would come in her own way.

"Well, I got customers, you know, men from the hotel that come out to my place for their needs. Sometimes Mizz Abby would tell them 'bout me if they asked, you know."

Faustus simply waited.

"So at the beginnin' of this season, it was her own boss that did the askin' and Mr. Birch himself come out for my company," she continued.

"You saw this Mr. Birch regularly?" he said.

"Couple times a week."

"And what changed?"

"Well, I done tol' Abby and she and me, we laughed about it and all. But then awhile ago Abby said that the Birches was thinkin' on gettin' rid of her. She been workin' for them for three seasons and they treated her good and she was mad.

"Abby knowed that Mizz Birch would rip the roof off if she knew her husband was off the porch with some nigger girl like me so she come up with this plan to get her share of money offen' him by sayin' she gonna tell the missus."

"Blackmail?"

"If'n that's what you call it."

"So did this Miss Abby confront Mr. Birch?"

"No, she too damn scairt to do it her own self so she asked me to do it an' I say uh-uh. I ain't gone mess up my business on doin' somethin' like that."

Faustus broke one of his own rules by skipping ahead.

"So you needed a go-between, someone to handle the negotiations?"

Carver stared at him for a moment, deciphering the words.

"We needed a man to do the threat, yeah. So's I knew this white man who, was, uh, well, I know he did things like that with white folks and we done set it up. He was going to tell Mr. Birch that he knew what was what and he would tell his wife unless he paid him not to. Then this white man was going to give the money to Abby."

"And the man was Mr. Bingham?"

"I ain't knowed his real name, but he the one dead for sure."

Faustus began to pace, an unconscious habit he undertook when trying to formulate questions or weigh information. The idea that a prostitute and a housemaid might concoct such a scheme was not inconceivable, but his experience with such folks in the past made him doubt that the women would shoot the man dead, and for what?

"On the night that this Mr. Bingham was killed, the night of the fire, my understanding is that you were not on the island."

The woman bowed her head.

"No, sir. That's not exactly right."

"No?"

"We was at the fair over this side, but then we went back cause Abby didn't want that man cheatin' us out our money."

"You knew when Mr. Bingham was to meet with Mr. Birch?"

"Yeah. An' we was there. Only hidin' round by Mr. Pott's boardin' house in the dark just watchin'."

"And what, pray tell, did you see?" Faustus' voice ratcheted up.

"The man, what you call Bingham, was at my place, back by the wood pile where Abby had tole' him."

"He was alone?"

"Yes, sir. All dressed up like some swell. Like some bidness man an all."

"And did Mr. Birch arrive while you were watching?"

"No, sir," Shantice said, but the quivering in her hands told Faustus there was more so he stood silently, waiting.

"But Mizz Birch did," she said.

"Mrs. Birch?" Faustus said, giving away his surprise.

"Yes, sir. We done heard someone walkin' up the road and walking hard. Then we seen Mizz Birch astridin' like a mad bull."

"And did she meet with Mr. Bingham?" Faustus asked.

"If'n she did, sir, we didn't see it. When we seen Mizz Birch come up we was scared and hid ourselves back in the bushes behind the boardin' house and then hightailed it back to the lake, sir."

"Before the fire?

"Yes, sir."

"And you never heard a gunshot?"

"No, sir."

Faustus took a second, assessing and processing the information and how it skewed his original hypothesis. Simplicity, he reminded himself. Rules of human behavior.

"Did you see anyone else there that night who might vouch for you, Mizz Carver, anyone at all?"

"No, sir. Wasn't anybody else. They was all over at the carnival."

Faustus had stopped his pacing. He had no reason not to believe her account, was in fact duty sworn to accept it as her attorney. At that point he went to the door and summoned McAdams. Marjory hesitated at first, searching the attorney's eyes for some clue. Now she had taken on the look of the student before the headmaster.

"I thank you for your candor, Miss Carver," Faustus said, turning to the house woman. "And we shall be in touch before the magistrate arrives."

"You gone get me free?" Carver asked in a voice touched with only the smallest tinge of hope.

"I will do my best, young lady," Faustus said, moving to leave. A thought, a recollection of a piece of information that Byrne had shared from his friends the binder boys, entered his head. He turned back to Carver.

"One more question," he said, and she looked up. "When you were watching this man, this Mr. Bingham, you said he was dressed like a business man. What made you believe that?"

"He was in fancy clothes. Not like some party or somethin'. But not like he was comin' to the Styx to do somethin' shady like. An' he was carryin' a bidness case. Like a leather case that would hold papers and such."

Faustus dwelt on the answer for a moment and went out the door.

CHAPTER TWENTY-ONE

WHEN BYRNE AWOKE, HE WAS FREEZING. The hard light of midday was in his eyes. His back was either on fire or frostbitten. He turned his head to the right and saw a wet wooden sideboard next to his face. He turned to the left and looked a dead fish in the eye. When he began to regain his sense of smell he closed his eyes again and hoped this was not hell.

The last thing he recalled was finding the road, a trail of crushed rock barely wide enough for a wagon. He'd been limping, holding his knotted shirt to his side for two hours. When one entire side of the shirt and one loosed sleeve became soaked in blood, he'd quit looking at the wound. On the road he'd meant to turn north, but his brain was too blurred and spinning to be sure he'd made the right selection. The sun suffered an eclipse, its center gone black, and when the rim of light around it came down over his head, he'd passed out.

"Michael! Michael Byrne. Can you hear me?"

Called by the devil, Byrne thought, hearing the words and expecting Lucifer himself. A face started coming into focus. Danny? Had he joined his brother in hell?

"Come on, son. Put some effort into it now," a familiar voice said. The intent eyes of Amadeus Faustus looked down on him.

"OK, boys. Let's get him down out of there and into the back of the bar," Faustus said. "Watch that wound on his side now."

With that, four men slid Byrne down out of a fish wagon loaded with red snapper and ice, carried him into the tavern, and laid him out on a table in back.

Faustus went to work without a word: soothing, questioning, or otherwise. He used a razor sharp knife to cut away pieces of the shirt still tied around Byrne's waist. He loosened the pants and stripped them off as well, probing with careful fingers around Byrne's rib cage and then his hip. A boy came in carrying a large wooden case.

"Put it just here, Adam, and get some water for this man if you please." Byrne looked at the case, trying to determine what might be coming. The box was labeled with a distinctive cursive lettering spelling Johnson and a red cross.

Faustus opened it and withdrew a bottle of liquid. He'd left the knot of Byrne's shirt in place, fastened there with both dried and sticky blood, and thus staunched some of the flow. Now Faustus pulled at it, pouring antiseptic over the area.

"Sssssss," Byrne hissed between his teeth.

"Easier to work with wounds on a corpse," Faustus said. "But I still prefer working on the living. Don't you, Mr. Byrne?"

"In this case, yes," Byrne said, his head coming more alert with the pain. His voice was raw and foreign to his ears.

With the wound exposed, Faustus took a dressing from the case and began dabbing at its edges.

"Fairly large caliber. Smaller than a musket ball but bigger than a handgun, although you've had a few hours to pucker a bit."

"Rifle of some kind," Byrne managed.

Adam returned with a beer mug full of water. Faustus directed the lad to pour some into Byrne's mouth. "Not too much now," he said without looking, concentrating instead on the entry wound.

The feeling in Byrne's throat was cool.

"Loss of blood and dehydrated," Faustus said. "You were lucky the fish wagon came along when it did. The driver said you were in an unconscious pile when he spotted you under a cabbage palm. Not quite like the gutters of your Lower East Side but still an ignominious spot to die. Can you roll onto your side, please?"

Again Byrne hissed at the pain when Faustus poked the corner of the antiseptic soaked swab into the hole in his back.

"I trust you know what you're doing, Faustus." Byrne said. "This isn't Appomattox."

"Ha! You're not in the hands of an amateur, my friend. And in fact I've twice read *Johnson & Johnson's Modern Methods of Antiseptic Wound Treatment*. I believe a copy came with the first aid kit."

When Faustus was done with the wounds he and the boy helped Byrne off the table and into a back room of the tavern. A cot was pushed against one wall and they lay him down on the old stained mattress. When he tried to close his eyes, the walls began to spin. The room was dark and dry and the temperature high. Byrne could feel the tingle of blood coming back into his skin.

"The wagon driver was smart enough to cover your side with the ice he had aboard. It probably kept you from bleeding out more than you did," Faustus said, sitting nearby in a straight-backed chair.

"The bastards tried to kill me," Byrne said, looking at the old Mason but seeing the faces of Ashton, McAdams, Pearson and Birch.

Faustus sat quiet for a moment, letting Byrne's anger seep out of the way.

"Who, exactly, are they?" he finally said. "And what do you think their motivation to kill a Pinkerton employed by the most powerful man in the state would be?"

When Byrne listed out the men on the hunting trip, Faustus seemed unable to let the names of Flagler's right-hand, the manager of the Poinciana and a banker of high esteem sit under the title of attempted murderers in his head.

"The guide, Ashton, did the dirty work, and I smashed his kneecap to pieces for his trouble," Byrne said.

"I heard he was brought into Dr. Lansing's early today," Faustus agreed. "The three others you've named brought him in on one of the pump carts. Some of the boys said it was quite a sight, a banker and a hotel big shot working the pump and perspiring like pigs, I believe they said."

Byrne wryly smiled at the vision.

"They described it as a hunting accident," Faustus said. "You've reason to believe differently?"

"He would have blown my head off if the damned alligator hadn't scared hell out of me first. The lizard was eight feet in front of me. No way Ashton was aiming at it and not me."

"Did you question Mr. Ashton as to his actions?"

"He was, what you might call, forthcoming, considering there was steel baton across his throat." Byrne said. "According to him, it was real estate. Said I was getting too nosey about some deal. What the hell would that mean? I haven't so much as considered buying a piece of land even if I had the money."

"But what are you getting your nose into?" Faustus said. "The shooting death of your own brother, a man, and excuse my bluntness here, who was known as a swindler and not just in the real estate field. Then there's your defense of a poor Negro prostitute arrested for said killing. And let's not forget your wooing of a prominent young woman. Don't deny it sir, I long ago learned to read the eyes of incipient love and the sprinklings of lust."

"She knew my brother."

Faustus raised his eyebrows.

"She admitted she knew him. And she's admitted being there when they found his body." The ache in his side was perhaps the lesser of two pains. "So what the hell else does she know about this whole affair, including who killed Danny?"

For several moments, Faustus sat mute. Then he leaned forward, putting his elbows on his knees and speaking in measured, clear statements of fact.

For the next hour he recounted verbatim his interview with Shantice Carver, her admission of the blackmail scheme, her co-conspirator Abby, and her observation of Mrs. Birch approaching Byrne's brother in the dark near the place his body was found.

"Whoa, whoa, whoa," Byrne interrupted. "Birch, did you say? Birch was the name of one of the Poinciana men on the hunt this morning. He was introduced as some kind of banker. And I recall his face from the city, a man who paid his way out of a prostitution raid at the Haymarket Dance Hall."

Faustus simply stared at Byrne out of the shadows.

"I don't believe in coincidence, my young friend. And I doubt that you, as a good investigator, do either."

"I'm not an investigator," Byrne said. "I'm a Pinkerton guard, as you and everyone else reminds me."

"Ha!"

"What ha?"

"I do have contacts in the north, despite my southern disposition. And my inquiries have resulted in an interesting description of a man with your name and physical appearance who was involved in some investigation of the most dangerous sort.

"You at one time took on the role of tracking the misdeeds of your own superiors and their political bosses. Highly placed and dangerous politicians at that."

Silence from the bed.

"In fact, rumor has it that a compromise was made. Your life may have been spared if and only if you left the city and never came back."

"Never was not a word that was used," Byrne said quietly.

"Nonetheless, I don't believe you when you say you're not a born investigator. And I don't believe that you can observe a moral and ethical misdeed without being pulled to make it right."

"What is this, the code of the Masons or something?" Byrne said, his voice sounding more cynical than he wanted.

"It is not just a code of Masons. It is a code of true men in a civilized society."

"You call this civilized?" Byrne said, sweeping his hand across the dingy room.

Faustus laughed. "Ah, the voice of a true New Yorker. Nothing exists outside of Kings County."

Byrne thought back to his friend Jack Brennan and his squad of young Pinkertons who'd never stepped outside the city, and he had to admit to Faustus' portrayal. He decided to change the subject.

"What else did Carver say she witnessed that night?"

"She denied seeing anyone else at the scene of the crime and swears she did not hear a gunshot nor did she see the fire begin."

"Did Marjory say anything? I'd sure as hell be surprised if she didn't know this Birch woman, if they're as prominent as they appear."

"She said she knew of her," Faustus said, but his voice betrayed him.

"And you think she's lying?"

"It's a very close society on the island. The separation between the daughter of Flagler's right hand man and the wife of a prominent banker would be thin at best.

"But I plan to speak with Mrs. Birch tomorrow to see if she has any of her own insights on the events described by Mizz Carver. And in addition, your information about your brother's new affinity for carrying his binder case was also confirmed by our client. She saw him with it on the night in question. So I shall also be visiting the mortician for another round of questions about its disappearance." Faustus stood. "For now I suggest you get some rest. A bullet wound can be quite debilitating if not given the time to heal and fight off infection."

With that the old Mason left the room, and Byrne soon fell into a fitful sleep with the images of gators and Tammany and a naked Marjory McAdams swimming through his head.

CHAPTER TWENTY-TWO

THIS TIME BYRNE WOKE WITH THE sound of clinking glass in his ears, the smell of stale beer and cigar smoke and hot cooking oil. A sudden anxiety came into his head—was he in New York, in the trash alley behind McSorely's? When he felt for the curb, he heard a moan. He was back in his mother's apartment, she was dying in pain, her face ashen, a tear glistening down a grayed cheek. He forced his eyes open, determined to help her. The wound at his side bit him hard and the moan came again, from his own mouth.

Reality. I was shot yesterday. I'm in Florida, in the back room of a tavern and there are slats of sunshine coming in low through the window, which means it's morning. Faustus is supposed to be here. We need to find out what Mrs. Birch knows. And shit, I was shot yesterday.

He swung his feet off the cot, sat upright and probed at the bandage Faustus had applied the night before. It was in place and not spotted on the outside, a good sign even though it still hurt like hell when he moved. Carefully, he pulled on a pair of clean pants and a cotton shirt that had been placed at the foot of the cot, his own ruined clothing gone from sight. When he felt he could stand, he did, while a bright light pulsed behind his eyes causing a bit of a swoon. He refused to go down. A minute, maybe two, and the dizziness passed. He moved to the door that opened to the barroom and went on through.

"Well, top o' the day, Mr. Byrne," said the woman at the bar, who was busy stocking beer mugs and bottles and any other thing that could create noises meant to penetrate a man's brain.

"Many a man has stumbled through that door in the mornin', sir, but you'd rank right up with the best of them for lookin' like an overrun dog."

"Aye, and to you," Byrne said, making his way to a stool at the rail and finding purchase with one haunch to steady himself.

Without comment the barkeep poured him an ale from a tapped keg and placed the mug and a hard'boiled egg in front him.

"Patti Graham's the name," she said, extending her hand. "This here works for hangovers, sir, so it can't be any harm to a gunshot wound neither."

Byrne shook the woman's fingers, and then sipped at the beer, a blessing in his throat. He took another.

"Heaven," he whispered.

"That's what they all say," the bartender said, pushing a lock of her blonde hair out of the way. "Hell, I bet Mr. Faustus last night that a bullet through the gizzard wouldn't put a good man down any more than a feisty night on the town.

"He said, Mr. Faustus that is, that he would be in this mornin' so take yer time, sir. That egg'll start you back to healin', guaranteed."

With the help of a fingerbowl full of shaved salt, Byrne had finished the first egg and was onto another by the time Faustus arrived.

"Now isn't that a fine sight to see? Belly up to the bar the very day after cheating the dark angel of death," he said.

"Maybe there's just magic in that Johnson & Johnson," Byrne said, feeling better with his second mug of beer.

"I see the clean clothes fit," Faustus said. "You can wash up out back next to the privy where there's a barrel of clean rain water. And since you're in such good shape, taking refreshment and all, I believe I'll be off to the undertakers and a possible visit with one Mrs. Birch on the island."

Byrne slipped off the stool, keeping the look of pain out of his face.

"Give me ten minutes then and I'll be right with you."

Faustus exchanged glances with the bartender, who only shrugged her shoulders.

"Your call, son," he said, slipping up onto Byrne's empty stool, and ordering a morning beer for himself.

Faustus and a limping Byrne were making their way down Clematis Street when they saw Maltby the mortician heading toward them.

"Well fancy that, I was just now heading to see you, Mr. Maltby," Faustus said. Maltby was less enthusiastic than when they'd first visited him and pointed out the discrepancies in Danny Byrne's autopsy.

"Yes, well gentlemen, I am on my way to the island on an urgent matter."

"Oh my," Faustus said. "I do hope one of our guests has not met an untimely death."

"No, sir. There's been an accident and I'm told a housemaid has fallen to her death down an elevator shaft."

"Really?" Faustus said. "And did they inform you of this woman's name?"

"Abigail Morrisette was the name they gave," Maltby said, information that, considering the station of the victim, seemed irrelevant. "She was a Negro woman who was employed there."

At the sound of the name, Byrne turned to look out over the lake to the Poinciana. Abby, he thought. Another witness dead? Had she known his brother too?

"Well then, in that case," Faustus said, "I do believe we're heading in the same direction. May we accompany you, sir?"

The undertaker was too flummoxed to object. All three men walked down to the nearby docks and boarded the ferry boat to the hotel. The group remained relatively silent on the short trip across the lake. Maltby was no doubt trying to figure out the angles; why would Faustus be interested in yet another death on the island? And would he again be asked to quash any questions over the matter. These things were best taken care of quietly.

Faustus and Byrne were turning questions of their own. What had Abby seen the night of the fire, and what did she see transpire between Danny Byrne and Mrs. Birch? Was it something that would have been worth killing her for?

When the ferry tied up at the dock on Palm Beach, Faustus and Maltby were the first ones off. Byrne lagged behind, leaning into his wound.

"Please, you two go ahead. There is a ride here for me," Byrne said nodding to the so-called Afromobile and its stoic driver parked at the side. "I'll follow when I catch my breath."

Faustus gave him a silent look: I know where you're going and be damned careful, it said.

At the concierge desk of the Royal Poinciana, Maltby's papers, written on Dade County Sheriff's stationary and authorizing him to remove the body of the victim, got them an escort to the basement of the northern wing of the hotel. Along the way Faustus, with an air of officialdom, asked questions of the concierge.

"Can you tell us, sir, when this unfortunate accident occurred?"

"Very early this morning, I'm afraid. Perhaps five or six."

"You're not sure of the exact time?"

"There were few people up at that hour other than early staff members, and as far as we know there were no reports of any sort of, well, screaming."

"Then who discovered the body?"

"I believe it came to our attention through one of the wait staff. He had encountered difficulty in getting the freight elevator to work for a delivery on the fifth floor, and when one of our maintenance men arrived to rectify the problem, well, there she was."

"I see," said Faustus. Maltby remained silent. "And who, may I inquirer, identified the unfortunate woman?"

"There was some difficulty at first," the concierge said. "There are so many housemaids and linen staff and such, and they all look the same."

Faustus raised an eyebrow in disdain, but the look was lost on the concierge. "I believe the original waiter was brought into the shaft and recognized her as a Miss Abigail Morrisette. Her records indicated that she was assigned to the Birch family, one of our more prominent seasonal guests. Mrs. Birch is quite upset."

It was the first time that the concierge gave any indication of empathy over the situation.

The men followed the concierge to the basement.

In the tight space, Faustus noted the presence of electrical wiring running under the floorboard above his head. The availability of electrical service inside of homes and structures was inconceivable even five years ago in the South, he knew, and would have been only a dream in frontier Florida before the arrival of Mr. Flagler. The group moved to a now open service door that led to the very bottom of the elevator shaft,

On the bare floor lay the crumpled body of a young Negro woman, perhaps in her early twenties, dressed in the typical maid's uniform of the day. Her face covered with what appeared to be a dinner table napkin. She could have been sleeping there but for the impossible angle of her right leg, which was folded like a hanger, the knee bent in the opposite direction from what would be normal.

Her left forearm was similarly broken, snapped at a midway point between the wrist and the elbow, forming a grotesque third bend in the arm.

Faustus crouched at the woman's head and removed the napkin. Abigail Morrisette's neck was obviously broken and a certain amount of rigor mortis had already set in. Pulled by gravity, the blood had drained from her face, already seeking the lowest parts of her body.

"That's enough for me." Maltby was watching over Faustus' shoulder. He turned to the concierge, who was looking up into the rising shaft, avoiding the two men's inspection. "I will require a thick blanket and two men with strong backs to remove the body to the mainland."

The concierge nodded. "Certainly. The sooner the better. We must get the elevator back in service before the luncheon rush."

But Faustus did not stand. Instead he took Abigail Morrisette's head in his hands and moved his fingers over her scalp, finding flat contusions from blunt trauma, but no unusual shapes such as the use of a blade or an obvious dent in the bone that some hand-held object might cause.

"Satisfied, Mr. Faustus?" Maltby asked.

Faustus raised one finger to him and took the woman's right hand in his own, straightened her frozen fingers and inspected her fingernails. On more than one occasion during the war he had been witness to the aftermath of rapes and other degradations visited on women of the South by Yankee soldiers. And although proof was rarely used to any legal remedy, there were times when a family took some comfort when Faustus was able to tell them that their daughter fought and scratched against such attacks. Removing a pen knife from his pocket, Faustus scraped under the dead woman's nails and looked closely at what he could only speculate might be a trace of powdered flesh.

He asked Maltby to assist him in turning the body over. The undertaker gave Faustus an angry look, but bent to help. Faustus carefully looked for obvious wounds or blood on the woman's clothing, but found nothing. But gripped in her left hand he discovered a matted and crushed wad of feather. Faustus was a student of the unique birds of Florida and was thus an opponent of the fashion of using their plumes to decorate women's hats. The wad of this feather held the pinkish tinge of the plume of a roseate spoonbill, one of the most uniquely colored wading birds of the state. How a maid would have one held tightly in her dead hand would be a question for another woman.

He stood. "I, sir, will require an introduction to Mrs. Birch."

The concierge knitted his brow and looked from Maltby to Faustus and then back to Maltby. The undertaker remained unambiguously silent.

"Very well," the bureaucrat said and then extended his palm toward the service door. "Shall we retreat?"

While Maltby attended to the removal of Abby Morrisette's body, Faustus was taken to the Birch apartment on the fourth floor. There would be a different excavation here, entailing a bit more tact and a lot less muscle.

With the concierge as his introduction, Faustus was greeted at the door by a young black woman, dressed just as the corpse downstairs. She was a replacement from the housemaid pool, and despite her age, which Faustus guessed at twelve or thirteen, she was already adept at greeting important white folk with deference and stoic servitude. Not once did she look up at the visitors.

"Yes, sir. Mizz Birch be out on the porch. I will tell her you are here."

The girl left them at the threshold. Faustus looked about the vestibule, sneaking glances around the corner at the collections of art pieces, cut glass objects and hand-carved furniture. A lot to lose, he thought to himself.

Within a suitable five minutes of waiting, a woman with the carriage of a tired old lioness approached, her hands folded in front of her large breasts and stomach. She was dressed in a dark conservative skirt that reached to the floor and a pristine white blouse with a high embroidered neck collar that rose up under her chin. Her face was inquisitive. Not unusual for a person being greeted by the coroner, yet her eyes were intent and steely and on full alert. If she had been grieving, it had not been with tears.

"Mrs. Birch, if I may," started the concierge. "This is Mr. Amadeus Faustus. He is working with the undertaker's office with our, uh, situation."

"Mrs. Birch," Faustus said, "My deepest condolences, madam. I understand that Miss Morrisette was a long-time employee and I hate to bother you at such a tragic time."

Faustus extended his hand and Mrs. Birch took it, just by the fingers, nearly touching the Masonic ring with her own thumb but never taking her eyes off his face.

"Have we met before, Mr. Faustus? In New York perhaps?"

"I don't believe so, ma'am. I certainly would have remembered."

"How is it, sir, that you know of my long-time employ and personal admiration of Miss Abigail?"

Faustus had his hat in his hand, and they had not yet been offered a chance to step inside.

"I've had the opportunity to speak extensively with one of Miss Morrisette's close friends, one Shantice Carver, who elucidated on her, Miss Morrisette's that is, close relationship to you and your husband."

Faustus saw the muscles in the woman's jaw tighten. "Mr. Conlon, unless you have any specific inquiries of your own, would you please leave us alone? I believe Mr. Faustus and I need to speak alone."

Not only was the concierge nonplussed by the request, he fairly bolted from the apartment with as much politeness as would not slow him down.

"Will you join me on the patio, sir?" Mrs. Birch said.

Faustus followed the woman through her expansive parlor and out through the French doors into the sunlight. When she sat in the big Adirondack chair Faustus noted there was a half-filled goblet of wine nearby. Mrs. Birch took a substantial draught from the glass before asking Faustus if he would join her.

"I will have a brandy if there's any available."

Birch rang an annoying silver bell and the young maid appeared.

"Bring us the bottle of brandy from the parlor bar and a glass for Mr. Faustus. And do bring more of my chateau, dear."

Faustus stood at the railing looking out on the deep green of the fairways beyond.

"Was Mr. Birch as fond of Abby as you?" he asked.

"Other than his use of her in procuring a whore for himself, no," Mrs. Birch said. "I doubt that he even noticed the girl in the three years she was with us. Though his obvious taste for Negro women leaves me to wonder if I was misled in that also."

Faustus blinked at the woman's bluntness. If she was drunk, it did not show. If she'd somehow obtained the news of her husband's philandering and was simply angered, he would use that to advantage.

"May I assume then, madam, that you are aware of your husband's, uh, dealings with the Carver woman?"

"Dealings? Is that the way you southern Masons refer to whoring and prostitution? Dealings?"

The maid returned, bringing the brandy and wine and bearing a look of embarrassment on her cheeks. She put the liquor down on the table and, forgetting to pour, started backing through the doors.

"Close the doors behind you, dear, if the conversation makes you uncomfortable," Mrs. Birch said with a chuckle.

Faustus filled her glass with wine and poured a substantial tumbler of brandy for himself. They both drank. Now it was his turn to be blunt.

"My understanding, Mrs. Birch, is that you were here on the island the night of the fire in the Styx. It has come to my attention that you were in fact in the woods that evening, seen in the company of a man known as Mr. Bingham, now deceased. If you will, madam, could you tell me about that meeting?"

Mrs. Birch took yet another draught of wine. "Would you like me to start before or after I shot the bastard in the throat and stuffed his bribery money into his offensive mouth?" she asked.

Byrne had a bicycle carriage driver take him to the northern entrance of the Royal Poinciana where he could enter through the side door. The night of the ball, Harris had given him a quick tour of the first floor where the executive suites were located, and it didn't take long for him to find the office of Mr. McAdams. He hesitated at the door, taking a deep breath against the pain in his side, then went into McAdams' rooms without knocking. Byrne knew the art of busting down doors of gambling and whore houses as a cop. You usually had to watch for the scrambling customers and employees scurrying out before they got caught in a lineup, but rarely did you have to be concerned that someone was going to take a shot at you or draw a blade. Byrne figured his confrontation with McAdams would be even more business-like. Yet the man and his colleagues had tried to kill him yesterday, so when he entered, his steel baton was out.

McAdams was caught sitting behind a large walnut desk on the other side of the room. The look on the man's face was probably quite foreign to him: surprise and fluster passed through his eyes and a dumfounded O shaped on his mouth. Byrne grabbed a wooden straight chair, swung it to the door and jammed its top rail under the knob. Flagler's architects had not yet adopted the habit of hanging office doors to open out instead of in and the chair would provide a lock that couldn't easily be broken.

"Well, my God, Mr. Byrne. How wonderful to see you, alive and well!"

Byrne took two long strides across the room and finished his approach with a whip of the baton. The whoosh ended with a crack across McAdams' desk top, shattering a porcelain figurine and sending a metal tipped ink pen flipping through the air until it stuck point first into the wallpaper to the left.

"Don't start, McAdams," Byrne said, his voice hard but in control. "Your plan to shut me up with a bullet in the Glades leaves you in a poor position to backpeddle now."

The rip of the baton had frozen McAdams with his knees flexed, hands still on either of the chair armrests, defenseless.

"Well," he said. "Obviously our Mr. Ashton overestimated the accuracy of his firearms skills. You were supposed to have bled out before we even got back to town."

"Hunting accident, eh?" Byrne said. McAdams was giving it up far too early for his liking.

"Something like that, yes," McAdams said. "But you weren't supposed to still be walking around asking questions."

McAdams had straightened his legs, maybe gaining confidence and Byrne knew better than to allow it. He poked the man in the chest with the baton, forcing enough pressure to McAdams' sternum to make it hurt, enough to make him stumble and sit back in his chair. A flash of fear came into McAdams' eye. This was not a man accustom to physical violence.

"Are you admitting that you tried to kill me?" he said, trying to show enough anger to jack up the fear factor. "Just because I know about this whole real estate swindle you guys have going?"

Byrne had no idea what Ashton had been talking about when he'd explained the motive for killing him out in the glades. He was bluffing. But you use the little you have to get more. It was one of Danny's old tricks and a detective's tactic. Turn their words back on them.

"We knew you were poking around in affairs that were none of your business," McAdams said, an air of control returning to his voice, the one he'd used on the handcar out to the glades. "It was our business, a quiet business, a quiet affair until other parties got involved. There is a way to do such things in a civilized manner."

"Like killing the messenger of bad news, sticking a wad of money in his mouth and then setting up some poor Negro housemaid to take the blame. That's civilized?"

"That was never supposed to happen," McAdams said. "Mr. Bingham was supposed to conduct himself in a straightforward manner. Sell the land documentation for the price agreed and walk away. It was a business proposition, nothing more."

Byrne was winging it now. He took the baton from McAdams' chest and began using the tip to flip over papers on the man's desk.

"You wanted the land. Bingham wanted the money. It should have been simple. Why kill him?"

"He was dead before we got there," McAdams said in a way that sounded like he was actually disappointed.

"We, Mr. McAdams?" Byrne said. "You mean Birch and Pearson? You must be talking about your co-conspirators because you were still on the train out of New York with me when he was killed."

"None of us killed him, Mr. Byrne. He was dead before anyone of us got there. The meeting was set up in the Styx because it was considered a safe place on that particular night when it was supposed to be empty. But when they arrived, Bingham had already been shot."

Byrne tapped the shaft of the baton again on the desk top, the armrests of the chair, the head rest only inches behind McAdams' skull.

"And why not you, Mr. McAdams? If you were the one to put this all together, why didn't you make the payoff yourself?"

"As you said, I was on the train. My duties are not easily discarded. And there was a deadline. The property had to be cleared and the paperwork signed or the deal was off. Bingham was the bearer of the deed and he'd been pushing the price higher and higher, trying to use the time constraint to make us barter."

"Sounds like a sharp businessman to me."

"He was a cheat and a bastard," McAdams said.

Byrne's baton crashed down on the desk, this time splitting a piece of the hardened walnut on the edge nearest to McAdams. He was not going to tell this man that it was his brother who was killed.

"But you still sent a woman to deal with him instead of doing it yourselves," Byrne said.

"I had no idea Marjory was going to take on the task herself," McAdams said. "I thought she was going to get Birch to do it."

Byrne froze at the admission. It was his turn for shock. He'd pieced together an assumption that Birch had sent his wife to make the land deal and that the prostitute and Abby Morrissette had gotten it all wrong. He was even entertaining the possibility that Danny had seen a chance to kill two birds with one meeting, a real estate swindle and a blackmailing at the same time.

The possibility that Marjory McAdams had anything to do with it was a blow.

"Marjory? You sent your own daughter to pull this off?"

"I already said I didn't send her," McAdams said. "But you underestimate my daughter if you think she lacks the wherewithal to carry out such a task. She is quite capable. And she proved so by acquiring the deed as expected."

"She has the land deed? This document you bought from Bingham that gives you title to the land that the Styx was built on?"

"Marjory and I kept in touch via the telegraph. She passed on business messages to me so she was aware of the timetable we were working against. She elected to take the matter into her own hands and paid Mr. Bingham for the deed. The fire was a fortunate accident that cleared the land."

Jaysus, Byrne thought. The man is actually proud of what he and his daughter had done, like it was some brilliant accomplishment, acquiring valuable land where a man lay dead. Again he let anger rule his hand and the baton whooshed down again with a ripping blow.

"A man has been killed, McAdams," Byrne snapped, raising his voice for the first time. "Peoples' homes and possessions burned. For a real estate deal?"

McAdams went quiet. Byrne could tell by the man's breathing that he was consciously trying to calm himself, like he might do in a boardroom during hard negotiations.

"You don't understand the ramifications," he said, his voice under control. "This island, in fact this state, is about to turn a corner. And the new avenues that open will make many men rich beyond their dreams."

"Wrong, McAdams. You don't understand the ramifications of a conspiracy to murder. It's a charge that will put you all in jail where riches don't spend well."

"Murder? My God man, there was no forethought of murder. That's not the way we do business."

"Right, you hire others to do that," Byrne said, swallowing the pain in his side rather than let McAdams see him wince.

"There is no proof of any such thing," McAdams said. "And besides I believe someone is already in custody for the murder of Mr. Bingham. As for your unfortunate hunting accident, Mr. Ashton is deeply sorry."

Byrne folded up the baton and slid it into his pocket. He would not need intimidation any longer. McAdams had said enough.

"We'll see what a judge has to say about that when Miss Carver's hearing is held tomorrow. I believe your cover-up of the crimes you have committed will be exposed."

McAdams folded his hands across his stomach in a classic pose of deep thought and let Byrne turn toward the door, but when the Pinkerton was halfway across the room he spoke again, this time in a voice of paternalism.

"We have many powerful friends and connections in New York, Mr. Byrne. In the tapestry of money and business and politics are found many crossovers, the reach of which are myriad and deep."

Byrne turned.

"I have no use for your money, sir. So I'm not interested in your bribery, or anything else you or your conniving family might offer."

He started toward the door. McAdams let him take two more steps.

"But do you have an interest in the whereabouts of your father, Mr. Byrne?" he said, his voice sounding self-assured, confident, and not a little greasy.

CHAPTER TWENTY-THREE

THE ARRAIGNMENT HEARING FOR ONE SHANTICE Carver on the charge of murder was to be held in the stuffy second-floor room of the jailhouse. Faustus was there early, standing at the foot the outside staircase, smoking a Cuban cigar and watching the procession of attendees climb the stairs.

The traveling judge, John E. Born, had ridden in his carriage from the town of Juno, where the Dade County seat was established. Faustus knew that Born had been newly appointed as the third county judge in the area by Gov. William Bloxham. He also knew that Bloxham was a staunch backer of Flagler and considered the railroad baron a land developer who would save the state from its present financial ruin. In Bloxam's first term as governor he'd sold four million acres of state land in the Everglades for twenty-five cents an acre to bolster state coffers, a real estate move only a true swampland-for-money entrepreneur could love. Faustus wondered about the new judge's integrity, whether he would owe his allegiance to the governor, and thus the Flagler powers on the island.

The night before, Byrne and Faustus shared what they'd each discovered. Mrs. Birch's admission to Faustus of firing the shot that killed Danny was hearsay. But Faustus put it out there first, unadorned, and had watched carefully as the muscles in Byrne's jaws tightened.

Byrne had put on his characteristic, internal and stoic face, and Faustus had waited an appropriate time in silence. "It was my duty to request that the woman turn herself in to the sheriff," he said at last.

"And?" Byrne said.

"If I can recall her words correctly, she simply stated 'My dear sir, we do not turn ourselves in. We hire the likes of you to avoid such messiness.'"

Byrne recounted his meeting with Mr. McAdams, explaining the real estate deal that Danny had somehow become involved with, and the fact that Marjory McAdams had been involved all along. Faustus stored all his newfound knowledge away. Today his goal was to have the charges against Miss Carver dropped, repercussions be damned.

Next up the staircase were the sheriff and his cadre of deputies. The fat man wore a tight but not unfriendly look on his face.

"Good day, counselor," he said to Faustus as he tipped his hat and climbed the stairs, his huge legs pumping like mechanical pile drivers. Faustus could nearly feel the shivering of the wooden structure beside him. Trailing behind the sheriff, almost as an afterthought, was man Faustus knew to be the attorney Marcus Willings, a real estate lawyer who had been appointed as the temporary prosecutor for the district. He was a civilized and studious man, given to bookish language and a also given to bend to the sheriff's wishes in all matters. His was simply to be Cox's puppet.

Next to arrive was a thin, bespectacled man that Faustus recognized immediately as the editor of the local *Gazetteer* newspaper whose creative nickname was "Town."

"Glad that you could come, Mr. Cryer," Faustus said.

"Not a problem, Mr. Faustus. It just so happens that I too am to face the judge this morning in a civil matter."

"A civil matter, sir?"

"The sheriff has filed suit against me and the newspaper for slander," Cryer said. "You do recall the crusade we led last year against the rampant crime threatening the city and Sheriff Cox's inability to handle the situation?"

"Yes, certainly," said Faustus. "I believe that at one point the man threatened to hickory whip you."

Cryer chuckled at the recollection. "But I am rather more intrigued by your message on the murder charge and your investigation, Mr. Faustus."

"Then my effort was not in vain, sir. Though I admit my motive for inviting you was to have the proceeding recorded by someone outside of the parties involved."

"Again, a role I take as a matter of duty. It is what we do."

At nine o'clock the first-floor door to the jail was opened and Shantice Carver was led out by a single deputy. She was dressed in the same clothing she'd worn when they arrested her days ago. With her head bent low and feet shuffling she looked like a lost soul heading for the gallows. Faustus stepped out. "Miss Carver. Pick your head up, my dear, you will be walking from this place in a short time as a free woman or my name is not Amadeus Faustus."

The woman's eyes met his, and their redness, their utter deadness, took Faustus back to a place on a battlefield in North Carolina in 1865 where he did not want to go, to faces that he had struggled mightily to forget.

"Please, my dear," he said. "Despite our circumstances in life, hope is not a dirty word."

The guard snorted and pushed Carver forward up the staircase. Faustus turned and looked across the street before heading up himself. Leaning against the rough hewn wall of a new dry goods store, Byrne was watching. He tipped his head to the old Mason. It was a sign to Faustus that steps had been taken to guarantee certain evidence had been secured as they had discussed the night before.

The sheriff's sparsely appointed office had been reorganized as an impromptu courtroom. A dozen cane chairs were arranged on the open floor facing Cox's desk as if expecting a crowd. Faustus knew this to be a ploy, only done for show. Citizens of the area were openly restricted from attending court proceedings by the sheriff ever since the lynching two years ago of the alleged killer of the property appraiser. In the past, when traveling judges came to conduct business, they said they merely assumed that the place was empty because no one in the community gave a damn about the cases he oversaw, or such would be their excuse if questioned. Sheriff Cox ran his own shop the way he deemed appropriate. Yet there was a twinge of consternation trying to hide in his fat face this morning as he straddled one of the now overburdened chairs and watched as the new judge sat behind the sheriff's personal desk.

"All right, gentlemen, let's get on with the matters at hand before the damnable sun begins to cook us like steamed vegetables," Judge Born announced, eschewing the typical "all rise" and all other formalities of courtroom decorum that Faustus was used to in his city experiences with the law.

"I am Judge John E. Born, the new circuit court representative. And for those of you who may find yourselves here on a regular basis, you should know that I don't take kindly to the use of my time for listening to manure shoveling, and I am not, and I reiterate, am not beholden to any proprietor, owner, county politician or railroad baron as the case may be in my rulings or interpretations of fact."

The judge looked up only once from his sheaf of papers during the pronouncement and that was when he'd used the phrase "railroad baron" as if to challenge anyone who might not interpret his meaning.

"I owe my allegiance only to the law, gentlemen," he then said. "And while I sit here, it is the law and justice that will be served."

Faustus heard the sheriff shift his weight, the cracking and groaning of the wooden legs of his chair rising in complaint.

"In the matter of Miss Shantice Carver who is being arraigned this morning on the charge of murder in the first degree," the judge said, looking at Carver.

"I assume, ma'am, that since you are the only female present that you are Miss Carver and I ask you to rise."

Both Carver and Faustus stood.

"Your honor," Faustus said. "My name is Amadeus Faustus and I will be representing Miss Carver in this matter, sir."

The judge lowered his reading glasses, peering over the top of the lenses for an uncomfortable length of time. If he was surprised that a southern lawyer would be representing a raggedy-looking Negro woman in a capital crime, or was taken by the sight of the well-dressed attorney towering over the small black prostitute, it did not show in his face.

"Excuse me for digressing, sir," he said instead. "But are you the same Amadeus Faustus of the 39th Regiment of the North Carolina Confederacy at Murfreesboro in the year of 1862?"

Faustus took in the judge's northern accent, his similar age, and the obvious scrutiny in his eye, but did not falter.

"The very same, your honor. I was an officer with the medical corps during the battle of Stone River."

The judge let time pass again.

"I sir, was with the Union Army under General William Rosecrans at the time," he said. "Your name and your actions during battle are legend, Mr. Faustus. For treating and saving the lives not only of your fellow soldiers, but those of wounded Union troops as well. I commend you sir, to your face."

This time the wood of the sheriff's chair stayed silent.

"Now then," the judge said, returning to his papers. "According to this document prepared by the sheriff's office, Miss Carver, who is employed by the Poinciana Hotel, is charged with the stabbing death of one Charles Bingham during an altercation on the island of Palm Beach.

"Said crime is alleged to have occurred on property next to Miss Carver's domicile where later was found a murder weapon, that being a knife.

"Further stated is the fact that Miss Carver is known to also be in the business of prostitution and that Mr. Bingham was a known customer, this being offered as motivation for the killing after an alleged argument over a transaction consummated by the individuals involved."

The judge looked up from his reading, his eyes this time focused on Sheriff Cox.

"This is your report sheriff and included is a finding by the local acting medical examiner as to the death of Mr. Bingham by stabbing, is that correct sir?"

"It is, your honor," Cox said.

The judge looked down at the papers again, offering nothing but a studied silence before looking up at Faustus.

"By your presence sir, I assume you have a rebuttal of these facts or is your client prepared to plead guilty to the charge?"

"I am only prepared to present the real facts, your honor," Faustus said, knowing he was overstepping his bounds, but hoping that the informality of the country court would give him leeway. "As the document before you is filled, sir, with lies."

The legs of the sheriff did not fail him. The big man came out of his chair as if he'd been goosed and he drew in a breath with which to power his indignation. But the judge beat him to the bark.

"Sit down, Sheriff Cox! You will have your turn," Judge Born snapped. "And Mr. uh, Prosecutor, Conlon. Be it understood that you represent the state at this hearing, not the sheriff." Conlon nodded.

The judge turned to Faustus.

"I do hope you have something of substance to back up such a statement, Mr. Faustus."

"I do, your honor."

"Be succinct, sir."

Faustus clasped his hands in front of him and with a voice devoid of emotion but unwavering in conviction, began to enumerate.

"First, your honor, after a close examination of the body of said Mr. Bingham, which I myself conducted in the presence of witnesses, the diseased did not die of a stab wound, but of a bullet, sir. And as is proven by the powder burns that still mark his throat, said bullet was fired at close range. Thus, the bullet entered the front of the neck at an upward angle and lodged in the third thoracic vertebrae."

Faustus then turned, ever so slightly, toward the sheriff.

"These facts, your honor, have been covered up by the sheriff's office in conspiracy with the appointed medical examiner. I submit, sir, that an independent examination by an expert of the court's choice will in fact come to the same conclusion that I have, your honor. As you well know sir, from your own afore mentioned military service, bullet wounds do not lie."

The judge remained impassive. Faustus continued.

"Secondly, sir, I have eye witnesses, including a manager of the Royal Poinciana, his assistant, a daughter of Mr. Flagler's vice president, a handful of residents of the community, and Mizz Carver herself, who will testify that when the body of the deceased was discovered, he had a roll of cash money stuffed, sir, into his mouth. That money, your honor, is neither included in the victims effects, nor is it in the sheriff's report. I bring it to your attention only to dispel the sheriff's convenient theory that the motive for Mizz Carver's so-called actions where monetary in nature."

The judge was now staring at the sheriff, his glare itself daring the man to stand again and refute Faustus' words.

"And thirdly, your honor, I have personally obtained a confession by the actual killer of the victim, who, to my face and in her own words, admitted that she shot said victim in the throat after confronting him over a blackmail attempt, she being the wife of a well-regarded Palm Beach banker who was a frequent patron of my client's, uh, services, sir."

Despite the explosive nature of the statements, the judge remained stoic, more thoughtful than was comfortable for either Faustus or the sheriff. But behind him, Faustus could hear the frantic scratching of a pen on paper and imagined the excitement that a journalist such as Mr. Cryer must be feeling.

"What say you, Mr. Conlon?" the judge finally said.

"Bullshit!" the sheriff bawled, yet he remained in his seat.

"I, I, I don't know, your honor," Conlon babbled. "I was just recently, your honor, apprised of the..."

"I see," said the judge, cutting the man off. "Although I do not doubt Mr. Faustus' abilities to medically assess a true bullet wound when he sees one, it should not be too difficult to find a coroner of ability and state sanction to confirm the manner of death of Mr. Bingham."

"Already buried," grunted the sheriff.

"Under whose authority?" said the judge.

"Seven day rule, your honor," replied the sheriff. "It's a city ordinance. A hedge against disease when we can't find next of kin."

"Another statement that is patently false, your honor," interrupted Faustus. "An associate of mine, a Pinkerton by standing, has secured the body of the victim despite attempts made last night by some unfashionably late and previously unemployed grave diggers to carry out orders to remove said body from Mr. Maltby's funeral parlor."

Despite himself, Sheriff Cox twisted his head to take in the visages of his deputies sitting in the back row of chairs. They in turn looked at one another, stupidly shrugging their shoulders.

"And your honor, said Pinkerton is in fact the true brother of the deceased, whose real name is Daniel Byrne," Faustus said, again in a clear and unemotional statement. "Being the only surviving relative of the deceased, Mr. Michael Byrne is outside at this moment, and he has rightfully claimed his brother's body. He will submit to an independent autopsy."

This time Sheriff Cox stood, staring at Faustus, his mouth open, a look of complete astonishment pulling down at the flesh of his face. "Pinkerton," he whispered.

Judge Born scratched a note for himself and again took a few moments. The temperature in the room was rising rapidly. The judge took a handkerchief from his coat pocket and mopped his brow. Almost as if he'd given permission, the sheriff followed in form.

"Right." The judge turned to Faustus. "And as to this confession, counselor, may I assume that you do not have said confession as a signed document or are you going to surprise us all even more?"

"No, your honor. Following the conversation with the suspect, I was dismissed from the room where the admission of guilt was made. And I believe, sir, that perhaps a statewide prosecutor may need to be empowered to delve into the matter as said suspect is an out-of-state resident."

"If I may ask a basic question, Mr. Faustus, in view of such incredible statements that you have made before this court. Have you any witnesses, sir, to vouch for your client at the time of Mr. Bingham's, uh, Byrne's demise?"

"At this point, your honor, I do not. As it stands, the only witness, a seasonal maid at the hotel and a friend of my client, has also been murdered. And I have reason to believe she was killed by the same hand that took the victim's life in this case."

Carver, who until that point seemed not to have listening, looked up at Faustus and pleaded with a single cry: "Abby?"

The room had gone silent but for the frantic scratching of the newspaper editor's pencil.

"By God, man, I must say you strain your own credibility with such statements, Mr. Faustus," said the judge. "Are you aware of this occurrence, Sheriff Cox?"

Cox was staring straight ahead, gathering himself, or perhaps simply burning.

"We were informed of an accidental death at the hotel this morning, your honor," the sheriff said with an emphasis on the word accidental. "I sent the coroner, uh, acting coroner, to retrieve the body, yes sir."

"And in the interest of the sheriff's upcoming investigation of said death," the judge said, looking from one man to the other. "Would you be willing, Mr. Faustus, to aid in that inquiry with whatever knowledge you have of the situation?"

"Quite simply, your honor, the deceased, Miss Abigail Morrisette, was a co-conspirator with my client in the blackmailing scheme. After the aggrieved woman confronted and killed Mr. Bingham, she discovered that her maid was involved, and in an attempt to silence her, pushed her down an elevator shaft.

"If the sheriff would inspect the suspect woman this day I believe he will find a set of scratch marks on the left side of her neck. If he takes traces of the skin matter from under the murdered woman's fingernails, he will find a similar match of skin and face powder consistent with the suspected woman's wounds. There seemed to be a bit of a cat fight, your honor."

At this point Faustus stepped toward the sheriff, removing an envelope from his inside coat and placing on the table before him.

"And this, sir, is a bird feather found in the hand of the dead girl. I believe you can easily match it to feathers missing from the suspect woman's hat."

"May we know the name of this out-of-state woman?" Cox asked, reaching out for the envelope.

"Do you plan to investigator her in this matter?"

Cox turned to the judge. "Considering what you have brought before this court, it would seem now that I must," Cox said, and Faustus could see the wheels turning in the man's head: the opportunity of holding power over one of the Flagler's guests, the use of such power to demean their haughty ways, or perhaps to be paid off for not doing the same.

"Then I should say, your honor, her name is Mrs. Roseann Birch," Faustus said, turning to the judge. "And now, your honor, since there is another viable suspect identified in the murder for which she is charged, I request that my client be released on bail, sir."

Judge Born watched the two men, bemused perhaps by Faustus' chess playing and Cox's transparencies.

"Bail will be set in the amount of ten dollars," he replied.

"Now hold on one damned second there, yer honor," Cox blathered, letting his street language slip through. "That cain't be right!"

The judge had endured enough and, in the absence of a gavel, banged his fist on the wooden table.

"Not only is it right, sir. It is just," he barked. "And it will also be just for me to summon a special prosecutor from Tallahassee to look into the whereabouts of the money Mr. Faustus has spoken of, the discrepancies of the medical report on the victim's death, and the attempts to withhold that information from this court and the legal system.

"You will find that a new day is dawning in the state of Florida, sheriff. Things will no longer to be done as usual. Welcome to the twentieth century, sir."

Cox stared at the judge, his back teeth grinding, the muscles in his jaw flexing, but still he was silenced by his chastisement.

"And as for you," the judge said, turning to Faustus. "You with your bevy of bombshells, I would ask one question that may seem basic, but must be entered in the record just the same. Motivation, sir? For a woman of social standing to engage in such heinous crimes."

Faustus simply raised his eyebrows in that way of his.

"We may be entering a new century, your honor, but as the playwright says, and it has ever been, Heaven has no rage like love to hatred turned, nor hell a fury like a woman scorned."

With the arraignment abruptly ended, Judge Born was quick to toss out the only other business of the day, the motion of a civil suit by the sheriff filed against the local newspaper editor. It would be, under the circumstances, superfluous at this point, the judge said. With that, he seemed to say a silent prayer and called an adjournment.

The parties involved all exited the room and descended the steps. Led by Faustus, who, after paying Shantice Carver's ten dollar bail, was at his client's elbow, trying to explain to the woman what had just transpired. The judge followed, trailed by the sheriff, who was whining vociferously about a miscarriage of justice. He in turn was being harangued by the newspaper editor, who was asking questions about what the sheriff intended to do about accusations of a double homicide on Palm Beach Island. Bringing up the rear was the sheriff's now-shy deputies and bailiff, who were in no hurry to incur their boss's wrath.

At the base of the staircase, Michael Byrne waited, cap in his hand despite the strong sun. When Faustus saw him, he tried to catch his eyes, to indicate that all had gone well. Faustus was worried about the steel baton he feared was concealed under Byrne's hat. To help deflect the possibility of violence, Faustus quickly turned to the judge behind him.

"If I may, your honor," he said. "I would like to introduce you to Mr. Michael Byrne, brother of the deceased victim. He has recently taken possession of the corpse in question and will both verify his identity and give permission for the new autopsy."

The judge nodded at Byrne but did not extend his hand.

"My sympathies for your loss, Mr. Byrne. It is my hope that this extraordinary affair can be sorted out and, be assured sir, that an investigation into the carriage of justice will be overseen."

Byrne bowed his head just enough to show respect, but not enough to lose sight of Sheriff Cox, who was glowering at him from the final step of the staircase.

"If there is anything else, Mr. Byrne, that needs to be brought to my attention, as if enough has not already been elucidated this morning, then do not hesitate to call on my office," the judge said.

"There is one thing, your honor," Byrne said, stepping in front of Sheriff Cox's before the man could take his final step off the staircase. "I would like my father's watch returned."

The metal baton flicked out from Byrne's hand like a stinger. Its tip caught the chain on Sheriff Cox's vest and froze there. The motion was too fast for the fat man, or perhaps he was already too stunned from the day's explosions to react.

"By God…" Byrne cut him off. "It is a Swiss made gold fob watch with blue-steel hands and my father's initials, CHB, engraved on the back."

The judge looked at the sputtering sheriff and held out his hand. Byrne lifted the watch out of the vest pocket with the tip of his baton. After the judge inspected the piece, front and back, he unfastened the chain and placed the watch into Byrne's hand. He winced, as if a terrible odor had just invaded his nostrils, spun on his heel, and walked away.

"By God, Byrne," Faustus said, uncharacteristically awed. "You never cease to amaze, my young friend."

"Nor do you, Mr. Faustus," Byrne said. "I trust that since Miss Carver has shed her leg irons, things went well upstairs?"

"As well as could be expected. Whether there will be any follow-through is yet to be ascertained. I doubt though that Sheriff Cox will be in authority for long. I do not think this particular judge is one to look the other way. But there is little we can do now except to wait, I am afraid, for justice to come around."

Shantice Carver was still standing at Faustus' side, trying to decipher perhaps from their faces and words just what the hell had just occurred. They, however, were both looking out across the lake, taking in the white shine of the Royal Poinciana glowing in sunlight.

"I suppose you are, by necessity, going to leave us now," Faustus said. "You are in possession of your brother's body, you can take him home. That was your purpose, was it not?"

Byrne kept looking out on the water.

"This state will need men like you, Mr. Byrne, to succeed."

Byrne still did not look at the elderly man. "You mean to build grand edifices to my ego?" he said. "To plunder and devour? To shift a natural beauty to a man-made one in our own concrete and glass image?"

Byrne closed his lips, realizing he was proselytizing in a manner that was foreign to him.

"Don't mock yourself, Michael," Faustus said. "You are a man of ethics and morality, and in your heart is a sense of justice that a society cannot exist without. The Flaglers and Birches and McAdams of the world can build sanctuaries unto themselves, but it takes men like you to build a civilization."

Shantice Carver stood next to the men, drawing a pattern in the sand with the worn toe of her work shoe, and they both seemed to recognize the piety that was being splashed around on all parts.

"I may take on your challenges someday, Mr. Faustus," Byrne finally said. "But for now, there is one final thing I do have to do."

"Yes," Faustus agreed, reaching out to shake Byrne's extended hand. "I suppose there is."

CHAPTER TWENTY-FOUR

ON TUESDAY MORNING MICHAEL BYRNE STOOD on the rail platform at the southern entrance to the Poinciana. He was dressed in his Pinkerton clothes, the trousers still a bit salt stained but the brogans cleaned and polished. He was there on Harris's orders to help Mr. Flagler aboard the train to New York.

It would be his final day of work. He had already tendered a resignation and would be accompanying his brother's body on a train later in the week. He watched the McAdamses, Birches, et al, boarding for their trip back home.

If a warrant had ever been issued for the arrest of Mrs. Birch, there was no one available or willing to present it. Rumor had it that Sheriff Cox had not been seen since Judge Born left him stammering in the street after the recovery of Byrne's watch.

Yet Mr. Flagler, accompanied as always by his entourage, walked imperiously from the hotel. At exactly nine-fifteen, after assisting his wife, he climbed aboard number 90. If he took note of Byrne, he did not let on. Byrne had no doubt that such a man would have been fully informed of the accusations against his inner circle and his guests. But he was a man who built things. The unraveling of human beings, their ethics, their motivations and their morality, were but the detritus left in the wake of his progress.

Mr. McAdams followed in Flagler's steps, his head held high and extending handshakes to those seeing off the travelers with manners as cordial and confident as always. He did not notice Byrne until his daughter veered away from his side and headed in the direction of the Pinkerton.

Byrne stood his ground when Marjory approached, her green eyes holding his, any shame buried, if it indeed ever existed.

"I'm off for the city, then, Michael," she said as if leaving a mate at summer camp. He kept all emotion out of his face.

"Do you have the deed to the former Styx land with you?" he said. It was the first time he'd seen her stumble.

"I have no idea what..."

"Kiss my Irish ass," Byrne said. "You've got Danny's valise and the papers to the property. Did he sign them before you got to the meeting or did you hold the pen in his dead hand to make his mark?"

Marjory McAdams stood silent, gathering herself, perfecting her words before she spoke. Byrne took it as a victory, but only for a few seconds.

"You have no idea, Michael, how it is to live in second place behind men who become rich and richer off your expertise and off your talent," she said.

"True," Byrne said and nothing more. Let them talk, just like on the streets.

"I'm sorry for the demise of your brother. He was actually a charming man in his own way."

She raised her chin even higher.

"He was not as demure as you when it came to lovemaking, and his business acumen was impressively aggressive, though in many ways flawed."

Byrne could imagine his brother in the same circumstance as he, standing naked with Marjory in the cool Atlantic. Danny would have taken what he wanted from this she-devil. She could delude herself all she wanted.

"So you screwed him and then tried to screw him," he said, matching her crudeness.

"My father knew Daniel was shopping the binder to the Styx land to the highest bidder. He knew the value. He had helped Mr. Flagler acquire most of this land himself."

They always have to justify when they're caught, Byrne thought, no different than any pimp, scofflaw or pickpocket on Broadway.

"Others found out about the deal," she said. "That ass Pearson, snooping through the telegrams. Then Birch wanted his share for lending my father the money to pay your brother's price for the binder. When I saw Roseann Birch heading into the Styx that night I knew they were going to double cross us. I was supposed to meet Daniel myself an hour later when the fair across the lake was in full swing."

"But Mrs. Birch was only avenging a stain to her honor," Byrne said.

Marjory lowered her eyes. "And so she did. Daniel was dead when I followed her into the woods that night. I heard the gunshot. I saw her run. She did not see me."

"But you saw Danny's body."

"Yes."

"And his valise?"

"It was just laying there. I found it," she said, a schoolgirl claiming finder's keepers.

"So you had it all. And paid nothing for it," Byrne said. "Why set the fire?"

"I pulled his body under the shed." She looked past Byrne's shoulder, seeing something in the night. "I smashed my lantern against the wood frame. I was only trying to burn away the signs of what had occurred, for everyone's sake, even the Birches. But the kerosene, it just, just...I never meant to destroy people's homes."

A tear had actually begun to form in her eyes. An actress to the end.

"Bullshit," Byrne said. "Your interest in Shantice Carver was only to make sure she hadn't seen you out there once you'd stolen the valise. You tried to get her away before she could talk and then weaseled your way between her and anyone who might interrogate her. You were protecting your own ass."

"I was protecting my father!" she said, raising her voice and letting in perhaps the first true emotion that he'd seen in her. "He needs someone to protect him, he needs a strong woman to watch out for him. But you wouldn't understand such a thing, Mr. Pinkerton! You wouldn't understand what families have to do for each other."

Byrne watched her eyes, wet and angry and so naïve about the world of people who lived outside of her own sphere.

"Everyone has a father," he said. "And when I get back to New York, yours will help me find mine, dead or alive. Your money, the Birch's money and influence, will help me whenever I need it. I'll rattle your skeletons until I'm satisfied that my family is reunited, even if it's in death. That is what happens when you do business with the devil."

When she looked into Byrne's face she saw something that scared her, the young woman who was never scared of anything.

"And remember, ma'am, my brother was a very sound and able man. Be sure you're not carrying part of my own family with you back to New York."

CHAPTER TWENTY-FIVE

LATE SEASON. ONE COULD FEEL IT in the rising humidity, the warmer nighttime temperatures, the bundles of cloud in the west. In the afternoon water vapor would rise from the heating soup of the Everglades until the clouds turned dirty and dark and could hold no more. As they moved east, lured by the cooler air over the ocean, the afternoon showers would come.

Today there was a gathering at the beach; the allure was a unique baseball competition. Carlo Santos, it was said, had been cajoled to challenge the mighty Pittsburgh Pirate slugger John Peter Wagner—in Florida to convalesce a leg injury at midseason—to a test of batting prowess and strength. Such a show-down had never occurred before, and there were more than a few discussions of the properness of pitting a white slugger against a Negro in such an endeavor. But harkening back to the myopic distinction of Santos's Cuban Yankees, it was pointed out that a Latin versus a white was not unduly provocative.

So it was that Santos and Wagner were standing bat to bat on the Palm Beach Island beach. The rules had been set: each man would face a pitcher who stood with his back to the ocean and delivered strikes to the batters over a home plate set in the sand. Each batter would receive ten pitches and have the chance to blast the ball into the sea. A set of judges standing out on the wharf would determine whose ball splashed down farthest out. Best out of ten would win.

The new manager of the Poinciana was posing as umpire and score keeper, the former manager having boarded a train for the north less than a week after both the Birches and the McAdamses had left the island. Judge John Born had posted a statement that "all men are equal under the law of the combined United States of America and if a crime has indeed been committed someone will eventually have to answer for said crimes."

Those with money had gone north to their respective homes in New York to await subpoenas that would never come. Michael Byrne had taken his brother's body back to the city and buried him next to his mother. All charges were dropped against Shantice Carver, but she was surreptitiously fired and moved back to be with her people in North Carolina.

On this day a home run derby was in progress. Women guests from the Breakers were carrying their parasols, and the men were still in their luncheon attire with boaters shading their eyes as they followed the long arc of baseballs as they catapulted off the ash wood of the hitters' bats, rose into the cerulean sky and then fell to splash without a sound in the distance. A white flag would be raised from the pier if Wagner's shot was longer, a black flag for Santos. Nearly everyone, including the daily staff at the Breakers, was in attendance. One spectator in particular was missing.

"Where Mizz Ida?" asked one of the laundry women who had gathered under the pier in the shadows.

"She said somethin' bout getting somethin' done down in the basement," said the one next to her. A black flag went up, a tally changed, and Santos took the lead six to four.

"I cain't believe she would miss her boy playin' this out," said one of the housekeepers.

"No, no. Here she come now," said the first one.

The maids made a prime spot for Ida May to stand. Her work dress was smeared with some kind of heavy dust and there was even a smudge of ash on her face, unusual for a woman known for her fastidiousness. She greeted the others, set her feet in the sand and then looked out at Santos, who was taking a few warm-up swings while Wagner was at bat. He made eye contact with Miss Fluery and a silent message was passed.

The patrons on the beach were all focused on Wagner, following the parabola as the professional put his tenth ball in the Atlantic at a distance yet unmet in the contest.

Carlos Santos didn't watch his opponent's hit, but concentrated instead on the sky behind them. He detected a curling spiral of black smoke rising directly above the beachfront hotel. A slight smile played at the corners of his mouth.

When he approached the makeshift plate, Ida May carried a look of glowing grace as she watched her Santos. One of her underlings turned to another and whispered: "Ain't like he's the holy spirit or sumthin'." The woman next to her cut her eyes to Mizz Fleury's face, knowing her colleagues' subject without asking.

"She seein' some kind of glory," she whispered back.

At the plate Santos dug his back foot into the sand and cocked his bat. He took one last look at smoke now pouring out of the dormered windows at the rooftop of the Breakers and then faced the pitcher. The ball cruised in at a nice level speed, perfect for creating a symbiotic energy between the now powerfully turning bat and the approaching orb. The shattering sound of bursting glass giving way to a ballooning internal heat and that of hard ash on a hard, leather wrapped baseball split their respective air simultaneously.

The patrons watched Santos' ball make a silent plop in the water, an obvious ten yards past Wagner's last attempt. Game over. Applause fluttered the beachfront air.

Ida May Fluery clapped too. Her adroit nose began to fill with the smell of dry plank wood charring in fire behind her. She did not see when the crowd's attention left the ballplayers, but their expressions of mild entertainment turned to surprise and excitement when they noticed the smoke and tongues of fire eating the luxurious Palm Beach Breakers. Ida May Fleury instead watched her boy come to accept a kiss of congratulations on his sweaty cheek. She knew by the rustle of women's skirts and the unaccustomed yelps of rich men's voices that, for one day at least, Eden was theirs.

On a clear and sunny day in 1903, the Breakers Hotel in Palm Beach burned to the ground. Hundreds of wealthy vacationers were forced out and lost their possessions to the fast moving flames. Since it was near the end of the tourist season, many simply returned to their true homes in the north.

Less than a year later, Henry Flagler had rebuilt the hotel and the soon-to-be-dubbed "snowbirds" returned the next winter. On February 1, 1904, the beachside hotel reopened to universal acclaim.

King, Jonathon.
The Styx

RECEIVED OCT - - 2015

CPSIA information can be obtained at www.ICGtesting.com
Printed in the USA
LVOW04s0002221015

459270LV00012B/87/P